how quaint the ways of paradox!

an annotated
Gilbert & Sullivan
bibliography

by

PHILIP H. DILLARD

The Scarecrow Press, Inc.
Metuchen, N.J., & London
1991

British Library Cataloguing-in-Publication data available

Library of Congress Cataloging-in-Publication Data

Dillard, Philip H.
    How quaint the ways of paradox! : an annotated
Gilbert & Sullivan bibliography / by Philip H. Dillard.
        p.   cm.
    Includes indexes.
    ISBN 0-8108-2445-0
    1. Sullivan, Arthur, Sir, 1842-1900--Bibliography.
2. Gilbert, W. S. (William Schwenck), 1836-1911--
Bibliography.   I. Title.
ML134.S97D5   1991
016.7821'4'0922--dc20   91-3763

In Appreciation

The author wishes to acknowledge and express appreciation for the extensive assistance received from the Interlibrary Loan Departments of Southern Utah University Library and Zimmerman Library, University of New Mexico. This service was, without exception, always cheerfully offered and professionally rendered. Without interlibrary loan, which gives access to literally millions of titles in libraries across the country, this annotated bibliography simply could not have been done. Interlibrary loan is indeed a jewel among library services.

I also wish to thank two departments of Southern Utah University for sharing resources during my writing of this book. The Department of Behavioral and Social Sciences allowed me to compose the material on their Macintosh computers, and the Utah Shakespearean Festival permitted the use of their LaserWriter for the printing of the camera-ready copy. I am sure that I monopolized their space and equipment more than I intended, and their forbearance is greatly appreciated.

While expressing gratitude, I do not wish to overlook my academic colleagues who during the research and preparation of this book probably heard and learned a whole lot more about Gilbert and Sullivan than they really wished to. Their support and encouragement were most helpful.

Finally, I appreciate the patience of my wife, Jill, during this long and often tedious undertaking. It was she who preserved the sanity in at least half the household by knowing when to ignore my frequent dark mutterings about computers and by knowing how to become conveniently "deaf" whenever I felt the urge to "... whistle all the airs from that infernal nonsense *Pinafore*."

Contents

Introduction

"How quaint the ways of Paradox!" sings Frederick in *The Pirates of Penzance.* And if any stage character should understand how "at common sense she gaily mocks," it is Frederick. For it is he who as a lad was apprenticed to a pirate band through the stupidity of a hard-of-hearing nurse who confused "pirate" for "pilot." No matter, for Frederick, always the slave of duty, has loyally remained in his abhorrent apprenticeship with the pirate band until today...his 21st birthday. Now out of his indentures he will devote himself heart and soul to the extermination of the pirates (whom he hates as a group but loves individually), after which he can lead a blameless life with his new love, Mabel. But, oh, horror! That Paradox! The disclosure is made that Frederick was born on the 29th of February in a leap year, making him a little boy of five when reckoned by his *natal* days. Being above all the slave of duty, Frederick sees no choice other than to return to the loathsome pirate band until he reaches his twenty-first *birthday*...in 1940! Beseeching the lovely Mabel to wait the 60 years until he is out of his indentures, Frederick then rejoins the pirate gang as they plot the death of Major General Stanley, the father of his beloved Mabel. Indeed, there are "quips and quibbles heard in flocks, but none to beat that paradox."

The Pirates of Penzance is one of 14 comic operas which brought fame and wealth to librettist Sir William Schwenck Gilbert (1836-1911) and composer Sir Arthur Seymour Sullivan (1842-1900). Known as the Savoy operas, these works blend fantasy with satire to form topsy-turvy worlds in which unlikely characters, caught in impossible situations, accept their absurd fates with good cheer, yet turning enough logical somersaults somehow manage to land on their feet! These comic operas wed Gilbert's remarkable skills with lyrics, satire, irony and humor to Sullivan's inexhaustible supply of lovely and appropriate melodies and harmonies. Now more than a century old, these operas today seem topical and dated; yet they have retained a robust popularity that seems to go on and on.

The Savoy operas, however, constitute but a portion of the creative output of these two men. Each of the artists had his own separate career before, during, and after the G&S partnership. W. S. Gilbert established an early reputation with his contributions of humorous verse to comic journals and productions for the British stage. By the time he met Sullivan, he had written and staged melodramas, farces, travesties, blank-verse tragedies, burlesques, and comic operas. Gilbert was to dominate the Victorian stage for 30 years with an output of over 70 works, of which only the Savoy operas were done in collaboration with Sullivan. As for Arthur Sullivan, he was hailed in his youth as the musical genius who would restore English music to greatness. He composed cantatas, oratorios, songs, hymns, incidental music, a grand opera, and comic operas with librettists other than Gilbert. Although Gilbert and Sullivan's fame over the past century rests predominately on their Savoy operas, their individual contributions are numerous and worthy of consideration.

Just as there continues to be a strong interest in Gilbert and Sullivan's creative works, there also remains a fascination with their stormy relationship. Perhaps never did two more antithetical personalities labor under such self-imposed stress and strain to produce such happy works. Gilbert seemed destined to be a thorn in the flesh of all who associated with him. Demanding, controlling, and combative, he was quick to take offense, prone to sue those who gave any offense, and slow to forgive and forget. Arthur Sullivan, on the other hand, was an easy-going social creature given to parties, to long vacations, to hobnobbing with royalty, to gambling, and to rather desultory work habits. In many ways, this was a most improbable partnership.

Arthur Sullivan yearned to be recognized for his "serious" music, but the wealth to support his lavish life-style came not from his oratorios but from the comic operas which many regarded to be beneath his dignity. Gilbert perceived himself as a serious dramatist and bristled when regarded as a cynical playwright who dabbled in formulaic trifles. Each man suffered long-term physical ailments, but each man suffered perhaps more deeply from the feeling that his artistic contributions were receiving short shrift. That a partnership of two such personalities could survive is remarkable and is in no small part due to the frequent intervention of Richard D'Oyly Carte. But even Carte's good offices could not forever prevail, and the infamous "carpet quarrel" which played itself out in the press and the courts was to exact a toll in bitterness. After this episode Gilbert and Sullivan produced jointly two more operas; the magic, however, was gone, and the last two operas were comparative "failures." Partners of more than 20 years, they stood together for one last time on a stage in 1898, not speaking to each other, never to meet again. In the final analysis, the two creators of some remarkably humorous lyrics and music seemed incapable of finding good humor between themselves.

While much of what Gilbert and Sullivan produced outside the Savoy operas has been forgotten or ignored by the general public, scholars continue to research the entire body of their works in an effort to assess the contributions and place in history of each man. The works by and about Gilbert and Sullivan in this book, therefore, cover the entire span of their separate and joint careers.

Posterity has judged neither Gilbert nor Sullivan alone to be a great master at his craft. Together, however, their talents became genius. Together they created the Savoy operas and achieved the long-lasting fame which has seemed so elusive for each man separately.

Around the world today, one may be sure, many of the Savoy operas are still taking to the boards, performed by amateur and professional groups alike. Whether the interpretation is traditional or modern, whether the treatment is conservative or hot, whether the medium is the stage, television or motion picture, and whether it is true G&S or "based loosely on" G&S-- many of Gilbert and Sullivan's comic operas continue to entertain and delight us. And legions of unrepentant Savoyards are grateful for that.

Philip H. Dillard
Southern Utah University
Cedar City, Utah

1. Biography & History

1. "Affairs of the Stage." *The New York Times* (August 31, 1884): 1.

   Responds to rumors about a new G&S opera by noting that so far only an outline of the unchristened work exists. Reports a disagreeable scene on the stage of the Lyceum Theatre when W. S. Gilbert walked out in high dudgeon, complaining that he was not being treated as an English gentleman.

2. Aldford, Edward. "Significant Changes in Gilbert's Lifetime." *The Gilbert and Sullivan Journal* 9. Part I: (January, 1966): 24-5; Part II: (September, 1966): 46-7.

   Contradicts the hoary myth that D'Oyly Carte productions kept exactly to the smallest detail laid down by Gilbert. Looks at some major changes in lines, songs, scenes, scenery, and interpretation of roles that Gilbert saw--and sometimes actively encouraged--in his lifetime.

3. Aldredge, James. "Two Bright Boys." *Music Journal* 19 (January, 1961): 74-5 +.

   Tells the story of two boys at the Chapel Royal choir school in 1856 competing very hard for the Mendelssohn Scholarship. Reveals that the loser was Joseph Barnby, who became one of England's great composers of church music, and the winner was--Arthur Sullivan.

4. Allen, Reginald. *Gilbert & Sullivan in America: The Story of the First D'Oyly Carte Company American Tour.* [s.l.] Gallery Association of New York State, 1979. New York: Pierpont Morgan Library. 26 p., illus.

   Recounts the superb achievement of theatrical production, coordination and management when four touring companies performed in more than 100 American cities in 1880. Includes the "catalogue of exhibition" of the "One Hundredth Anniversary Exhibition," Pierpont Morgan Library.

5. _____. "Move Over, Verdi!" *Opera News* 25 (February 4, 1961): 8-13.

   Traces the popularity of the G&S operas from their original first performances, speculates on the effect that the expiration of Gilbert's copyright will have on productions, and considers the operas that might lend themselves to modern stagecraft and full-color television.

6. _____ . *Sir Arthur Sullivan: Composer and Personage.* In
collaboration with Gale R. D'Luhy. New York: Pierpont Morgan
Library, 1975. xxviii, 215 p., illus., facsim., bibl., index.

Presents the life of Sir Arthur Sullivan as seen through the archival
materials, supplemented by autograph manuscripts and letters,
printed scores, librettos, posters, drawings, photos and memorabilia,
which form the G&S Collection at the Pierpont Morgan Library.

7. Archer, William. "Conversation VI. With Mr. W. S. Gilbert." *Real
Conversations.* Recorded by William Archer. London: William
Heinemann, 1904. p. 107-31. Illus.

Reports a conversation at Gilbert's home that reveals the playwright's
attitudes toward hunting animals, the ingenuity of older plays versus
the "new drama," his admiration for Robertson as a stage-manager, his
chagrin at being labelled a "cynic librettist," and many other aspects of
writing, producing, and judging dramatic works.

8. Atkins, Sidney H. "The Autograph Score of *The Mikado.*" *The Gilbert
and Sullivan Journal* 9. Part I: (September, 1969): 248-49; Part II:
(January, 1970): 274.

Describes the handwritten manuscript (reproduced in photographic
facsimile) and discusses Sullivan's transcribing techniques, work
habits, recording of Gilbert's words, and the interaction between
librettist and composer.

9. Baily, Leslie. *Gilbert and Sullivan, Their Lives and Times.* (A Studio
Book). New York: Viking Press, 1974. 119 p. Illus, bibl., index.

Traces the story of the men and their partnership as G&S create
comic operas based on lyricism, geniality, and mock-heroic satire.
Looks at their separate artistic efforts which have not fared well.
Concludes that G&S stand on two rocks as classics: (1) expression of
something basic in the Anglo-Saxon character, and (2) adherence to
sheer professionalism. Includes a chronology.

10. Baker, George. "Dissertation on the Orchestra." *The Gilbert and
Sullivan Journal* 9 (September, 1966): 28.

Itemizes the various musical instruments Sullivan required for his
opera orchestrations and discusses the possibilities and results of
variations in the orchestra pit and recording studio.

11. _____. "Frederic Clay--A Friend of Both." *The Gilbert and
Sullivan Journal* 9 (January, 1970): 270-71.

Tells how it was to Clay that we owe the first meeting of G&S and
portrays the composer's character and achievements. Speaks of
Sullivan's deep affection for Clay and emotional upset at his death in
1889.

12. Baker, H. Barton. "The New Theatres." *The London Stage: Its History and Traditions From 1576 to 1888.* London: W. H. Allen, 1889. Vol. II, p. 271-97.

Documents the mania for theater building in the last part of the 19th century, discusses the theaters in which Gilbert's plays appeared (Gaiety, Court, etc.), and looks at the G&S combination at the Opera Comique and Savoy Theatre.

13. Bargainnier, Earl F. "W. S. Gilbert and American Musical Theatre." *Journal of Pop Culture* 12 (Winter, 1978): 446-58.

Examines the impact of the G&S operas on America and looks at Gilbert's influence on the structure of musical plays and the writing of stage lyrics in modern times. Notes that Gilbert's satiric libretti have inspired many American writers to emulate his craftsmanship.

14. Barker, Frank Granville. "Sullivan, Arthur." *The Dictionary of Composers.* Edited by Charles Osborne. London: The Bodley Head, 1977. p. 335-38.

Follows Sullivan's musical development in early life, mentions his early works not with Gilbert, assesses G&S as being the oddest couple Fate ever brought together, notes the run of successes of the operas in spite of their weaknesses, and concludes that it was the tragedy in Sullivan's life that he succeeded in a genre that he rather despised.

15. Barnby, Muriel. "My Letters from Gilbert and Sullivan." A special interview with Claude F. Luke. *The Strand Magazine* 72 Part I (December, 1926): 642-46; Part II (January, 1927): 52-7.

Talks of Miss Barnby's early memories of Sullivan, whom she called "Uncle Arthur," and Gilbert, and of the letters they wrote to her and other members of her family. Reprints portions of the letters.

16. Barrington, Rutland. *Rutland Barrington, A Record of Thirty-Five Years' Experience on the English Stage.* By Himself. With a preface by Sir William S. Gilbert. London: Grant Richards, 1908. 270 p., front., illus., ports.

Presents an autobiographical account of Barrington's acting career, including his major roles in most of the G&S operas. Reminisces about the great triumvirate--G&S and Carte--and relates many anecdotes about rehearsals, performances, and social life.

17. _____. *More Rutland Barrington.* London: Grant Richards, 1911. 233 p. Illus. with plates.

Continues the account of Barrington's career when, in 1908, Mrs. D'Oyly Carte initiated a series of Savoy revivals. Tells of various roles in several G&S operas as well as plays by other authors.

18. _____. "W. S. Gilbert." *The Bookman* 40 (July, 1911): 157-61. Illus.

Reminisces, upon Gilbert's death, that to those who knew him intimately there was as much to love as to admire, and that though Gilbert could be stern almost to harshness, he could be generous in giving help when needed. Shares Barrington's impressions as he got to know Gilbert, the man, as distinct from Gilbert, the author.

19. Berger, Fred. "Accord and Discord, Ltd." *Coronet* 48 (June, 1960): 20+.

Gives a brief history of Gilbert, the playwright, and Sullivan, the composer, noting their backgrounds, their separate successes prior to partnership, their great flair for success in D'Oyly Carte's Savoy Theatre, and the breakup of the team from a trifling argument over carpet expenses.

20. Blackburn, Vernon. "Arthur Sullivan." *The Fortnightly Review* LXIX. New Series. (January 1, 1901): 81-5.

Puts on record a memorial to Sullivan's genius in a very personal paper. Assesses several of the G&S operas and comments on Sullivan's character as a person and artist.

21. Bodley, J. E. C. "The Late Sir A. Sullivan." *The Athenaeum* No. 3814 (December 1, 1900): 730.

Recounts a brief anecdote about Sir Arthur's charm and musicianship in the wake of much discussion about his European reputation.

22. Bond, Jessie. *The Life and Reminiscences of Jessie Bond, The Old Savoyard, As Told to Ethel MacGeorge.* London: John Lane, 1930. xii-xiv, 243 p. Illus. with 15 plates, index.

Presents an autobiographical account of the "twenty years without a break" that the actress played in G&S operas. Describes what it was like to work with Gilbert, who wrote parts with her in mind, and Sullivan, a man of many kindnesses. Explains why she quit the theater for the domestic life.

23. Bradley, Ian. "Trial by Piracy for G&S." *New Society* 61 (September 9, 1982): 426-27.

Observes how, following the demise of the D'Oyly Carte Opera Company, the Savoy operas are becoming a middle-class art form. Examines modern treatments in Broadway and television productions and contrasts those with the traditional approach.

24. Brahms, Caryl. *Gilbert and Sullivan, Lost Chords and Discords.*
London: Weidenfeld & Nicolson, 1975. 264 p., illus. (some color),
index.

Follows the lives and careers of these two disparate creative talents
through all their successes and problems. Portrays the personality of
each, as Sullivan "swans" into a room and Gilbert growls and
intimidates. Looks at the remarkable products which brought G&S
fame almost in spite of themselves.

25. Braun, Charlotte E. "...Right Good Partners, Too!" *The Etude* 64
(November, 1946): 624+. illus.

Traces the events leading to the partnership between the literary man
and "Mr. Music." Looks at their joint successes and the artistic clouds
forming. Notes how their association re-established English musical
comedy and left a legacy of witty lyrics and charming music.

26. _____. "The Savoyards; Gilbert and Sullivan, Fathers of
Modern Musical Comedy." *Forum* 105 (February, 1946): 505-09.

Identical to "...Right Good Partners, Too!" See 25.

27. Bridgeman, Christopher Vickry. "Arthur's Chapel Royal Days." *The
Musical Times* XLII (1901). Reprinted in *Great Composers Through
the Eyes of Their Contemporaries.* Otto Zoff, editor. New York: E. P.
Dutton, 1951. p. 385-87.

Reminisces about Sullivan's days (from 1854) as junior chorister at
Chapel Royal, St. James. Tells of his pure soprano voice, his sense of
humor, and his devotion to music, as recalled by one who was a
classmate and close friend.

28. Bristol, Lee Hastings, Jr. "Sullivan, Hymn Tune Composer." *The Hymn*
18 n. 4 (1967): 101-3.

Points out the importance of the hymn-writing aspect of Arthur
Sullivan's career, noting that he wrote 56 hymn tunes and is
represented well over 400 times in 78 hymnals in the first half of the
20th century.

29. Brown, H. Rowland and Rowland Grey. "The W. S. Gilbert of His Own
Letters." *The Cornhill Magazine* 52 (February, 1922): 159-76.

Draws from approximately 100 of Gilbert's letters to reveal the
human side of the genius. Notes that this born letter-writer was
truly fond of corresponding with those congenial to him, and that
he conducted the whole of his business affairs and of his very
considerable landed estate without outside assistance. Prints
samples from the letters to show his easy style.

30. Brown, James D. and Stephen S. Stratton. "Sullivan, Sir Arthur
    Seymour, Kt." *British Musical Biography: A Dictionary of Musical
    Artists, Authors and Composers Born in Great Britain and Its Colonies.*
    Reprint of the 1897 edition by William Reeves, London. (Da Capo Press
    Reprint Edition). New York: Da Capo Press, 1971. p. 400-1.

    Gives a thumbnail sketch of Sullivan's musical career and lists his
    works by category of cantatas and oratorios, operas and plays,
    orchestral, and songs.

31. Browne, Alexander P. "Sir Arthur Sullivan and Piracy." *North
    American Review* 148 (June, 1889): 750-60.

    Chronicles the battles Gilbert and Sullivan fought in the absence of
    international copyright laws as *Pinafore* and *Pirates of Penzance* were
    being performed in hundreds of American theaters. Examines the
    decisions of the American courts and the resultant loopholes.

32. Browne, Edith A. *W. S. Gilbert.* (Stars of the Stage Series). London
    and New York: John Lane, 1907. x, 96 p., illus., plates, bibl.

    Follows Gilbert's career from the writing of the *Bab Ballads* through the
    penning of his plays to his work with Sullivan in creating "our national
    opera." Bases much of the information upon interviews with Gilbert.
    Includes a list of his plays.

33. Bulloch, John Malcolm. "W. S. Gilbert's Father." *Notes and Queries*
    171 (December 19, 1936): 435-39.

    Describes and tells the life story of W. S. Gilbert's remarkable father
    who, beginning at age 53, wrote over 30 books. Provides a
    chronologically arranged and annotated list of Gilbert senior's works.

34. Carr, J. Comyns. "Arthur Sullivan. A Personal Note." *The Fortnightly
    Review* LXIX. New Series. (January 1, 1901): 85-7.

    Dedicates the article to the personality of the artist, noting that in
    Arthur Sullivan the man and the artist were woven of one fabric and
    that Sullivan was naturally endowed with the gift of friendship and
    social charm.

35. _____. "The Work of the Theatre." *Some Eminent
    Victorians, Personal Recollections in the World of Art and Letters.*
    London: Duckworth, 1908. p. 281-92. Illus.

    Reminisces about Sullivan's measure of social fascination, the ease with
    which the composer invented melodies, the strain of ill-health, and
    the touching solemnity at his funeral.

36. Carte, Bridget D'Oyly. "Great Opera Houses: The Savoy Theatre." *Opera News* 29 (December 12, 1964): 26-9. Illus.

   Traces Richard D'Oyly Carte's efforts to bring G&S into collaboration, his troubles with the directors of the Opera Comique, and his building of the Savoy Theatre. Describes the breaks with custom and the innovations of his 1881 design. Follows the history of the Savoy beyond the deaths of the triumvirate.

37. Cellier, Francois Arsene and Cunningham Bridgeman. *Gilbert and Sullivan and Their Operas; With Recollections and Anecdotes of D'Oyly Carte and Other Famous Savoyards.* Reprint of the 1914 edition published in Boston by Little, Brown, & Co. New York: Blom, 1970. xxiii, 443 p., with 63 portraits and other illus., and 6 facsimile letters.

   Provides reminiscences with accounts of first performances of the operas and anecdotes of singers and others. Part I is by Mr. Cellier, who died before completion of the book; Part II is by Mr. Bridgeman.

38. "*Charity.*" *The New York Times* (February 18, 1880): 5.

   Prints a short letter from W. S. Gilbert protesting the unauthorized production of a rewritten version of *Charity.* States Gilbert's powerlessness, because of copyright laws, to prevent the play's production in its debased condition.

39. Cole, Hugo. "A Source of Innocent Merriment: 100 Years of G&S." *Country Life* 157 (April 7, 1975): 986.

   Offers a nostalgic look back at G&S, notes the changes in modern versions, recalls Gilbert's careful working out of movement, gesture and position in his productions, and exhibits a fondness most of all for the elegant, gay, moving music.

40. Cooke, James Francis. "Destiny and Genius." *The Etude* 72 (June, 1954): 11+. illus.

   Shows how the amazing genius of Gilbert and Sullivan seemed destined to be combined from the very beginning of their association in the production of some of the most successful operettas of all times.

41. Copley, I. A. "Tennyson and the Composers." *Musical Opinion* 101 (September, 1978): 504-12.

   Uses correspondence between Tennyson and Sullivan to show the personal nature of the composer's relationship with the poet from 1866 to 1870 when the two stayed on good terms despite artistic disagreements. Shows the correspondence resuming in 1891 after a long gap.

42. Dark, Sidney and Rowland Grey. *W. S. Gilbert, His Life and Letters*.
London: Methuen; New York: George H. Doran, 1953. ix, 269 p., illus.,
8 p. of plates, bibl., index.

Follows Gilbert from youth through his journalistic phase, his early
plays, the crowning years in the theater, and his last days, using
passages from his letters and works to portray the man and the artist.
Includes appendix containing "Lost Babs."

43. Davis, Graham. "The Changing Face of *Patience*." *The Gilbert and
Sullivan Journal* 9 (September, 1967): 115-16.

Documents changes in costume and scenery that occurred within
seven months of the premier of *Patience* (1881) and follows the
opera through 1957 as various changes in characters, sets and
style came about.

44. _____. "Recollections of the 'Thirties." *The Gilbert and
Sullivan Journal* 8 (September, 1961): 72-3.

Shows how the old order of Savoyards was changing, notes the
departure of Henry Lytton and the "deputizing" of Martyn Green,
and recalls the restricted opportunities for opera-going then.

45. _____. "Recollections of the 'Forties." *The Gilbert and
Sullivan Journal* 8 (January, 1962): 88.

Recounts briefly the activities of performers and performances of
the comic operas in London in the 1940's decade.

46. _____. "Recollections of the 'Fifties." *The Gilbert and
Sullivan Journal* 8 (May, 1962): 108.

Offers a look back at the performers and performances of the
D'Oyly Carte productions by one whose own performances had
reached 644.

47. "Declining '*U. S. S. Pinafore*.' " *The Literary Digest* 49 (July 25, 1914):
153-54.

Discusses the attempts at "Americanizing" *Pinafore* and G&S's efforts
to thwart this practice. Recounts a discussion that allegedly took place
between Gilbert and an American impresario and also Sullivan's reply
to the trade-union American musicians who sought higher pay.

48. Dicey, Edward. "Recollections of Arthur Sullivan." *The Fortnightly
Review* LXXVII. New Series. (January 2, 1905): 74-87. Also printed
in *The Living Age* (February 4, 1905): 272-82.

Writes about his intimate acquaintance with Sullivan, dwells on the
artist's character, and attempts to explain the causes of mis-
conceptions about Sullivan's leading a Bohemian life.

49. Dole, Nathan Haskell. "Sir Arthur Sullivan, 1842-1900." *Famous Composers.* Third Edition, revised and enlarged. New York: Thomas Y. Crowell, 1929. p. 639-66. Illus.

Shares Sullivan's reminiscing about his ancestry and his childhood, follows him through his youth to his first success (*The Tempest* music), looks at his activities and work before partnership with Gilbert and runs through the events of the Savoy era and up to his death.

50. Edwards. F. G. "Sir Arthur Seymour Sullivan." *Dictionary of National Biography*, XXII (Supplement). Edited by Sidney Lee. London: Smith, Elder, 1909. p. 1241-46.

Details the life of Sullivan as a musician and composer, emphasizing the "more serious side" of his career. Covers his honors, awards, commissions, appointments, and serious music accomplishments as well as his contribution to comic opera with Gilbert. Lists his musical compositions.

51. Emmerson, George S. *Arthur, Darling: The Romance of Arthur Sullivan and Rachel Scott Russell (From Her Love Letters).* London, Ont., Canada: Galt House, 1980. xi, 139 p., illus., plates, facsims., maps, bibl., index.

Draws from the letters of Rachel Scott Russell and her sister, Louise, to reveal the close relationship of the young composer to the Scott Russell family, to show the degree to which Rachel commanded his devotion, and to disclose the progress and end of the long, tortured, and often beautiful affair (1864-70).

52. Ewen, David. *The Book of European Light Opera.* New York: Holt, Rinehart & Winston, 1962. 297 p.

Provides background historical information and synopses for 12 of the Savoy operas (excluding *Thespis* and *The Grand Duke*) scattered throughout this book which covers many other works and composers. Includes a chronology of European musical theater and a list of selected recordings.

53. _____. "Sir Arthur Sullivan." *The Lighter Classics in Music; A Comprehensive Guide to Musical Masterworks in a Lighter Vein by 187 Composers.* New York: Arco Publishing, 1961. p. 299-311.

Discusses the irony (fitting for a G&S opera) that the comic opera music which Sullivan viewed with such self-apology has made him an immortal. Tells the plot and history of the most popular operas and mentions the vast repertory of Sullivan's serious music, of which hardly more than two songs have retained their popularity.

54. An Eyewitness. "The Fracas at the Opera Comique." *The Theatre*. New
    Series. III (September 1, 1879): 85-7.

    Identifies the directors of the Comedy Opera Company and tells of a
    quarrel between them and D'Oyly Carte and the author and composer,
    resulting in the uproar when a number of roughs invaded the theater
    during a production of *Pinafore*. Describes the reactions of individuals
    and the aftermath of the fracas.

55. Fellowes, Myles. "Flowers That Bloom in the Spring." *The Etude* 71
    (March, 1953): 12-3 +. illus.

    Recounts the details, from an interview with producer-director S. M.
    Chartock, concerning the formation of the American Gilbert and
    Sullivan Company, and reveals Chartock's attitudes towards the G&S
    operas, the approach to their performance, and their suitability for
    American audiences.

56. Ferguson, William C. *A History of the Savoy Company*. First published
    in 1940 under the title: *Savoy Annals*. 1950 edition. Philadelphia, Pa.:
    Savoy Company, 1951. viii, 135 p., illus, ports., plates.

    Gives a brief history of G&S and of Alfred Reginald Allen, founder of the
    Savoy Company. Tells of the founding of the company and portrays its
    history through its chronological record of productions from 1901
    through 1950. Includes indexes listing executives, players and dates,
    financial records, necrology, and general register.

57. Findon, B. W. *Sir Arthur Sullivan and His Operas*. London: Sisley's
    Ltd., 1908. 198 p., front., plates, ports.

    Follows Sullivan's life and career from youth through his attainment of
    continental fame. Looks at his hymns, cantatas, oratorios, the comic
    opera period, the Savoy successes, his work as conductor, the Royal
    English Opera effort, his character as a man and artist, and his death.

58. _____. *Sir Arthur Sullivan: His Life and Music*. Reprint of the
    1904 edition published by James Nisbet and Co., London. New York:
    AMS Press, 1976. 214 p., ports.

    Revised in 1908 as *Sir Arthur Sullivan and His Operas*. See 57.

59. "The First Gilbert and Sullivan Film: A Technicolor *Mikado*." *The
    Illustrated London News* 194 (January 14, 1939): 59. Illus.

    Gives a synopsis of and scenes from the technicolor film *The Mikado*,
    produced by Geoffrey Toye with the D'Oyly Carte Opera Company.

60. Fitz-Gerald. S. J. Adair. *The Story of the Savoy Opera in Gilbert and Sullivan's Days*. With an introduction by the Rt. Hon. T. P. O'Connor. Reprinted from the 1925 edition published by D. Appleton, New York. New York: Da Capo, 1979. xiii-xx, 239 p., front., illus. (facsims.), ports.

Tells the origin of the operas and gives details of their production, successes, and problems. Contains many anecdotes about those who participated in the production of the operas and early plays. Includes a list of the original cast of each opera.

61. French, Owen. "Sorcery in Manchester; The Company in the North. *100 Years of D'Oyly Carte and Gilbert and Sullivan*. 1975? p. 10-11? (unpaged). Illus. See 143.

Gives the history of the D'Oyly Carte Opera Company in the North of England from the first appearance of Mr. Carte in 1878 through 1971.

62. Ganzl, Kurt. *The British Musical Theatre, Vol. I, 1865-1914*. London: The Macmillan Press Ltd., 1986. x, 1196 p., index.

Gives year-by-year production details, interspersed with historical notes, for British light musicals, including G&S operas. Lists adaptations, such as *The Swing Mikado*, *The Hot Mikado*, and *The Black Mikado*, as well as TV/video/film versions.

63. "Gilbert, Sir William Schwenck." *British Authors of the Nineteenth Century*. Edited by Stanley J. Kunitz. New York: H. W. Wilson, 1936. p. 247-48. Illus. (port.), bibl.

Tells Gilbert's life story from infancy through 1877 when as an already noted playwright he met the composer Arthur Sullivan. Continues telling of his career with Sullivan and notes how Gilbert, a man of violent temper, quarreled with his partner and D'Oyly Carte. Judges the most remarkable thing about the work of G&S is its vitality.

64. "Gilbert, Sir William S(chwenck) 1836-1911." *The Reader's Encyclopedia of World Drama*. Edited by John Gassner and Edward Quinn. New York: Thomas Y. Crowell, 1969. p. 358-9. Illus., bibl.

Recalls Gilbert's circuitous path to the theater, identifies his early farces and burlesques, and summarizes the G&S opera era. Notes that this master of intricate verse patterns and pungent commentator was not destined to be remembered as a "legitimate" dramatist, but that his serious plays deserve close attention.

65. "Gilbert, Sir William Schwenck (1836-1911)." *The New Theatre Handbook and Digest of Plays*. Edited by Bernard Sobel. New York: Crown Publishers, 1959. p. 313.

Offers a one-page biography listing plays and operas, and comments on the wit and finish of his dialogue and lyrics.

66. "Gilbert, W(illiam) S(chwenck) 1836-1911 (Bab)." *Contemporary Authors.* Edited by Frances C. Locher. Detroit, Mich.: Gale Research, 1982. Vol. 104, p. 166-67.

Supplies a brief entry about Gilbert's career, noting that through the witty comic operas he and Sullivan achieved popularity that neither equaled in separate careers. Lists works.

67. "Gilbert, W(illliam) S(chwenck) 1836-1911." *McGraw-Hill Encyclopedia of World Drama.* Stanley Hochman, Editor-in-Chief. New York: McGraw-Hill Book Co., 1984. Vol. 2, p. 296-309. Illus., bibl.

Gives a brief biography of this English poet, columnist, dramatist and librettist. Summarizes each of the 14 G&S comic operas, discussing story line, themes, and musical numbers. Lists publications under the headings of G&S operettas, plays, editions, and criticism.

68. "Gilbert, William Schwenck (1836-1911)." *The Oxford Companion to the Theatre.* Edited by Phyllis Hartnoll. Fourth Edition. New York: Oxford University Press, 1985. p. 334-35.

Tells briefly of the collaboration with Sullivan on the Savoy operas, the unhappy nature of the partnership, and Gilbert's early efforts at writing burlesques and extravaganzas. Notes that, although he wrote almost up to his death, only the librettos for Sullivan have survived.

69. "Gilbert, W(illiam) S(chwenck), 1836-1911." *Something About the Author; Facts and Pictures About Authors and Illustrators of Books for Young People.* Edited by Anne Commire. Detroit, Mich.: Gale Research, Vol. 36, p. 77-96. Illus., ports., bibl.

Presents in summary form the career and writings of Gilbert. Describes in a year-by-year history the highlights of his print and theatrical career, using frequent quotes from Gilbert and others. Lists adaptations and recordings of his works.

70. Gilbert, W. S. "An Appeal to the Press." *The Era Almanack.* (1878): 85-6.

Explains why the author does not invariably avail himself of the advice of dramatic critics, why a play as presented the first night never represents the author's intentions with unimpeachable accuracy, and how critics could learn of the variables in stage production that circumvent the author's intentions.

71. _____. "A Hornpipe in Fetters." *The Era Almanack.* (1879): 91-2.

Answers critics' comparisons of French and English dramatic literature and discusses the very serious restrictions under which British authors write, specifically how they are bound by Victorian standards on sexual morality while the French are not.

72. Gilbert, W. S. "An Autobiography." *The Theatre*, New Series. I
    (April 2, 1883): 217-34. Reprinted in *W. S. Gilbert: A Century of
    Scholarship and Commentary*, John Bush Jones, ed., 1970. p. 51-60.
    See 386.

    Presents Gilbert's own account of his life from age 19 through the
    performance of *Iolanthe*, with his assessment of some of his works.
    Puts the date of his first appearance in print at 1858, talks about his
    contributions to magazines, and writes of his early plays and work with
    Sullivan.

73. Glasstone, Victor. *Victorian and Edwardian Theatres, An Architectural
    and Social Survey*. Cambridge, Mass.: Harvard University Press, 1975.
    136 p., with 210 illus. (8 in color)., bibl., index.

    Describes and shows the prominent British theaters of the late
    1800's, including those used to stage various G&S productions--
    Gaiety, Opera Comique, Royal English Opera House, Haymarket, and,
    of course, the electrically lighted Savoy, which opened with *Patience*
    in performance.

74. Goldberg, Isaac. "Gilbert and Sullivan in America." *The American
    Mercury* 11 (May, 1927): 78-83.

    Recalls how the author became a confirmed Savoyard (and a "trifle
    cracked"), and documents the feverish rage, starting with *H. M. S.
    Pinafore*, for American productions of G&S operas in America, the
    court proceedings against American "pirates," and the history of the
    various G&S operas in the USA.

75. _____. *The Story of Gilbert and Sullivan, or, The 'Compleat'
    Savoyard*. Reprinted from the 1928 edition published by Simon and
    Schuster, New York. New York: AMS Press, 1970. xviii, 588 p., illus.
    (incl music), plates, ports., facsims. (incl music), bibl., index.

    Provides a detailed biography and analysis of those two "human
    antonyms," the dissonant personalities of Gilbert and Sullivan as they
    created, produced, fought and reconciled their way through a
    remarkable partnership. Discusses the development and merits of the
    G&S operas and examines the separate works and careers.

76. Goodman, Andrew. *Gilbert and Sullivan at Law*. Rutherford, N.J.:
    Fairleigh Dickinson University Press, 1983. 246 p., illus., bibl., index.

    Examines the early career of Gilbert, the unsuccessful barrister, and
    continues with an account of him as a private and frequent litigant,
    busily suing actors, managers, critics, and the Americans who pirated
    his works.

77. _____ . *Gilbert and Sullivan's London.* Edited and
    presented by Robert Hardcastle. New York: Hippocrene Books, 1988.
    192 p., illus., bibl., index.

    Takes us on "tours" of London's districts to show sites, streets, hotels,
    theaters, houses and statues that figured in the lives of G&S, whose
    lives spanned the transformation of London from small center to large
    city. Gives details of the Gilbert-Sullivan-Carte endeavors and links
    them to the London environs in which they occurred.

78. Green, Martyn. *Here's a How-de-do, My Life in Gilbert and Sullivan.*
    New York: W. W. Norton, 1952. 283 p. Illus., plates, index.

    Gives an autobiographical account of Green's association with the D'Oyly
    Carte Opera Company from 1922 until 1951. Tells the histories of bits
    of performance business invented by Green that have become part of
    tradition, and shares the life backstage and onstage.

79. "The Grievances of the Dramatists." *The Theatre.* New Series. II
    (March 1, 1879): 71-5.

    Raises criticism of the British stage and gives the gist of a letter from
    W. S. Gilbert in which he lists grievances against managers and the
    system of borrowing plays from the French.

80. Grossmith, George. "Sir Arthur Sullivan: A Personal Reminiscence."
    Pall Mall Magazine XXIII (February, 1901): 250-60. illus.

    Recalls the actor's association with Sullivan over a 12-year engagement
    with G&S at the Opera Comique and Savoy theatres, and relates
    anecdotes that reveal the composer's craftsmanship, work techniques,
    and personal traits.

81. _____. *A Society Clown.* (Arrowsmith Bristol Library).
    Bristol: J. W. Arrowsmith, 1888. 192 p.

    Provides an autobiographical account of the actor's life and career on
    the stage. Devotes one chapter to his association with G&S, recalling
    the dynamics and styles of the two, the roles that Grossmith played,
    and incidents that occurred during his years performing the Savoy
    operas.

82. Grossmith, George, et al. "Recollections of Sir W. S. Gilbert." *The
    Bookman* 40 (July, 1911): 162-65. Illus.

    Grossmith, Jessie Rose, Edward German, and C. H. Workman look
    backward upon the life of the late W. S. Gilbert, commenting on his
    personal traits and professional deportment. Recount anecdotes that
    show Gilbert's wit, his provocative nature when rubbed wrong, and his
    kind word, patience and forbearance for any one who tried.

83. Hansl, Eva and Helen L. Kaufmann. "Sir Arthur Sullivan, A British Peer of Song." *Minute Sketches of Great Composers*. Illustrated by Samuel Nisenson. New York: Grosset & Dunlap, 1932. p. 76-7. Illus.

Gives a one-page biography of the man who was to become the idol of England, telling of the 25 years when G&S were flint to each other's steel.

84. Harris, Roger. "Sullivan's *Romance*." *The Gilbert and Sullivan Journal* 8 (September, 1965): 303.

Tells of Sullivan's composing *Romance for String Quartet* in his first month at Leipzig at age 16. Describes the form of the short work, which takes only three minutes to perform, and its first publication--more than 100 years later.

85. Hartley, Mildred Howson and Jane W. Stedman. "The First Josephine." *The Gilbert and Sullivan Journal* 9 (May, 1970): 290-91.

Relates the story of Emma Howson, who in 1878 created the *H. M. S. Pinafore* role of Josephine, which she was to sing 702 times during her career.

86. Hauger, George. "Victorian Musical Theatre." *Opera* 29. Part I: (February, 1978): 135-39; Part II: (March, 1978): 266-69.

Describes the great productive growth in Victorian musical theater (Part I) and discusses a number of works with poor music and mechanical plots (Part II), noting the exception of Gilbert and Sullivan's lasting works which inspired a horde of imitators.

87. Hawes, Arthur. "The First *Cox and Box*." *The Gilbert and Sullivan Journal* 9 (January, l967): 69-70.

Tries to unravel the often conflicting testimony of Sullivan's biographers as to the exact date of the first performance of *Cox and Box*. Provides a sequence of performances which are authenticated by press reports.

88. Hibbert, Christopher. *Gilbert & Sullivan and Their Victorian World.* New York: American Heritage Pub., 1976. 279 p., illus, bibl., index.

Examines the origin, the story of the writing and scoring, the production, and the reception of each of the operas. Shows how the misalliance of contentious Gilbert and congenial Sullivan was held together for two decades, partly because of D'Oyly Carte's talent and influence. Reveals the Victorian lives behind the masterworks.

89. Hibbert, H. G. "Concerning Gilbert and Sullivan." *A Playgoer's Memories*. Prefatory note by William Archer. With 12 illustrations. London: Grant Richards, 1920. p. 259-67.

Looks back on the nature of the G&S partnership, Gilbert's choice of actors and his autocratic stage management style, the involvement of D'Oyly Carte, and revivals of G&S operas since the closing of the Savoy.

90. Hilton, George W. "*The Mikado* American Copyright, 1885." *The Gilbert and Sullivan Journal* 8 (May, 1963): 167-68.

Reports how D'Oyly Carte fought legal and business battles to secure the American rights to *The Mikado*, how Americans produced the opera anyway, and how the judges' decisions cost G&S untold sums in American royalties.

91. _____. "*The Symphony in E.*" *The Gilbert and Sullivan Journal* 9 (September, 1969): 250-52.

Recalls that Sullivan composed a single symphony early in life and gives the history and criticism of this work which was first performed at the Crystal Palace in 1866.

92. Hobbs, Frederick. "The Savoyard Saga." *The Etude* 53 (April, 1935): 197-98.

Describes the talents and contributions of the producing genius (D'Oyly Carte), the versatile melodist (Sullivan) and the word artist (Gilbert). Shows how they gave us clean fun plays that were strictly British yet enjoyed around the world.

93. Hollingshead, John. *Gaiety Chronicles*. London: Archibald Constable, 1898. xvi, 493 p., 47 p. of plates, index.

Recounts the history of the Gaiety Theatre from 1868 through 1886, during which time Gilbert's *An Old Score* and *Robert the Devil* were staged, and the first G&S collaboration, *Thespis*, premiered. Lists all the pieces performed at the Gaiety during this period.

94. How, Harry. "Mr. W. S. Gilbert." *Illustrated Interviews*. London: George Newnes, 1893. p. 1-16. Illus.

Describes Gilbert's "miniature kingdom" estate and the interior of his house, and repeats Gilbert's telling of his life history from his early days as a barrister, the writing of his plays, the first meeting with Sullivan, and the success of their comic operatic work.

95. Hughes, Gervase. "Sullivan 1962." *Opera* 13 (January, 1962): 8-13. Illus.

Considers Sullivan's early career, the decade of the 'eighties as the G&S heyday, the three generations of D'Oyly Cartes guarding the rights to the Savoy operas, and the balance of the D'Oyly Carte stewartship in faithfully preserving Gilbert's (but not necessarily Sullivan's) intentions.

96. Hunter, Ralph. "Assignment: Gilbert & Sullivan." *Music Journal* 18 (June/July, 1960): 14+.

Tells of the decisions required in planning a new complete G&S album for R. C. A. Victor (*A Gilbert and Sullivan Song Book*). Shows concerns for being true to the spirit of G&S while presenting their music with a fresh feel to modern audiences.

97. Hyman, Alan. *The Gaiety Years.* London: Cassell, 1975. xiii, 230 p., 16 p. of plates, illus., ports., bibl., index.

Tells the history of the "Old Gaiety" (1868-1886), which opened with a production of Gilbert's *Robert the Devil,* and the Gaiety under the "Guv'nor" George Edwardes until its closing in 1915. Gives some information about the early days of G&S.

98. _____. *Sullivan and His Satellites: A Survey of English Operettas 1860-1914.* London: Chappell, 1978. 224 p., illus., bibl., index.

Concentrates on the people who created the operettas--the composers, librettists and lyric writers, the actors and actresses, and the leading impressarios of the period. Includes index of operettas, and the theaters and years for the first-night performances of the 14 G&S operas.

99. "In the Days of *Iolanthe.*" *The Etude* 44 (November, 1926): 820.

Gives the abbreviated facts about how Sullivan, heart-broken upon the death of his beloved mother, composed and rehearsed *Iolanthe,* and how he conducted the premiere even as he learned that he had just become financially ruined.

100. Jacobs, Arthur. *Arthur Sullivan: A Victorian Musician.* Oxford and New York: Oxford University Press, 1984. xvi, 470 p., illus., 16 p. of plates, bibl.

Depicts the varied activities of Arthur Sullivan and shows the Victorian social, political, and musical environment. Documents the daily occurrences in Sullivan's life, reveals the man's personal side, and follows his movements in society.

101. _____. "The Secret Diaries of Sir Arthur Sullivan." *High Fidelity and Musical America* 27 (May, 1977): 46-50. Illus.

Draws from diaries to show that Sullivan pursued the active but clandestine sex life of a Victorian bachelor. Recounts his relationships with the Scott Russell sisters and Mrs. Ronalds, his affairs with the mysterious L.W. and D. H., and his decline in health and sexual activity at about age 50.

102. Jellinek, Hedy and George. "The One World of Gilbert and Sullivan." *Saturday Review* 51 (October 16, 1968): 69-70. Illus.

Reveals that the Savoy operas, despite being difficult to translate due to Gilbert's special brand of satire, have been performed internationally. Tells of the immensely popular German-language production of *Der Mikado (oder Ein Tag in Titipu)* and follows the history of G&S in Russia, Hungary, Italy, Japan, and a number of other countries.

103. Joseph, Tony. "D'Oyle Carte in Bristol, 1879-1969." *The Gilbert and Sullivan Journal* 9 (January, 1970): 268-69.

Chronicles the history of the Savoy operas in Bristol, England, from the time when *H. M. S. Pinafore* was first performed in 1879. Evaluates performances and trends from the early days through the war years and into the late 1960s.

104. _____. *George Grossmith: Biography of a Savoyard.* Bristol: Published by the Author, 1982. x, 212 p. Illus., ports., bibl., index.

Details the life and career of Grossmith from boyhood to piano entertainer, to his premiering on stage as J. W. Wells in *The Sorcerer,* through his starring in major roles in G&S operas 1877-1889, and into the later years until his death in 1912. Relates much about what transpired on and off stage during his Savoy opera years.

105. Joslin, Peter. "Church Hymns With Tunes." *The Gilbert and Sullivan Journal* 10 (Autumn, 1974): 123-24.

Relates how Sullivan witnessed the establishment of a new style of hymn-singing over 25 years and notes his contributions.

106. "Kings of Comic Opera." *Life* 33 (December 22, 1952): 49-53. Illus. (some color), ports.

Uses the occasion of the production of the film biography *Gilbert and Sullivan* to review the historic facts of the G&S partnership, to record the reign of three generations of D'Oyly Cartes, and to ponder the changes to come with the expiration of the last copyrights.

107. Klemm, G. "Failures That Triumphed: *H. M. S. Pinafore.*" *The Etude* 53 (July, 1953): 394.

Relates how the music for *Pinafore,* written in great pain by the suffering Sullivan, had some trouble in establishing itself. Tells how the capriciousness of the weather kept audiences away until Sullivan's special music arrangement at the Covent Gardens Promenade Concert sparked public interest.

108. Lamb, Andrew. "*Cox and Box*--A Postscript." *The Gilbert and Sullivan Journal* 9 (January, 1968): 132-33.

Uses diary entries to throw light on the question of the date of the firs performance of the Burnand/Sullivan *Cox and Box.* Summarizes a series of articles which have to some extent rewritten the history of *Cox and Box* upon the centenary of Sullivan's first comic opera.

109. _____. "Gilbert and Sullivan and the Gaiety." *The Musical Times* 112 (December, 1971): 1162-64.

Describes the Gaiety Theatre and its ambitious, innovative manager, John Hollingshead, at the time of the 1868 opening with Gilbert's *Robert the Devil.* Relates the events of the 1871 Christmas season when G&S produced their first collaborative work, *Thespis,* a hastily put together, short-run enigma that disappeared from the repertory.

110. _____. "Gilbert and Sullivan for Dancing." *The Gilbert and Sullivan Journal* 10 (Spring, 1973): 32-3.

States that the 19th century was the great age of dance music and documents that from each of the G&S operas (except *Thespis*) up to five dances were published in the form of the galop, the quadrille, the waltz, and the polka.

111. _____. "Sullivan as Opera Critic." *The Gilbert and Sullivan Journal* 9 (May, 1970): 288-89.

Recounts the one occasion on which Arthur Sullivan acted as a newspaper's opera critic, writing an unsigned and unfavorable review for *The Observer.* Judges the tone and authority of Sullivan's only musical criticism ever published in a newspaper.

112. _____. "Sullivan, Sir Arthur (Seymour)." *The New Grove Dictionary of Music and Musicians, Vol. 18.* Edited by Stanley Sadie. London: Macmillan Publishers Ltd., 1980. p. 355-64, illus (incl. music), bibl.

Provides detailed history of Sullivan's early career and the period of his professional maturity. Assesses his posthumous reputation and looks at the comic operas. Provides a list of his works by category (hymns, orchestral, choral with orchestra, etc.).

113. _____. "Sullivan's Continental Journeys, 1867." *The Gilbert and Sullivan Journal* 9 (May, 1967): 96-7.

Clarifies points about Arthur Sullivan's two trips to Europe in 1867, correcting names and events erroneously recorded by his biographers.

114. Lauterbach, Edward Stewart. *"Fun" and Its Contributors: The Literary History of a Victorian Humor Magazine.* Unpublished Ph.D. Dissertation. University of Illinois, 1961. 326 p.

Traces the history of *Fun* (1861-1901), the rival of *Punch,* shows how its humor depended on puns and word play, and notes how it served as a cradle for men such as W. S. Gilbert, Ambrose Bierce, and others.

115. Lawrence, Arthur. *Sir Arthur Sullivan; Life Story, Letters, and
     Reminiscences.* With critique by B. W. Findon and bibliography by
     Wilfred Bendall. Reprint of the 1899 edition published by J. Bowden,
     London. New York: Haskell House, 1973. xii, 340 p., illus. ports.,
     facsims (incl. music).

     Follows Sullivan from boyhood through his career and lifetime.
     Provides abundant anecdotes from people who had known Sullivan.
     Includes assessment of Sullivan as a composer by B. W. Findon and an
     appendix listing all of Sir Arthur's works.

116. Lawrence, A. H. "Sir Arthur Seymour Sullivan." *The Strand Magazine*
     XIV (1897): 649-58. Illus., ports., facsims.

     Presents an illustrated interview with Sullivan in his 56th year.
     Covers the composer's career from young musical student through his
     work with Gilbert. Records some of Sullivan's observations, interests
     and opinions.

117. Lawson, Winifred. *A Song to Sing-O!* Foreword by Sir Malcolm
     Sargent. London: Michael Joseph, 1955. Illus, index.

     Gives an autobiographical account of the actress who joined the D'Oyly
     Carte Opera Company in the 1920's and sang many leading G&S roles
     in England, including performances at the rebuilt Savoy, and later
     with the Sadler's Wells Company in Australia and other parts of the
     world.

118. Lingg, Ann M. "The Immortal 'Trifles' of Gilbert & Sullivan." *The
     Etude* 69 (May,1951): 20-2+. illus.

     Explains why, just as there will always be an England, there will
     always be Gilbert and Sullivan. Analyzes the operas' appeal, gives a
     brief history of the two artists' collaboration and break-up, and notes
     the popularity of the operas through WWII.

119. _____. "The Immortal 'Trifles' of Gilbert & Sullivan."
     Reader's Digest 58 (June, 1951): 84-8.

     Abbreviated version of the article which appeared in *The Etude.* See
     118.

120. Lytton, Henry A. *The Secrets of a Savoyard.* Foreword by Rupert
     D'Oyly Carte. Reprint of the 1922 edition published by Jarrolds,
     London. (Da Capo Press Music Reprint Series). New York: Da Capo
     Press, 1980. 191 p. Illus., plates, facsim., bibl.

     Provides an autobiographical account of the actor who played major
     roles in the G&S operas from 1884 through 1901 and after 1909.
     Shares memories of G&S and Carte. Summarizes the stories of all the
     G&S operas except *Thespis* and *The Grand Duke.*

121. Mackinlay, Sterling. "Comic Opera, Gilbert and Sullivan; Savoy Opera and Tradition." *Origin and Development of Light Opera.* Philadelphia: David McKay Co., 1927. p. 226-48.

Examines what manner of men Gilbert and Sullivan were, and chronicles their separate and joint careers. Looks at the Savoy tradition after the famous "carpet quarrel."

122. Macqueen-Pope, W. *Gaiety, Theatre of Enchantment.* London: W. H. Allen,1949. 498 p., illus., 32 p. of plates, index.

Chronicles the history of the Gaiety Theatre and the plays, the actors, the directors and managers from 1868 through WWII. Shows G&S involvement with *Thespis* in 1871 and in other contexts. Provides a list of plays performed at the Gaiety through its existence.

123. Mander, Raymond and Joe Mitchenson. *The Lost Theatres of London.* London: Hart-Davis; New York: Taplinger, 1968. 572 p., illus. with 56 p. of plates, maps.

Provides history and description of "lost theatres" which still exist as buildings although no longer used for their original purpose. Covers the Gaiety and the Opera Comique of Gilbert and Sullivan association as well as 26 other theaters. Includes list of architects.

124. _____. *A Picture History of Gilbert and Sullivan.* Foreword by Bridget D'Oyly Carte. London: Vista Books, 1962. 160 p., illus.

Presents 382 photos, portraits, drawings, posters, and other illustrations of W. S. Gilbert, Arthur Sullivan, Richard D'Oyly Carte, and myriad actors and scenes from the plays and operas from 1868 to 1962. Includes a brief biography of each of the famous triumvirate.

125. _____. *A Picture History of the British Theatre.* (Hulton's Picture Histories). London: Hulton Press, 1957. 160 p., illus.

Covers, through words and pictures, the pageant of the British theater from the 1570's through 1957. Part V deals with the Victorian era (1837-1901) and, while not mentioning G&S, illustrates the milieu in which they worked.

126. _____. *The Theatres of London.* Illustrated by Timothy Birdsall. London: Hart-Davis; New York: Hill & Wang, 1961. 292 p., illus., map.

Gives opening dates, seating capacity, description of the building, and identification of plays produced in the Savoy and more than 50 other London theaters between 1663 and 1959. Includes alphabetical list of architects.

127. Marek, George R. "Gilbert and Sullivan Never--Well, Hardly Ever--Got
     Along." *TV Guide* 32 (March 17-23, 1984): 18-19. Illus, port.

     Tells of the first meeting between G&S, the durability of the joy of
     Gilbert's timeless wit and Sullivan's winged, singable melodies, the
     differences in their personalities, and the repeated quarrels of these
     humorists who proved to be humorless.

128. Matlaw, Myron. "Gilbert, Sir W[illiam] S[chwen(c)k] (1836-1911)."
     Modern World Drama, An Encyclopedia. New York: E. P. Dutton,
     1972. p. 293-94. Ilus.

     Lists Gilbert's frothy but clever and amusing plays, discusses the
     25-year G&S period, lists the comic operas and notes the
     playwright's autocratic and waspish temperament.

129. Matthews, Betty. "*Onward, Christian Soldiers;* A Centenary." *The
     Musical Times* 113 (December, 1972): 1232. Illus. with music
     facsim.

     Explains how and when the words and music to *Onward, Christian
     Soldiers* came to be written. Describes the first performance of the
     hymn and discusses Sullivan's two collections of hymns in which he
     harmonized or arranged some and added some of his own.

130. Matthews, Brander. "Notes on W. S. Gilbert." *Papers on Playmaking.*
     New York: Hill and Wang, 1957. p. 292-95.

     Surveys Gilbert's career as civil servant, unsuccessful barrister,
     contributor to humorous magazines, writer of burlesques and other
     plays in prose and blank verse, and creator of librettos with Arthur
     Sullivan and other composers. Links Gilbert to the influence of his
     elders and betters among dramatists.

131. "Memoir of George Grossmith." *The Theatre* . New Series V (June 1,
     1885): 309-10. Illus. (port.).

     Presents a brief biography of the actor from his 1869 debut as a
     public entertainer through his appearances in all the G&S operas
     produced at the Opera Comique and Savoy Theatres. Lists his parts in
     the operas and the dates of production.

132. "Memoir of Miss Jessie Bond." *The Theatre* . New Series V (February
     2, 1885): 94-5. Illus. (port.).

     Presents a brief biography of the "singing soubrette" from her debut
     as a vocalist, to her first appearance on the dramatic stage as Hebe in
     H. M. S. Pinafore, and through her playing important original parts in
     the G&S operas. Assesses her qualities, attributes, and achievements.

133. Miller, James Nathan. "The Partnership That Couldn't Be." *Reader's Digest* 122 (March, 1983): 66-71. Illus.

Tells the story of the G&S saga, one of the theater world's longest-running successes but personally a story that ended in disaster for the odd couple of Victorian theater. Looks at the personalities and histories of the *word man* and the *music man*, and shows how these two celebrities joined to produce an astoundingly successful music machine, only to lose it to incompatibility.

134. "Mr. Grossmith, Jun." *The Theatre*. New Series. III (November 1, 1879): 216. Port.

Provides background on Grossmith's early career and tells how, against the opposition of the directors of the Opera Comique, he appeared as J. W. Wells in *The Sorcerer*. Judges that the young actor's success admitted of no doubt, and outlines his career through 1879.

135. Mullen, Donald (compiler). *Victorian Plays; A Record of Significant Productions on the English Stage, 1837-1901*. New York: Greenwood Press, 1987. 444 p.

Lists alphabetically hundreds of London theater productions, including W. S. Gilbert's serious plays. Includes dates of performances, names of theaters, and lists of casts. Does not include Gilbert's comic operas, burlesques, or travesties.

136. "Musings--G&S." *Blackwood's Magazine* 317 (June, 1975): 567-69.

Uses the 100th anniversary of *Trial by Jury* to think about that extraordinary, quarrelsome duo. Considers the life of Sullivan, who more than Gilbert keeps the operas going today, and the fact that the Savoy operas are a monument to Victorian music.

137. "My Maiden Brief." *The Cornhill Magazine* VIII (December, 1863): 725-32.

Describes the young barrister's first courtroom brief, defending a woman accused of purse stealing. Tells how, when found guilty, the client hurled her boot at the attorney, missing him but hitting a reporter, and surmises this to be the cause of unfavorable newspaper reviews of his defense speech. (Published anonymously but later attributed to Gilbert.)

138. Nettleton, George Henry. "A Visit to Sir William S. Gilbert." *The Nation* 93 (August 3, 1911): 96-7.

Reminisces about a visit in which Gilbert professed his interest lay primarily in his serious poetic dramas. Reports Gilbert's extraordinary sensitiveness to adverse criticism and discusses his remarkable attention to details.

139. Nicol, P. G. "A Century of Staging." *The Gilbert and Sullivan Journal* 10 (Spring, 1975): 143-44.

Documents the staging of *Trial by Jury* from 1876 in regard to its London and provincial performances, touring companies, revivals, principal actors, and gaps in its production.

140. _____. "Dealers in Magic and Spells." *The Gilbert and Sullivan Journal* 10 (Spring, 1977): 272-73.

Chronicles the 100-year history of performances and performers of *The Sorcerer* on its centenary, and notes the periods of "slumber" for the piece.

141. _____. "Some Early Players." *The Gilbert and Sullivan Journal* 9 (September, 1970): 319-20.

Gives an account of some of the prominent players who contributed to the lengthening history of the G&S operas after the original Savoyards. Discusses Isabel Jay, C. H. Workman, Walter Passmore, and others.

142. Nicoll, Allardyce. "The Theatres: 1850-1900." *A History of English Drama 1660-1900. Vol. V.: Late Nineteenth Century Drama 1850-1900.* Cambridge: The University Press, 1962. p. 215-28, 378-81.

Lists theaters and music halls (with pertinent dates) in London and environs, and includes a handlist of plays with dates, records of the Lord Chamberlain's manuscripts, and published editions.

143. *100 Years of D'Oyly Carte and Gilbert and Sullivan.* (Cover title: *D'Oyly Carte Centenary 1875-1975*). London: s.n., 1975? 125 p., illus. (some color).

Gives, opera by opera, an illustrated history with lists of original casts and photos of the principal actors from *Trial by Jury* through *The Grand Duke* (1875-1896) and then of revivals and productions through 1975. Presents half a dozen short essays by G&S authorities.

144. Overton, Grant. "Great Partnership." *Mentor* 16 (February, 1928): 1-10. Illus., ports.

Gives an illustrated history of the G&S partnership from their first meeting in 1870 through their successful collaborative works to *The Grand Duke* when the partnership was dying as a result of contentious correspondence.

145. Palmay, Ilka. "At the Savoy Theatre." Translated by Andrew Lamb.
     The Gilbert and Sullivan Journal 9. Part I (May, 1972): 417-19;
     Part II (September, 1972): 439-40.

     Tells the history of the celebrated prima donna who appeared in
     The Grand Duke no fewer than 175 times. Recalls how the
     association with G&S came to be and gives insights into the
     personalities of the pair.

146. Pearson, Hesketh. "Further Quarrels of W. S. Gilbert." *The Listener*
     LVIII (September 5, 1957): 347-48. [Part II. See 150]

     Reviews Gilbert's extremely touchy personality and passion for
     confrontational straight dealing which landed him in many quarrels.
     Uses his private papers to document the final rumpus between
     Gilbert and the D'Oyly Carte management, his indignation over opera
     revivals, and his conflict on behalf of his adopted daughter, Nancy
     McIntosh.

147. _____. *Gilbert and Sullivan. A Biography.* New York and
     London: Harpers, 1935. 317 p., 3 p. of plates, bibl., index.

     Deals with the lives and personalities of each artist separate from the
     other and as a member of the librettist/composer team.

148. _____. *Gilbert: His Life and Strife.* New York: Harper,
     1957. 276 p., illus. with 8 p. of plates, index.

     Follows the life and career of "Bab" from his earliest writing of verse
     through his triumphs and troubles as writer/dramatist, his
     collaboration with Sullivan, his ordeal with gout, and his place as
     villain/hero in the British theater.

149. _____. "Private Papers of W. S. Gilbert." *Theatre Arts* 41
     (December, 1957): 70-1+. Illus.

     Explains how an examination of Gilbert's private papers turned up
     several aspects of the G&S partnership hitherto unrecorded and how
     they contradicted several previous assumptions. Provides details of
     the "carpet quarrel" as revealed by these fresh facts.

150. _____. "The Quarrel and the Carpet." *The Listener*
     LVIII (August 29, 1957): 307-8. Illus. [Part I. See 146]

     Uses information culled from Gilbert's private papers to give a
     detailed history of the issues, events, and repercussions of the quarrel
     over the price of a carpet for the auditorium of the Savoy Theatre.
     Tells how intercession brought the team together but without
     harmony.

151. _____. "William Schwenck Gilbert." *Lives of the Wits.*
New York: Harper & Row, 1962. p. 191-208. Port., bibl., index.

Starts by noting there was never the slightest likelihood that W. S.
Gilbert would be anything but a thorn in the flesh, and continues on
to tell his life story through his unhappy childhood, his quarrels, his
personal touchiness, his grievances against colleagues, his long-held
grudges, his need for financial success, and the relative calm of his
later years.

152. Pounds, Courtice. "My Stage Memories." *The Gilbert and Sullivan
Journal* 10 (Spring, 1981): 426-27.

Recounts how the tenor became a member of the chorus of the
D'Oyly Carte Opera Company at the Savoy Theatre and went on to
create the role of Colonel Fairfax and later Marco Palmieri.
Relates his first meeting with Arthur Sullivan and an amusing
incident in connection with Rutland Barrington.

153. Prestige, Colin. "Boxes, Coxes and Bouncers." *The Gilbert and
Sullivan Journal* 9 (January, 1967): 71-2.

Identifies the various performers, performances, and interpretations
of *Cox and Box,* including some in which the Sullivan brothers --
Arthur and Frederic--played the two title roles. Discusses the name
change of the celebrated farce, *Box and Cox,* to that milestone in
Sullivan's career, *Cox and Box.*

154. _____. "D'Oyly Carte and the Pirates: The Original New
York Productions of Gilbert and Sullivan." *Gilbert and Sullivan,* James
Helyar (ed.), 1971. p. 113-48. See 354.

Traces the history of each comic opera as it was "pirated" on stage in
America, reveals the American audacity in "Americanizing" the plots,
and shows the Savoyards' vigilance in trying to prevent the piracy.

155. _____. "Frederic Sullivan, Thespian." *The Gilbert and
Sullivan Journal* 9. Part I: (September, 1971): 372-74; Part II:
(January, 1972): 402-3.

Explores the brief stage career of Arthur's older brother, noting that
Frederic died in 1877 before he could consolidate the fame which he
had won so near the end of his short life. Quotes passages from Press
critiques to assess his talent and potential.

156. _____. "*The Gondoliers*--Feelings of Pleasure." *The Gilbert
and Sullivan Journal* 8 (January, 1965): 267.

Looks back at the historic evening when *The Gondoliers* opened in
1889--an evening of rapture unrestrained before the harmony of the
partnership was to be shattered in the courts of law.

157. _____. "Ten Battles Off Spithead." *The Gilbert and Sullivan Journal* 10 (Spring, 1978): 289-94.

Looks at ten legal actions that D'Oyly Carte and G&S took against the Comedy Opera Company for the right to perform *H. M. S. Pinafore* in London. Includes details of the fracas with 50 roughs who forced their way into the theater just as the duet, "Things are seldom what they seem," was being sung.

158. _____. "With One Brain: A Centenary Survey of *Trial by Jury*." *The Gilbert and Sullivan Journal* 10 (Spring, 1975): 141-42.

Traces the unassuming approach to the publicity for and first appearance of *Trial by Jury*, and considers the ability to create operas "from one and the same brain" to be one of the signal factors accounting for the success of G&S in their later partnership.

159. _____. "*The World* and the New World." *The Gilbert and Sullivan Journal* 10 (Autumn, 1977): 275-76.

Examines the critique by *The World*, a serious and high-minded weekly journal, of *The Sorcerer* (1877) and its opinions about the limitations of the librettist and composer in doing this "unambitious" work.

160. "Recollections of *Ivanhoe*." Told to Manuel Weltman. *The Gilbert and Sullivan Journal* 8 (September, 1965): 302-3.

Records the recollections of Miss Lily Howard, a cast member of the 1891 production of Sullivan's grand opera, *Ivanhoe*. Tells how she met D'Oyly Carte and Sullivan, and how she came to sing in the opera.

161. Rees, Terence. "Sullivan's Royalty Contracts." *The Gilbert and Sullivan Journal* 10 (Spring, 1973): 7-8.

Uses the archives of Metzler/Cramer publishers to give details of Sullivan's royalty contracts and his selling outright several compositions, plus one opera *The False Heiress* (which he apparently bought back and later staged as *The Sapphire Necklace*.).

162. _____. "The Wanderings of Wilfred." *The Gilbert and Sullivan Journal* 10 (Autumn, 1973): 56-7.

Traces the history of Sullivan's attraction to Sir Walter Scott's writings, Sullivan's composition of the opera *Ivanhoe*, and its subsequent record of performances and revivals.

163. Rickett, Edmond. "Certain Recollections of W. S. Gilbert: The Author
     of *The Mikado*, et al., Was a Difficult Director." *The New York Times*
     (April 1, 1934): Section 10, p. 1-2.

     Tells of this musical director's first becoming acquainted with W. S.
     Gilbert in 1904 doing *The Fairy's Dilemma* and speaks of the
     librettist's methods, which were not endearing, and his extra-
     ordinary faculty for composing stage pictures. Tells how his very
     appearance at rehearsals was terrifying to his victims due to his
     autocratic manner and forbidding personal demeanor.

164. Rollins, Cyril and R. John Witts. *The D'Oyly Carte Opera Company in
     Gilbert and Sullivan Operas: A Record of Productions, 1875-1961.*
     Foreword by Bridget D'Oyly Carte. London: Michael Joseph, 1962.
     xii, 186 p., illus. with plates, append., discog., index.

     Provides a detailed record of original London productions and
     revivals, summary of touring companies in Great Britain, Canada, and
     America, listings of staff personnel of the D'Oyly Carte Opera
     Company, and compilation of sound recordings made under D'Oyly
     Carte supervision.

165. Ronalds, Mary Teresa. *Victorian Masque: The Love Story of Arthur
     Sullivan.* London: Macdonald & James, 1975. 268 p.

     Presents a historical romance (fiction) loosely based on the facts of
     Sullivan's life.

166. Rowell, George. "The Merchant of Manchester." *The Gilbert and
     Sullivan Journal* 10 (Spring, 1974): 81-3.

     Tells of Sullivan's scruples about and participation in the commercial
     theater as he composed his first theatrical score for Chadles Calvert's
     The Merchant of Venice and notes how this led to a commission to
     work with Gilbert on *Thespis.*

167. _____. "A New and Original Comic Opera." *Theatre in the
     Age of Irving.* Totowa, N.J.: Rowman and Littlefield, 1981. p. 77-92.

     Gives the history of Gilbert and Sullivan's separate contributions
     to the German Reed Gallery of Illustration program and their joint
     efforts with D'Oyly Carte. Recalls Gilbert's forceful hand in control-
     ling standards of performances, his character-drawing in the evolving
     form of the operas, and Sullivan's enormous contributions to the
     sustained enchantment of the atmosphere.

168. Rowland-Entwistle, Theodore and Jean Cooke. "Sullivan, Sir Arthur
     Seymour (1842-1900)." *Famous Composers* (Brief Biographies
     Series). London: David & Charles, n.d., p. 112-13.

     Gives a one-page biography of this son of an Irish clarinettist. Lists
     Sullivan's main compositions.

169. Sanders, L. G. D. "Jenny Lind, Sullivan, and the Mendelssohn
     Scholarship." *The Musical Times* 97 (September, 1956): 466-67.

     Tells of the involvement of Jenny Lind in establishing the
     Mendelssohn Scholarship and of Arthur Sullivan, a 14 year old
     chorister of Her Majesty's Chapels Royal, who became the successful
     candidate in 1856. Uses correspondence to track Sullivan's progress
     at the Leipzig Conservatory until 1861.

170. Scholes, Percy A. "Sullivan, Arthur S." *The Mirror of Music 1844-
     1944*. London: Novello, Oxford University Press, 1947. Vols. I and
     II, p. 233; 383; 472; and various other pages.

     Presents the story, dispersed throughout the two volumes, of
     Sullivan's career in music with and without Gilbert. Builds a record of
     a century of musical life in Britain as reflected in the pages of the
     Musical Times.

171. Searle, Muriel V. "The Other Sullivan." *Musical Opinion* 96 (March,
     1973): 290-91.

     Observes that serious music, Sullivan believed, was his life's calling,
     yet fickle posterity has never taken him seriously. Traces his life and
     musical career through his compositions apart from and in the G&S
     operas. Notes that perhaps in a sense Sullivan did achieve his
     ambition by making light music *good* music.

172. Shenker, Israel. "Lately of London, Gilbert and Sullivan Make a TV
     Treat." *Smithsonian* 14 (March, 1984): 104-14. Illus., port.

     Chronicles the highlights of the G&S collaboration, the demise of the
     D'Oyly Carte Opera Company, and the $14 million George Walker
     Productions television series that ran on PBS.

173. Short, Ernest. "Gilbert and Sullivan Comic Opera, 1871 Onwards."
     Sixty Years of Theatre. London: Eyre & Spottiswoode, 1951.
     p. 48-60. Illus., plates.

     Examines the individual talents and contributions of Gilbert and
     Sullivan to the artistic products of their partnership and notes how
     the pair restored respect to the English stage. Looks at the staying
     power of the comic operas in the post-WWI era.

174. "Sir Arthur Sullivan, 1842-1900." *Great Composers 1300-1900*.
     Compiled and edited by David Ewen. New York: H. W. Wilson, 1966.
     p. 363-67. Illus. with port., bibl.

     Develops through different periods of his life the biography of this
     "genius of the comic opera" and comments on his successes and
     failures. Emphasizes his contributions to the comic operas with
     Gilbert, but also notes that he did not abandon his activities as a
     "serious" musician. Lists principal compositions classified by type of
     work.

175. "Sir Arthur Seymour Sullivan As an Old Friend Knew Him." *Argosy* 73
     (February, 1901): 1161-67.

     Records the memories and impressions of Sullivan by one who
     counted 25 years of friendship with the composer. Tells of Sullivan's
     pleasure-giving nature, his deep religious feelings, his manner of
     composing, and the fortuitous collaboration with W. S. Gilbert.

176. "Sir William Gilbert and Sir Arthur Sullivan." *National Geographic*
     XCV (April, 1949): 538-39.

     Tells how the G&S operas are as British as roast beef and Yorkshire
     pudding, even though no more oddly assorted pair of artists ever
     collaborated together. Gives a brief career biography of Gilbert,
     Sullivan, and D'Oyly Carte during their light opera period.

177. "Sir William Schwenck Gilbert." *The Dictionary of National Biography,
     The Concise Dictionary*, Part II, 1901-1950. London: Oxford
     University Press, 1961. p. 170.

     Presents a concise, compressed history of Gilbert's life and career,
     listing the titles and dates of his writings and the pertinent events of
     his life.

178. Smalley, George W. "English Men of Letters, Personal Recollections
     and Appreciations." *McClure's Magazine* XX (January, 1903):
     296-306.

     Discusses, among other writers, W. S. Gilbert (p. 302-4), noting his
     celebrity both for humor and ill-humor. Considers those antithetical
     aspects of his personality that brought such public attention, and
     states that the stage owes Gilbert much for his clear conception about
     what he wanted and his firm resolve to do it his way.

179. Stedman, Jane W. "Cousin Hebe: Who Was She?" *The Gilbert and
     Sullivan Journal* 10 (Spring, 1978): 295-96.

     Investigates why Jessie Bond replaced Mrs. Howard Paul in the role of
     Hebe in *H. M. S. Pinafore*. Looks at Gilbert's development of that role
     and at Mrs. Paul's departure.

180. _____. "Kitty's Cookery Book: or, The Gilberts at Table."
     The Gilbert and Sullivan Journal 10 (Spring, 1973): 5-6.

     Describes Lady Gilbert's 1914 cookbook and notes dishes of
     biographical interest (those named for operas, opera characters, and
     prominent personalities). Tells how Gilbert's notorious sweet tooth
     was provided for.

181. "The Story of The Lost Chord." Mentor 16 (February, 1928): 16-17.
     Illus. with ports.

     Reveals how Sullivan composed The Lost Chord as a musical
     monument upon the death of his brother, Frederic. Tells how the
     notes scribbled during the death watches became the song of Mrs.
     Ronalds, whose rendition would bring tears to the eyes of the
     composer.

182. "Sullivan and the Union." The Etude 43 (1925): 620.

     Relates briefly the story of Sullivan's handling of American bandmen's
     demands for higher wages and how, taking the gentle hint from
     Sullivan, they agreed not to charge extra.

183. Sullivan, Herbert and Newman Flower. Sir Arthur Sullivan: His Life,
     Letters, and Diaries. With an introduction by Arnold Bennett. New
     York: George H. Doran, 1927. xii, 393 p., illus. with 31 plates (2 in
     color), ports., facsims., bibl., index.

     Presents a detailed biography of Sir Arthur that draws much of its
     information from his letters and diaries as well as the reminiscences
     of his nephew, Herbert, whom Sir Arthur adopted after the death of
     brother Frederic. Lists Sir Arthur's works as compiled by the
     British Museum.

184. "Sullivan, Sir Arthur Seymour." Baker's Biographical Dictionary of
     Musicians. Seventh edition. Revised by Nicolas Slonimsky. New
     York: Schirmer Books, 1984. p. 2245-46. Bibl.

     Discusses Sullivan's life in regard to his musical works, listing and
     commenting on his major compositions. Includes bibliography.

185. Sutton, Lindsay. "Great Names of the Savoy." The Gilbert and Sullivan
     Journal 9 (January, 1969): 201-2.

     Catalogs some of the great names of the Savoy, starting with the
     original five Savoyards--Barrington, Grossmith, Bond, Temple and
     Brandram. Looks at later Savoyards who made memorable
     contributions to the G&S world of comic opera.

186. Sutton, Max Keith. W. S. Gilbert. (Twayne's English Authors Series).
     Boston: Twayne, 1975. 150 p., bibl., index.

     Shows the range of the works of W. S. Gilbert, who wrote over 70
     works for the stage as well as many short stories, verses, reviews, and
     prose sketches. Deals with Gilbert's early journalism, his plays
     without Sullivan, and the recurrent themes and patterns of action in
     the operas. Includes a chronology.

187. Swayne, Egbert. "Sir Arthur Sullivan as a Boy." *Music* 18 (July, 1900)
      219-32. Illus. (ports.).

      Tells the early-life history of this small, dark, curly-haired boy whose
      singing was noted for its sweetness. Shows how everything in the
      chapel boy's life turned upon music, using excerpts from his letters
      home to indicate both his bent toward hard work and his lighter side.

188. Traubner, Richard. "A Most Ingenious Paradox." *Opera News* 48
      (March 17, 1984): 11-13.

      Notes the 1982 demise of the D'Oyly Carte Opera Company, that
      custodian for over a century of G&S authenticity, and gives a history of
      the company's recent troubles. Prepares us for new interpretations
      and radical rethinkings of the G&S classics.

189. _____. "The Savoy Tradition." *Operetta, A Theatrical
      History.* Garden City, N.Y.: Doubleday, 1983. p. 149-85. illus.

      Follows the careers and examines the artistic products of Gilbert and
      Sullivan from the German Reed entertainments into the remarkable
      D'Oyly Carte Savoy Theatre span of production and popularity, and
      then into the post-partnership years of decline.

190. Trewin, J. C. "Savoy Theatre Centenary." *Illustrated London News*
      269 (October, 1981): 69-70.

      Recalls the highlights of the Savoy's history from its opening in 1881,
      noting the productions of the G&S operas, the reconstruction of the
      theater in 1929, and the D'Oyly Carte Opera Company's revivals.

191. "W. S. Gilbert." *The Bookman* 33 (July, 1911): 463-65.

      Relates several stories which show the readiness of Gilbert's wit and
      the popularity of the catchy lines from the often pirated *Pinafore*.

192. Wade, Wyn and Barbara. "Sullivan and Miss Violet." *The Gilbert and
      Sullivan Journal* 10 (Autumn, 1977): 276-77.

      Tells briefly the life story of Violet Zillah Beddington, who at the age
      of 21 became acquainted in Lucerne with a composer in his
      fifties--Sullivan--and turned down his proposal of marriage.

193. Walbrook, H. M. *Gilbert & Sullivan Opera, A History and a Comment.*
      With a foreword by Sir Henry Wood. Illustrated by H. M. Bateman,
      W. H. Holloway, etc. London: F. V. White, 1922. 154 p., iii, 2 p. of
      plates, illus., bibl.

      Traces the chronological succession of the operas with attention to
      the casting, staging, plots, and reception by critics and audiences.
      Assesses the place these works of wit and harmony hold in the hearts
      of Englishmen.

194. Walker, Richard. "The D'Oyly Carte Company in Wartime." *The Gilbert and Sullivan Journal* 8. Part I (January, 1965): 260-61; Part II (May, 1965): 287-88.

Notes that wars come and go, but that the D'Oyly Carte Opera Company goes on forever. Recounts their activities during the 1939-1945 period.

195. Watson, Iain. "Royal Command." *The Gilbert and Sullivan Journal* 10 (Autumn, 1976): 230-32.

Gives details of the presentation of *The Mikado* in September, 1881, for Queen Victoria at her holiday home, Balmoral, and presents a brief history of Her Majesty's Opera House, Aberdeen, from 1872 to1906.

196. Wearing, J. P. *The London Stage 1890-1899: A Calendar of Plays and Players.* Vol. I: 1890-1896; Vol. II: 1897-1899 and index. Metuchen, N. J. : The Scarecrow Press, 1976. 2 vols., 1229 p.

Presents in chronological order the first-night playbills relating to some 30 major London theaters. Playbills include full title, genre, author(s), name of theater, date and length of run, cast members, and production staff. Gives citations for contemporary reviews.

197. Wells, Walter J. *Souvenir of Sir Arthur Sullivan, Mus. Doc. M. V. O.; A Brief Sketch of His Life & Works.* London: George Newnes, Ltd., 1901. viii, 106 p., illus., facsims (music).

Relates Sullivan's musical talents as a youth, his first successes in London, his association with Gilbert and D'Oyly Carte, the G&S method of work, the success of the operas in England and America, his contribution to the Leeds Festival, and his later works. Lists Sullivan's works.

198. Welsh, R. S. "How *The Lost Chord* Came to be Composed." *The Etude* 56 (July, 1938): 471.

Summarizes the dramatic circumstances of the death of Sullivan's brother, Fred, and the way in which verses of Adelaide Proctor struck a magical note in the composer's soul, resulting in *The Lost Chord*, which rose to heights of fame which Sullivan did not dream of when composing it.

199. White, Eric Walter. *A History of English Opera.* London: Faber and Faber, 1983. 472 p., illus., 32 p. of plates, index.

Develops the history of serious and comic operas in England from the 17th century through the 20th. Devotes one chapter to Gilbert and Sullivan and some national opera schemes of their time. Includes appendix giving the rules and regulations of the Royal English Opera.

200. White, Eric Walter. (compiler). *A Register of First Performances of English Operas and Semi-Operas from the 16th Century to 1980.* London: The Society for Theatre Research, 1983. vi, 130 p.

Presents by annual chronological arrangement the first performances of English operas and light operas. Lists works under name of composer, gives date and name of theater, and supplies name of librettist and occasional short notes. Lists the separate and joint G&S works.

201. _____. *The Rise of English Opera.* Introduction by Benjamin Britten. New foreword by the author. Reprinted from the 1951 edition published by The Philosophical Library, New York. New York: Da Capo, 1972. vi, 335 p., illus., 32 p. of plates, bibl., index.

Presents a sketch of the history of English opera, examines its position today, and discusses the G&S operas in a chapter on abortive national opera schemes to reform the British theater. Includes appendices listing first performances of English operas.

202. Willeby, Charles. "Arthur Seymour Sullivan." *Masters of English Music.* Unabridged republication of the 1893 edition. Boston: Longwood Press, 1977. p. 1-102. Illus, facsims.

Chronicles the life and career of England's most representative musician. Notes his devotion to the money-making lighter and smaller forms of the art to escape the drudgery of teaching. Reviews his involvement in the G&S operas, and analyzes *The Golden Legend, Ivanhoe,* and other serious music.

203. "William Schwenck Gilbert." *The Ridpath Library of Universal Literature.* John Clark Ridpath, Editor-in-Chief. New York: Fifth Avenue Library Society, 1899. Vol. 11, p. 234-37.

Presents a biographical summary, lists major dramatic works, and gives excerpts from his *Bab Ballads* and from *The Wicked World.*

204. Williams, Henry B. "Adapting *Box and Cox.*" *The Gilbert and Sullivan Journal* 9 (January, 1967): 68-9.

Examines the origins, development, and curious history of the Burnand/ Sullivan work, *Cox and Box.* Observes that the new talent that Sullivan found in himself as a composer of comic opera music would eventually demand a librettist of equal genius--W. S. Gilbert.

205. Williams, Richard. "Sail On, *Pinafore.*" *House Beautiful* 95 (July, 1953): 103-4+.

Celebrates the diamond jubilee by retelling the story of how *Pinafore* came to be, how Sullivan worked on the score while in great pain, how Gilbert took complete control of the production, and how the opera became a sensation in England and America.

206. _____."Sullivan and Gilbert." *House Beautiful* 92 (October, 1950): 121+

Tells, upon the 50th year since Sullivan's death, the events of the composer's last few years of life. Discusses his ill health, his feelings of ambivalence about doing "serious" work, the rupture with Gilbert, and the way posterity has considered G&S as equals.

207. _____. "The Town of Titipu Celebrates Its 60th Birthday." *House Beautiful* 87 (August, 1945): 26+

Uses the occasion of the 60th anniversary of *The Mikado's* premiere to discuss its origin, the British nature of the opera that was only costume-deep Japanese, the huge success at the Savoy, and the transporting of a whole company of actors to New York to thwart the American "pirates."

208. Wilson, P. W. " 'It's Greatly to His Credit,' All Agree." *The New York Times Magazine* (November 15, 1936): 12-13. Illus.

Recalls, upon the centenary of Gilbert's birth, the life story of the playwright/librettist who inherited an ill-tempered accuracy from his father. Tells how the tactless young Gilbert failed at law and went on to write ballads, plays and comic operas. Looks at what held the curt, exacting Gilbert and the smooth, easy-going Sullivan together to create the famous operas.

209. Wilson, Robin and Frederick Lloyd. *Gilbert and Sullivan: The Official D'Oyly Carte Picture History.* 1st Edition. New York: Knopf, 1984. 216 p., illus, bibl., index.

Contains photographs, drawings, posters and program materials illustrating G&S operas from the earliest times to the disbanding of the D'Oyly Carte company in 1982.

210. Wolfson, John. *Sullivan and the Scott Russells: A Victorian Love Affair Told Through the Letters of Rachel and Louise Scott Russell to Arthur Sullivan, 1864-1870.* (A Headlion Book). Chichester: Packard, 1984. x, 130 p., illus., bibl.

Draws from approximately 200 love letters from sisters Rachel and Louise Scott Russell to Sullivan to reveal aspects of his personal life during this emerging phase of his musical career.

211. Wood, Roger. *A D'Oyle Carte Album; A Pictorial Record of the Gilbert and Sullivan Operas.* 2nd edition. First published in 1953. Foreword by Bridget D'Oyly Carte. London: Adam and Charles Black, 1958. 68 p., illus.

Presents 82 b&w photographs made in the 1950's of the people carrying on the G&S tradition. Depicts actors and scenes from 11 operas as well as the D'Oyly Carte organization. Summarizes the history and plot of each of the operas.

212. "Work of Gilbert." *The Nation* 92 (June 1, 1911): 562.

   Notes the death of Sir W. S. Gilbert, playwright and librettist, lists his works of poems, plays and operas, and calls him one of the brightest ornaments of the Victorian stage.

213. Wyndham, H. Saxe. *Arthur Seymour Sullivan (1842-1900)*. New York and London: Harper, 1926. xi, 276 p., illus. (music).

   Presents a straightforward chronological account of Sullivan's life, including his collaboration and relationship with W. S. Gilbert.

214. Young, Percy M. *Sir Arthur Sullivan*. New York: W. W. Norton, 1971. xiii, 304 p., illus. (incl music), 16 p. of plates, bibl., index.

   Details Sullivan's life and musical development as he became the white hope of English music, and documents the phases of Sullivan without Gilbert, Sullivan with Gilbert, and Sullivan versus Gilbert. Includes catalog of works with index.

2. Analysis & Criticism

215. Adams, William Davenport. *A Book of Burlesque; Sketches of English Stage Travestie and Parody.* London: Henry and Co., 1891. 220 p. Illus. with ports.

Points out Gilbert's contribution to burlesque, with discussions of his works scattered throughout this book under headings of burlesque of faerie, Shakespeare, modern drama, and opera.

216. _____. "Mr. Gilbert as a Dramatist." *Belgravia* 45 (October, 1881): 438-48.

Calls attention to the extreme neatness of Gilbert's prose dialogue and his verse-production, and selects passages to show this skill. Makes judgment of his serious works written in blank verse, and ranks some of his plays as first class, deserving to bring fame for his invention and perfection of two new species of dramatic writing.

217. Aldford, Edward. "Ancestors of the Operas." *The Gilbert and Sullivan Journal* 9 (May, 1969): 230.

Shows how Gilbert borrowed freely from the stock-pot of his early plays, noting how *Our Island Home* is the parent of both *Pinafore* and *Pirates of Penzance.* Tells how *Iolanthe* is indebted to earlier plays in which Gilbert learned the ABC's of his craft.

218. _____. "Master of the Muse." *The Gilbert and Sullivan Journal* 9 (September, 1971): 381-82.

Extrapolates from observations about librettists in general to form an image of W. S. Gilbert, the dominant personality in the creation of the Savoy operas.

219. Allen, Reginald. "Cox and Box and Bouncers." *The Gilbert and Sullivan Journal* 9 (September, 1967): 116.

Uses correspondence and other documentation in an effort to establish the date of the first performance of *Cox and Box* (1866) and notes the low estate to which F. C. Burnand fell in his stubborn defense of his opinion on the matter.

220. Anonymous. "Mr. Gilbert as a Dramatist." *The Theatre*, (June 26, 1877): Reprinted in *W. S. Gilbert: A Century of Scholarship and Commentary*, John Bush Jones, (ed.), 1970, p. 7-16. See 386.

Reviews the selections in *Original Plays* and evaluates Gilbert's works as readable books as well as staged dramas, judges his considerable command of pure, strong English, and notes his problem with purpose and meaning.

221. Anonymous and "M. B." "Review of The Bab Ballads." *The Athenaeum*, No. 2163 (April 10, 1869). Reprinted in *W. S. Gilbert: A Century of Scholarship and Commentary*, John Bush Jones, (ed.), 1970, p. 3-5. See 386.

Describes the *Bab Ballads* as the dreariest and dullest fun, lacking in real humor and geniality, wooden , and containing not a single thread of interest, and yet curiously capable of a better impression at a second or third glance.

222. Archer, William. "*The Chieftain.*" *The Theatrical 'World' of 1894*. London: Walter Scott, 1895. p. 339-42.

Critiques *The Chieftain* (libretto by F. C. Burnand) as a childish and feeble story, redeemed only by Arthur Sullivan's masterful music. Rates Sullivan as the most polyglot composer who is able to write, with grace and felicity, music in any language under the sun. Includes a playbill.

223. _____. "*The Grand Duke.*" *The Theatrical 'World' of 1897*. London: Walter Scott Ltd., 1897. p. 67-73.

Judges *The Grand Duke* to have two distinct themes, neither of which is satisfactorily worked out. Contends that the opera remains delightful entertainment even though its conception and workmanship do not rank with the best of its predecessors.

224. _____. "*His Excellency.*" *The Theatrical 'World' of 1894*. London: Walter Scott, 1895. p. 289-98.

Critiques *His Excellency*, with its simple and ingenious plot, as a nearer approach to true comic opera as anything Gilbert has done. Notes the absence of the supernatural and "ingenious paradoxes." Looks at Gilbert's cynicism, his being neither a story-teller nor a character-creator, and his remarkable literary faculty. Includes a playbill.

225. _____. "Mr. W. S. Gilbert." *English Dramatists of To-day.*
London: Sampson, Low, Marston, Searle & Rivington, 1882.
p. 148-81. Reprinted in *W. S. Gilbert: A Century of Scholarship and
Commentary,* John Bush Jones, (ed.),1970, p. 17-49. See 386.

Gives a contemporary assessment of W. S. Gilbert as standing foremost
among his contemporaries, examines Gilbert's successes, documents
weakness in his use of blank verse and lack of growth and
development among his characters, and calls the G&S operas the most
characteristic productions of the English stage of the time.

226. "Arthur Sullivan." (Contemporary Portraits, New Series--No. 22).
Dublin University Magazine 94 (October, 1879): 483-91. Illus. with
ports.

Follows the life and career of Sir Arthur through an analysis of his
musical compositions, starting with his *The Tempest* and ending with
his *The Light of the World.* Emphasizes his work separate from the
G&S partnership. Notes the honors bestowed upon him during his
lifetime.

227. Ashley, Leonard R. N. "Gilbert and Melodrama." *Gilbert and Sullivan,*
James Helyar (ed.),1971. p. 1-6. See 354.

Traces and examines the use and abuse of melodrama by W. S. Gilbert,
who himself was something like a character out of melodrama. Shows
that Gilbert, who wrote more than 15 melodramas, mocked the
melodrama throughout his career by using it as the basis for
exaggerated plots and characters.

228. Atkinson, Neville. "A Dying Cult." *Musical Opinion* 90 (July, 1967):
568.

Ponders the persistent popularity of the G&S operas, which have a
super-abundance of Gilbert's nonsense words, a heavy reliance on
cliche, and a killing predictability. Concludes that it is the very
mediocrity and the consistent writing to formula which account for
the extraordinary success of the Savoy operas.

229. Baker, George. "Sullivan Subtleties." *The Gilbert and Sullivan Journal*
9 (May, 1972): 424.

Gives an example of Sullivan's constructional and technical skill from
The Emerald Isle. Cites the music to the entrance of The Lord
Lieutenant as proof of Sullivan's wit, but notes that this is often
erroneously attributed to Edward German, who completed the work
after Sullivan's death.

230. Bargainnier, Earl F. "*Charity*: W. S. Gilbert's 'Problem Play.' " *South Atlantic Bulletin* 42 (November, 1977): 130-38.

Examines *Charity*, the most un-Gilbertian of more than 70 plays, and the reasons for its failure. Labels it essentially a melodrama with a "problem" theme imposed on it. Notes how it was denounced as immoral, and how it anticipated the problem plays of Pinero and Shaw. Cites passages that offended Victorian audiences.

231. _____. "Mr. Gilbert and Mr. Shaw." *Theatre Annual* 31 (1975): 43-54.

Reviews the generally disapproving tone of Shaw's statements about Gilbert's works, and critics' opinions that, although Shaw was snooty toward Gilbert, he was deeply influenced by him. Looks at Gilbert's influence in method, techniques and devices that were used over and over by Shaw, and identifies four principal areas of similarity between their works.

232. _____. "The Operatic Extravaganzas of W. S. Gilbert." *Theatre Annual* 34 (1979): 67-86.

Tells of Gilbert's being the recognized heir of J. R. Planche ́ (1796-1880) and the only one who advanced the form of the extravaganza. Defines *extravaganza* and *burlesque*, lists and gives examples from Gilbert's works, and notes his farewell to the burlesque-extravaganza form with *The Pretty Druidess*.

233. _____. "*Ruddigore*: Gilbert's Burlesque of Melodrama." *Gilbert and Sullivan*, James Helyar (ed.),1971. p. 7-15. See 354.

Shows how Gilbert's original plot for *Ruddigore* is a burlesque of melodramatic plot, convention and characterization. Identifies some of the standard devices and stage conventions that Gilbert burlesques, such as artificial rhetoric, abduction of the heroine, the secret of birth, the patriotic appeal, and others.

234. _____. *W. S. Gilbert and Nineteenth Century Drama.* Unpublished Ph.D. Dissertation. The University of North carolina at Chapel Hill, 1969. 557 p.

Studies Gilbert's career as author and director and his role in the changing drama of the time. Relates how his 71 stageworks cut a cross-section though 19th century theatrical types: burlesque-extravaganza, pantomime, farce, comedy, comedy-drama, melodrama, blank-verse tragedy, and comic opera.

235. Baring, Maurice. "Gilbert and Sullivan." *The Fortnightly Review.* New
     Series. 118 (September, 1922): 422-36.

     Claims that Sullivan's lighter music is so essentially British that, while
     popular, it has taken years to gain serious recognition, and that
     Gilbert's verses, while not great, are neat, lyrical and rhythmical
     enough to be set to music. Quotes from the operas to show the G&S
     combined talents.

236. Beatty-Kingston, Wm. "*Iolanthe; or, The Peer and the Peri.*" *The
     Theatre.* New Series. I (January 1, 1883): 20-8.

     Expresses disappointment as well as surprise, in a critique of
     Iolanthe, that Gilbert's pathos smacks of anger, a passion altogether
     out of place in a "fairy opera," and that his politics are bitterly
     aggressive. Notes symptoms of fatigue in Gilbert's writing but rates
     Sullivan as being without a rival in Europe with his inexhaustible vein
     of melody.

237. _____. "*The Mikado; or, The Town of Titipu.*" *The Theatre.*
     New Series. V (April 1, 1885): 186-90.

     Critiques *The Mikado* upon its premiere as being an extravaganza of
     the old Savoy type. Notes the characteristics of the opera, which are
     ingenious and frequently funny. Praises the author's rhyming, dialogue
     and witticisms. Evaluates the stars, the musical score, and the
     scenery.

238. _____. "*Patience; or, Bunthorne's Bride.*" *The Theatre.*
     New Series. III (June 1, 1881): 352-56. Illus.

     Critiques *Patience* as produced at the Opera Comique. Summarizes
     the plot, praises the sustained humor of W. S. Gilbert, the "quaintest
     and neatest of Latter-Day Paradoxists" and commends Sullivan for the
     high class of compositions which are rife with sweet spontaneous
     melody.

239. _____. "*The Pirates of Penzance; or, The Slave of
     Duty.*" *The Theatre.* New Series. V (February 21, 1885): 80-2.

     Critiques the D'Oyly Carte production of *Pirates of Penzance* with an
     exclusively juvenile cast at the Savoy Theatre in December, 1884.

240. _____. "*Princess Ida; or, Castle Adamant.*" *The
     Theatre.* New Series. III (February 1, 1884): 75-80.

     Critiques G&S's Respectful Operatic Per-version of Tennyson's
     "Princess" as a "great go," likely of success, yet revealing symptoms of
     fatigue in both the words and music. Calls the story dull, deficient in
     incident, and quite forlorn of surprises, and judges the words of some
     songs to be painstaking twaddle and the music rather commonplace.

241. _____. "*Princess Toto.*" *The Theatre* . New Series. IV
     (November 1, 1881): 297-300.

     Critiques the 1881 comic opera (with music by Frederick Clay) to be
     in every respect a meritorious work. Claims the chief charm is
     Gilbert's air of homely and simple consistency that pervades the
     sayings and doings of his quaint personages. Judges Clay's music to be
     melodious but lacking in appropriateness to the absurdities of a comic
     opera.

242. Becker, Philip. "New Light on Three Tower Songs." *The Gilbert and
     Sullivan Journal* 9 (September, 1970): 312-13.

     Examines a full score of Sullivan's *The Yeomen of the Guard* to reveal
     words and music for songs not generally known to exist. Analyzes the
     character and scoring and recommends inclusion in future recordings.

243. Beckerman, Michael. "Arthur Sullivan, *Haddon Hall,* and the Iconic
     Mode." *Comparative Drama* 22 (Spring, 1988): 1-20.

     Analyzes why *Haddon Hall,* with music by Sullivan and libretto by
     Sydney Grundy, has failed to recapture the stage in spite of
     enthusiastic reviews during its initial run of 214 performances.

244. Beerbohm, Max. "A Classic in Humour." *The Saturday Review* XCIX
     (1905): 696-98. Reprinted in *W. S. Gilbert: A Century of Scholarship
     and Commentary,* John Bush Jones, (ed.), 1970. p. 61-7. See 386.

     Evaluates a "new" edition of *Bab Ballads* and pronounces W. S. Gilbert
     not a poet, but a delicious versifier. Probes the quality of silliness
     that distinguishes the *Bab Ballads* as a whole.

245. _____. "Mr. Gilbert's Rentree (and Mine)." *The Saturday
     Review* 97 (May 14, 1904): 619-20.

     Critiques *The Fairy's Dilemma* (1904) as boring and 20 years too late
     to be contemporaneous parody. Notes that, although "Bab" is full of
     intrinsically humorous ideas, his prose is dull and heavy. States that
     without music and Gilbert's verse, the machinery of the humor
     creaked for the reviewer.

246. Binder, Robert. "Gilbert's Other Princess." *The Gilbert and Sullivan
     Journal* 10 (Autumn, 1978): 313-17.

     Critiques and tells the theatrical history of *Princess Toto,* the 3-act
     comic opera by Gilbert with music by Frederick Clay. Concludes that,
     although "the other princess" no longer takes the boards, she makes a
     significant step in Gilbert's development as comic opera librettist.

247. Blom, Eric. "Sir Arthur Sullivan." *The International Cyclopedia of Music and Musicians.* 9th Edition. Oscar Thompson, Editor in Chief. Robert Sabin, Editor, 9th Edition. New York: Dodd, Mead, 1964. Vol. 2, p. 2148-50.

Evaluates Sullivan's musicianship and craftsmanship, notes influence of Schubert and others on the G&S opera music, compares Sullivan to other composers, and discusses his varied musical compositions. Provides a catalog of his works for the theater, grand opera, ballets, incidental music, and oratorios and cantatas.

248. Boas, Guy. "The Gilbertian World and the World of To-day." *English* 7 (Spring, 1948): 5-11.

Starts with a look at the relatively "safe" age of Victorian Englishmen, examines Gilbert as an entertainer who, with no axe to grind, rescued musical comedy from vulgarity, debunks the notion that he was cruel when his only purpose was to make people laugh, and assesses the respective contributions of Gilbert and Sullivan to the operas.

249. Booth, Michael R. "Research Opportunities in Nineteenth-Century Drama and Theatre." *Gilbert and Sullivan,* James Helyar (ed.), 1971. p. 17-23. See 354.

States that theater criticism and scholarship should examine not just the dramas of the time, but the relationships among an audience, its theater, and its dramatists. Raises questions about 19th-century audiences, theater economics, historical judgments, acting as technology, and production technology.

250. Bowman, Walter P. "Gilbert Without Sullivan." *Literary Onomastics Studies* 5 (1978): 3-13.

Focuses on Gilbert's use of names of persons and places in the *Bab Ballads,* and tells how the humor is enhanced by alliteration, meter and rhyme. Shows how, in the comic operas, Gilbert "plagiarizes" his own writings and explains how he gives us a lively presentation of Victorian social and political life. Reprints *The Yarn of the "Nancy Bell"* and *Ellen McJones Aberdeen.*

251. Boyer, Robert D. *The Directorial Practice of W. S. Gilbert.* Unpublished Ph.D. Dissertation. The Ohio State University, 1970. 141 p.

Develops the directorial techniques used by Gilbert in the preparatory and rehearsal stages, shows his general artistic principles and philosophy, and reveals his methods of casting and his techniques of collaboration with Sullivan and other associates.

252. _____. "No Offense Intended: W. S. Gilbert and the Victorian Public." *Theatre Studies* 18 (1971-72): 65-74.

Credits the Savoy operas for destroying public tastes for crude and improper works that stigmatized English theater for the middle class. Discusses the problem of the playhouse, censorship, and the maintenance of good taste on the part of G&S. Concludes that Gilbert's knighthood testifies to his conservative standards as well as to his contributions to the English stage.

253. Bradley, Ian. "Gilbert and Sullivan and the Victorian Age." *History Today* 31 (September, 1981): 17-20. Illus.

Shows how the characters and plots of the Savoy operas provide rich source material for the historian of Victorian Britain, gives examples of the operas' parody of several leading figures and most institutions, and notes that Gilbert's wide-ranging satire was gentle and affectionate.

254. Brailes, Robert. "Colonel, Major, and Duke." *The Gilbert and Sullivan Journal* 9 (September, 1967): 117.

Pictures the bachelors of the 35th Dragoon Guards in *Patience* as they sit in their jolly officers mess, and analyzes the three personalities which catch the eye--Colonel Calverley, Major Murgatroyd, and the Duke of Dunstable.

255. _____. "Dummkopf's *Troilus and Cressida* " *The Gilbert and Sullivan Journal* 10 (Spring, 1973): 11.

Conjectures on Gilbert's use of *Troilus and Cressida*, which he probably had never seen, in his *The Grand Duke*, and raises questions about the casting.

256. Bryant, Sir Arthur. "Perennial Delight." *100 Years of D'Oyly Carte and Gilbert and Sullivan*, 1975?, p. 4-5? (unpaged). Illus. See 143.

Describes the Victorian era in which the Savoy operas first appeared, reports how in the cynical twenties they had little place, examines the happy union of Gilbert's unerring sense of the absurdity of human nature and Sullivan's magical gift of setting words to music, and predicts the operas will be alive in 2075.

257. Buckley, Francis J. "The Music of *Cox and Box*." *The Gilbert and Sullivan Journal* 9 (January, 1967): 70-1.

Makes the point that *Cox and Box* is the music of a fun-loving genius of 24 (Sullivan) who was too diverted by the farcicalities of the plot to trouble about the lyrical shortcomings of the libretto. Looks at his musical contributions that made the little argosy almost awash with melodic booty, ripe for future looting.

258. Burleigh, Diana G. "A Point Little Considered." *The Gilbert and Sullivan Journal* 8 (September, 1965): 307.

Debates whether *The Yeomen of the Guard* is a tragedy, using salient points from Aristotle's definition of tragedy to analyze Jack Point's character and the unities of time, place and action.

259. Burton, Nigel. "*The Yeomen of the Guard*: Apogee of a Style." *The Musical Times* 129 (December, 1988): 656-59. Illus. with ports. and music.

Observes a sudden and unforeseen maturing of Sullivan's style in *Iolanthe* (1882) and traces the process of inserting "serious" elements into the "comic" style until this stylistic fusion was consummated in *The Yeomen of the Guard* (1888). Analyzes stylistic elements and concludes that Sullivan's art had reached its apogee in *Yeomen.*

260. Buxton, Mark. "*Princess Ida* and *Ruddygore*." *The Gilbert and Sullivan Journal* 8 (September, 1965): 301.

Explores reasons why the two operas have had a relative lack of success in their original runs and in modern repertoires. Identifies Gilbert's discounting the drawing power of Grossmith and Barrington by giving them small parts as a factor in the original *Princess Ida.*

261. "Can Gilbert and Sullivan Be Jazzed?" *The Literary Digest* 63 (1919): 29-30.

Raises the issue of suitable interpretations of the G&S comic operas, imagines performers such as Al Jolson and Eddie Cantor as Koko or the Mikado, and gives suggestions for those who would produce the Savoy operas for modern audiences.

262. Cardullo, Burt. "The Art and Business of W. S. Gilbert's *Engaged*." *Modern Drama* 28 (September, 1985): 462-73.

Analyzes Gilbert's intentions in *Engaged*, a savage satire on a society devoted to the pursuit of money. Gives examples of Gilbert's use of disjuncture, contradiction, and reversal. Explains in what ways *Engaged* is both farcical and yet more like verbal comedy than farce.

263. Carrdus, Kenneth. "The Duke's Song in *Patience*." *The Gilbert and Sullivan Journal* 9 (May, 1967): 98-9.

Consults manuscripts in the British Museum to locate and print the missing words to No. 4 song which Sullivan had apparently torn out of Act II in *Patience.*

264. Carrdus, Kenneth and Ian Bartlett. "Sullivan Restored." *Musical Opinion* 90 (May, 1967): 449+.

Shows the process of reconstruction of the vocal line of a lost Sullivan song in *Patience*, given the orchestral accompaniment and Gilbert's lyrics. Raises questions about why Sullivan cut the song and the ethics of rescuing a song which the composer has discarded.

265. Carroll, Charles Michael. "Barataria: An Elusive Operatic Utopia or, The History of Sancho Panza on the Lyric Stage." *Opera Journal* 7 (1974): 7-23.

Documents the evolution of Cervantes' novel, *The Ingenious Gentleman Don Quixote de La Mancha*, through various adaptations, and mentions, in passing, W. S. Gilbert's opera, *The Gondoliers*, whose sub-title *The King of Barataria* was borrowed from Cervantes but which is peopled with his own concept of a topsy-turvy never-never land.

266. Cattermole, Jessie. "Gilbert's Bow in *Fun.*" *The Gilbert and Sullivan Journal* 8 (January, 1962): 93.

Summarizes Gilbert's first few contributions to *Fun* in November, 1861, and notes that the drawings are excellent while the humor seems rather cheap to modern taste.

267. Cecil, David. "Introduction." *The Savoy Operas*. London: Oxford University Press, 1962. Vol. I, p. vii-xvii. See

Points out that the unique Savoy flavor comes from the blending of fantasy of the nonsensical kind to satire, depending on the strict logical working out of a preposterous hypothesis. Notes how sentimentality is incompatible with satire and thus is quickly deflated by Gilbert. Critiques Gilberts weaknesses, such as inconsistency and insensitiveness to taste, and the strength of his satire.

268. Chesterton, G. K. "Gilbert and Sullivan." *The Eighteen-Eighties, Essays by Fellows of the Royal Society of Literature*. Edited by Walter de la Mare (1930). Reprinted in *W. S. Gilbert: A Century of Scholarship and Commentary*, John Bush Jones, (ed.), 1970, p.183-205. See 386.

Analyzes the attitudes of the British people during the epoch and describes how the Gilbertian "nonsense" fits in so well. Traces the influence of the *Bab Ballads* upon the Savoy operas.

269. _____. "The Impenetrability of Pooh-Bah." *The Living Age*
272. Seventh Series LIV. (January 27, 1912): 247-49.

States that Englishmen appreciated Gilbert's satires without
appreciating what he was making fun of--themselves. Uses *The
Mikado* as a symbol of how Gilbert pursued and persecuted the evils of
modern England, but notes that the opera was once forbidden in
England because it was thought to be a satire on Japan.

270. Clinton-Baddeley, V. C. "The Poet & The Theatre." *Words For Music.*
Cambridge at the University Press, 1941. p. 125-47.

Discusses, among others, W. S. Gilbert as an admirable writer of words
(but not a major lyric poet) who combined wit with grace. Gives
examples of songs from the operas to illustrate how he wrote witty
rhythmical words that, with Sullivan's music, had an influence on the
restoration of English song.

271. _____. "W. S. Gilbert." *The Burlesque Tradition in the
English Theatre After 1660.* London: Methuen; New York: Barnes &
Noble, 1952. Reprinted by Methuen Library Reprints, 1973.
p. 114-20.

Calls Gilbert not a satirist, but an extravaganza writer deriving from
Planche. Shows that burlesque was a powerful ingredient in Gilbert's
art, identifies the operas which are comedies salted with burlesque,
and concludes that his circuitous manner stood in the way as a
burlesque writer, but even so, his contribution is great.

272. Coe, Charles N. "Wordplay in Gilbert and Sullivan." *Word Study* 37
(February, 1962): 6-8.

Comments on the effects that Gilbert achieves with rhetorical devices
and figures of speech. Gives examples from his comic operas to
illustrate his use of proverbs, puns, homonyms, cliches, alliteration
and hyperbole.

273. Cole, David C. "The Policy of Contentiousness: Some Non-Literary
Factors Contributing to Gilbert's Theatrical Success." *Gilbert and
Sullivan,* James Helyar (ed.), 1971, p. 25-31. See 354.

Documents how Gilbert's pugnacity and intimidation tended to earn
his plays a more favorable hearing than they might otherwise have
received. Recounts Gilbert's private, public and court battles
against his critics.

274. Cole, David W. "Gilbert's *Iolanthe*." *The Explicator* 29 (April, 1971): Item 68.

Gives a brief note to explain the faery queen's puzzling declaration to Parliament that Strephon shall end the cherished rights you enjoy on Wednesday (Friday?) nights.

275. _____. *W. S. Gilbert's Contribution to the Freedom of the Stage*. Unpublished Ph.D. Dissertation. The University of Wisconsin, 1970. 260 p.

Shows how Gilbert violated Victorian taboos and contended with the official censor and those self-appointed guardians of the public values--the drama critics. Identifies the factors that enabled Gilbert to succeed in spite of his violation of taboos.

276. "*Comedy and Tragedy*." *The Theatre*. New Series. III (March 1, 1884):143-44.

Reviews Gilbert's Original Drama, in One Act (1884) as a capital little play, summarizes the plot, discusses the acting and stage management, and counters opinions antagonistic to the play by other critics.

277. Cook, Albert. "Gilbert · Dodgson · Butler in Nineteenth-Century Britain." *The Dark Voyage and the Golden Mean, A Philosophy of Comedy*. New York: W. W. Norton, 1966. p. 113-36.

Describes the still-royalist and aristocractic empire under Queen Victoria, explains how Gilbert and others discussed social class problems, and takes examples from the G&S operas to show how Gilbert treated appearance and reality to present people in paradox with the mask they wear in society.

278. Cook, Dutton. "*The Palace of Truth*." *Nights at the Play; A View of the English Stage*. London: Chatto and Windus, 1883. p. 90-3.

Critiques Gilbert's "fairy comedy" as an enchanted edifice that, aimed at the dignity of comedy, nearly approaches the early extravaganzas of Planche. Outlines the plot and judges that the literary value of the play may not be sufficient to overcome the dramatic deficiencies.

279. _____. "*Pygmalion and Galatea*." *Nights at the Play; A View of the English Stage*. London: Chatto and Windus, 1883. p. 136-39.

Notes that Gilbert's plots have been found void of interest and his characters lacking in vitality, but that he has displayed an inventiveness with themes not of his devising. Outlines the plot of and critiques *Pygmalion*, which is written in blank verse that is rarely melodious but often terse and bright enough.

280. _____. "*The Wicked World.*" *Nights at the Play; A View of the English Stage.* London: Chatto and Windus, 1883. p. 171-73.

Explains the plot of and critiques Gilbert's fairy comedy, judging it to display considerable ingenuity but to be essentially unsuited for dramatic purposes. States that the long speeches are tedious, the lack of action is oppressively manifest, and the blank verse is sufficiently fluent but "unillumed" by poetic thought.

281. Cooper, Martin. "The Fickle Philistine." *Opera News* 32 (April 20, 1968): 8-12. Illus, port., music.

Appraises Arthur Sullivan as a composer who vacillated between parody and religiosity. Looks at the richness of his harmony, his skill as a contrapuntist, and his efforts at serious composition. Judges Sullivan to be a victim of the British Philistinism of the 19th century.

282. Cottis, Eileen F. "Gilbert and the British Tar." *Gilbert and Sullivan,* James Helyar (ed.), 1971, p. 33-42. See 354.

Looks at drama's treatment of the British Tar as noble savage in whiteface, and compares Gilbert's treatment and techniques to those used in 28 cited plays between 1695 and 1864.

283. Cunliffe, John W. "W. S. Gilbert (1836-1911)." *Modern English Playwrights, A Short History of the English Drama from 1825.* New York: Harper & Brothers, 1927. p. 25-8.

Points out that while Gilbert's earlier comedies of the 1870's were of no permanent signficance, his immense intellectual and artistic superiority was clear in the genre of the comic opera. Uses passages to illustrate how he poked fun at folly and asserts that his satire opened the way for more profound criticism of national life by other playwrights.

284. Danton, George H. "Gilbert's *Gretchen.*" *The Germanic Review* 21 (April, 1946): 132-41.

Gives the plot for *Gretchen,* for which Gilbert acknowledged his debt to Goethe's *Faust* theme, analyzes Gilbert's interest in good and evil, looks at contemporary and modern criticism, and concludes that Gilbert, a class-conscious squire-Tory Victorian gentleman, manifestly never felt the scope of the cosmic forces and titanic strivings of the *Faust* story.

285. Darlington, W. A. *The World of Gilbert and Sullivan.* New York: Thomas Y. Crowell, 1950. xiii, 209 p., illus.

Provides a study of G&S with concentration on Gilbert's contributions and temperament. Evaluates Gilbert's stagecraft, skill with language, and weakness for puns.

286. Davis, Graham. *"Ages Ago* and Seventeen Years Later." *The Gilbert and Sullivan* Journal 8 (January, 1965): 263.

Looks at the *Ruddygore* angle in Gilbert's 1869 German Reed piece, *Ages Ago,* and identifies recognizable resemblances and parallels between the two works.

287. Davis, Reginald G. *In Defence of Gilbert's Ladies.* With a foreword by A. H. Godwin. London: Published by the Author, 1927. 48 p.

Defends, with a staunch Victorian mind-set, the many excellent qualities of Gilbert's female characters who usually have been viewed as simpering maids or crotchety spinsters. Discusses the redeeming points of the female roles in chronological order of the operas in which they appear, and ranks them from most to least favorites.

288. Degen, John A. "Gilbert and the Limerick." *Victorian Poetry* 25 (Spring, 1987): 87-93.

Documents how Gilbert made use of limericks in pure or varied form in the Savoy operas, and explains why their existence has often escaped general notice.

289. DeVoto, Bernard. "G. & S. Preferred." *Harper's Monthly Magazine* 178 (May, 1939): 669-72.

Concludes that the G&S collaboration is one of the highest reaches of 19th-century literature, comments on the quality of intelligence of the works, and claims the greatness of the Savoy operas is that they exist as a dream that is aware of itself.

290. Dingley, R. J. "Gilbert's *Patience." The Explicator* 45 (Winter, 1987): 33-34.

Claims that Gilbert was clearly inviting ribald speculation with his reference to the style of the Bishop of Sodor and Man (Sod. & Man?) in Colonel Calverley's patter song in *Patience.*

291. DuBois, Arthur E. "W. S. Gilbert, Practical Classicist." *Sewanee Review* 37 (January, 1929): 94-107.

Traces the path by which W. S. Gilbert, neither a romanticist nor a realist, became inevitably a classicist. Shows how Gilbert's traits of classicist, humorist and businessman combined to create his success.

292. Dunhill, Thomas F. *Sullivan's Comic Operas: A Critical Appreciation.* London: Edward Arnold; New York: Oxford University Press, American Branch, 1928. 256 p., illus. with music.

Examines Sullivan's musical compositions to defend him against the frequent charges that he was either a negligible writer of music for the uncultured or a genius who frittered away his talents upon ephemeral rubbish such as the G&S comic operas.

293. Duployen, Richard. "Musical Characterisation in *Iolanthe*." *The Gilbert and Sullivan Journal* 9 (January, 1969): 199-200.

Notes that even the critics who snub Sullivan recognize the qualities of the music in *Iolanthe*. Identifies the splendid characterization which can be divided into fairy music, pastoral music and peer's music, and discusses each of these as it appears in the opera.

294. _____. "The Three Princesses." *The Gilbert and Sullivan Journal* 9 (September, 1971): 376-77.

Analyzes how Gilbert adapted Tennyson's poem "The Princess" to his first play, *The Princess,* and into the eighth G&S collaboration, *Princess Ida.* Shows how in Gilbert's "respectful perversion" it was necessary to be unfaithful to Tennyson's work, and yet how he and Sullivan sometimes captured the essence of it.

295. Dyson, J. Peter. "*Waiting for Godot* and *The Mikado:* The Game of Time." *English Language Notes* 18 (September, 1980); 46-8.

Shows how a scene in Samuel Beckett's *Godot* has both verbal and structural links, incorporating a series of dramatic attitudes and procedures, to a scene in the earlier *Mikado.* Establishes Beckett's debt to the form of theater popularized by Gilbert.

296. Eden, David. *Gilbert and Sullivan: The Creative Conflict.* Rutherford, N.J.: Fairleigh Dickinson University Press, 1986. 224 p., illus., bibl., index.

Demonstrates that Gilbert's libretti have a significant autobiographical content that Freudian theories can elucidate, and analyzes Sullivan's musical personality. Points to the differences and difficulties of this creative partnership.

297. "Editorial." [The Mortality of Opera]. *Music and Letters* 41 (July, 1960): 207-10.

Asks what the qualities are that guarantee success for any opera, looks at the curious failures of operas by some great composers, and examines the interesting case of Arthur Sullivan, who saw himself as a serious composer but who was regarded by contemporaries as a composer of trifles--the comic operas.

298. Ellis, James D. *The Comic Vision of W. S. Gilbert.* Unpublished Ph.D. Dissertation. The University of Iowa, 1964. 424 p.

Shows how Gilbert developed a form of fantasy and inversion and created fairy realms or topsy-turvy worlds in which unlikely characters are caught in impossible situations. Reveals how Gilbert discovered a supply of humorous situations by observing the disparity between personal desire and public necessity.

299. _____. "The Counterfeit Presentment: Nineteenth-Century Burlesques of *Hamlet*." *Nineteenth Century Theatre Research* 11 (Summer, 1983): 29-50.

Observes that only in the 19th century did the sub-genre of theatrical burlesque flourish both in print and on amateur and professional stages. Looks at burlesques of *Hamlet* and discusses (among others) Gilbert's clever parody, *Rosencrantz and Guildenstern* (1874).

300. _____. "The Unsung W. S. Gilbert." *Harvard Library Bulletin* 18 (April, 1970): 109-40. illus.

Identifies and reprints with illustrations some of the poems that were never included in any edition of the *Bab Ballads*. Gives background information on the poems and insights into the personality of W. S. Gilbert, the remarkable humorist with little or no sense of humor.

301. Ellis, Theodore Richard III. *The Dramatist and the Comic Journal in England, 1830-1870.* Unpublished Ph.D. Dissertation. Northwestern University, 1968. 396 p.

Demonstrates that many playwrights, including Gilbert, wrote for humor magazines for supplementary income and creative freedom. Traces the playwrights' associations with various comic journals, contrasts humorous treatments to account for the disparity in styles, and examines the relationship between drama and comic journalism.

302. Ewart, Gavin. "Was W. S. Gilbert a Greater Poet Than W. B. Yeats?" *London Magazine* 7 (December, 1967): 29-46.

States that the words Gilbert wrote could not have been better for their purpose, and quotes from the *Bab Ballads* and various operas to show that Gilbert, whose verse sometimes suffered from the rhyme-at-any-price syndrome and whose love songs are only averge Victorian, was nonetheless one of the great comic geniuses of his century and the best poet of his kind England ever produced.

303. Ewen, David. "Sullivan." *Music for the Millions; The Encyclopedia of Musical Masterpieces.* New York: Arco Publishing, 1945. p. 562-64.

Evaluates Sullivan, never an innovator in music, as scholarly and lacking inspiration in his "serious" works but witty and fresh in his comic operas. Cites Dunhill's analysis of Sullivan's style in the opera scores and discusses *The Mikado* in regard to the manner in which the music throughout is neatly characterized.

304. _____. "W. S. Gilbert and 'That Topic of the Age.' " *Gilbert and Sullivan,* James Helyar (ed.), 1971, p. 53-61. See 354.

Tells of Gilbert's spirited battle to end "that topic of the age"--the degradation of the English stage. Examines the deficiencies in actors, authors, managers, and audiences, and looks at Gilbert's consistent efforts to gain control over these elements.

305. Ferrall, Edwin W. "Characters Anonymous." *The Gilbert and Sullivan Journal* 9 (September, 1971): 382-83.

Asks where in literature and theater are there so many important personages unidentified except for their position or occupation as exist in the G&S operas. Looks at several characters whose complete identity is never revealed.

306. _____. "Contraltos--First and Last." *The Gilbert and Sullivan Journal* 9 (January, 1969): 197-98.

Searches for the relative eminence that Gilbert gives the "elderly ladies" of his operas through analysis of the placement of conralto songs. Concludes that whatever else Gilbert did to his "elderly ladies," he made them prominent.

307. Filon, Augustin. "Gilbert." *The English Stage, Being an Account of the Victorian Drama.* New York: Dodd, Mead, 1897. p. 139-55.

Compares Gilbert with Robertson and describes the "naive" irony of the *Bab Ballads,* the cruelness of the farce, *Engaged,* the fantasy of *The Palace of Truth* in which Gilbert is thoroughly at home, and the characteristics of several other Gilbert plays and Savoy operas.

308. Fischler, Alan B. *"Modified Rapture": The Comedy of W. S. Gilbert's Savoy Operas.* Unpublished Ph.D Dissertation. The University of Rochester, 1987. 624 p.

Posits that Gilbert cleaned up not just the theater, held in low esteem by Victorian audiences who believed in subordinating self (and erotic aspirations) to society, but comedy itself. States that his aim was to provide his post-theistic audiences not with ridicule, but rather a catharsis of their misgivings about accepting flawed human authority as a substitute for Providence.

309. Fisher, Judith L. "W. S. Gilbert: The Comedic Alternative." *When They Weren't Doing Shakespeare: Essays on Nineteenth-Century British and American Theatre.* Edited by Judith L. Fisher and Stephen Watt. Athens: The University of Georgia Press, 1989. p. 280-98.

Analyzes Gilbert's *Engaged* to show how this compound of comedy, melodrama and farce is an acerbic wit unlike the comedies of Robertson, Byron and Albery. Points out that Gilbert demands that we see the play as an artifact, that while other wits played with life, Gilbert played with art.

310. Fitzgerald, Percy. "Mr. Gilbert's Humour." *The Theatre.* New Series. IV (December 1, 1881): 339-41.

Analyzes Gilbert's art of humor as lying in a vein of extreme earnestness--a soi-disant simplicity--which attends on such absurdly far-fetched requests. States that Gilbert educated his audiences to his allusions which are so fine they would have gone over people's heads a few years earlier.

311. Flatow, Sheryl. "Risky Business." *Opera News* 51 (May, 1987): 18-20+. Illus.

Discusses the gamble associated with adapting classics, of rewriting and modernizing beloved and enduring works. Uses as examples various modern adaptations of *The Mikado* (*The Hot Mikado, The Swing Mikado*) and *H. M. S. Pinafore* (*Memphis Bound*).

312. Fludas, John. "Nothing Sacred." *Opera News* 43 (March, 1979): 8-9+.

Looks at Gilbert's early, benign desecrations of popular operas of his day and details how his libretto for *Pretty Druidess* (1869) was a burlesque of Bellini's *Norma*. Shows how Gilbert brought grace, wit and true satire to a genre that was generally condemned as "trashy."

313. Ford, Adrian. "The Background to *Princess Ida*." *The Gilbert and Sullivan Journal* 8 (January, 1964): 206.

Looks at the uniqueness of the G&S opera *Princess Ida* and examines the issues of woman's role, Tennyson's aim, and Gilbert's writing of the libretto. Notes discrepancy of interpolated musical numbers and the "tightening" of lines for production.

314. Freeport, Andrew. "Under the Thumb-Screw." *The Gilbert and Sullivan Journal* 8 (January, 1962): 90.

Reviews *The Yeomen of the Guard* to point out that the characters are real, complex people, not the usual Gilbertian puppets, and that the opera is about people and the effect the Tower has on their lives, not about the edifice itself.

315. Frymire, Jack. "Savoy in the Blood." *Music Journal* 26 (March, 1968): 50-1+. Illus.

Observes the influences of G&S on modern musical comedy. Quotes passages from *Oklahoma* to show parallels and similarities between that and *The Mikado*, and discusses *South Pacific, Bye Bye Birdie*, and *Carousel* to indicate structural analogies with some G&S operas.

316. Frymire, Jack and Virginia. "The Savoy Opera: Museum Piece or Modern Parody?" *The Music Journal* 23 (March, 1965): 61+. Illus.

Questions whether the operas, whose charm lies in the parody of Queen Victoria's England, should be presented as exquisitely embalmed museum pieces or in modern versions. Compares two production treatments and concludes that both win, and that the question of style *versus* updating need never arise in G&S.

317. Fulkerson, Richard. "Gilbert's Great Expectations." *Dickens Studies Newsletter* 7 (March, 1976): 12-5.

Tells how Gilbert was the only London playwright in the 19th century to attempt a dramatic version (*Great Expectations*, 1871, never published) of Dickens' famous work, gives a brief sketch of Gilbert's treatment, and analyzes why the play was not a success.

318. Fuller-Maitland, J. A. "Sir Arthur Sullivan." *The Cornhill Magazine* 83 (March, 1901): 300-9.

Considers Sullivan's musical career, begun with a work which at once stamped him as a genius and to which level he rarely rose again. Notes his contribution in helping Englishmen acquire the habit of listening with respect to English music. Points out it was through the astonishing vogue of the comic operas that he got a hearing for English music.

319. Garson, R. W. "The English Aristophanes." *Revue de Litterature Comparee* XLVI (April-June, 1972): 177-93.

Discerns parallels between Aristophanes and W. S. Gilbert through analysis of the themes of some of the Savoy operas. Shows the importance, for both writers, of extravagant fantasy, political satire, theater reform, literary parody, and words as toys. Predicts immortality for both as long as society continues to throw up shams.

320. George, John C. G. "Wilfred Shadbolt's Deleted Song." *The Gilbert and Sullivan Journal* 8 (September, 1961): 76.

Provides from Gilbert's draft manuscript the full version of a lyric, "The kerchief on your neck of snow," that had been intended for Shadbolt. Notes that Sullivan had set it to music, but the music is not now known to exist.

321. "Gilbert, Author of *Pinafore*." *The American Review of Reviews* XLIV (July, 1911): 98-9. Illus.

Notes the death of Sir Gilbert at age 75 on May 29, 1911, and quotes articles from *The Spectator* and *Nation* to estimate Gilbert's works and place in the theater.

322. "Gilbert Without Sullivan." *The Living Age* 270 (July 1, 1911): 50-53.

Judges Gilbert to be short of "Aristophanic" and not a poet to English ears, but possessed of a true ear for lyrical values and the audacity in fitting sense (or nonsense) to sound. Says that the *Bab Ballads*, in spite of their sameness, exhibit the lyricist at his best. Remarks on the high standards he set himself and on the difficulties of the form of drama through which he steered successfully.

323. Godwin, A. H. *Gilbert & Sullivan; A Critical Appreciation of the Savoy Operas*. With an introduction by G. K. Chesterton. Reproduced from the original edition published in 1926 by J. M. Dent, London. Port Washington, N.Y.: Kennikat Press, 1969. xx, 299 p.

Treats the G&S operas analytically and points out aspects of their structure and their characters. Reviews the plots of the 13 G&S operas (excluding *Thespis*) and examines the satire, humor, and logic of Gilbert and Sullivan.

324. Goldberg, Isaac. *Gilbert and Sullivan, A Handbook to the Famous Operas*. (Little Blue Book No. 476). Girard, Kans.: Haldeman-Julius Co., 1923. 87 p.

Shows the first appearance of the peculiar Gilbertian outlook in the *Bab Ballads*, notes how the sham-hating Gilbert aims his shaft at prince or peer alike, and analyzes themes, plots, and characters of the various operas. Tells of Sullivan's veritable genius for translating Gilbert's words into music.

325. _____. *Sir William S. Gilbert, A Study in Modern Satire. A Handbook on Gilbert and the Gilbert-Sullivan Operas*. Boston: Stratford Publishing, 1913. 156 p.

Discusses satire as an ingredient of comic opera and analyzes Gilbert's prose and verse plays and the famous operas. Regards G&S as reformers of the stage and estimates their place in contemporary comic opera.

326. _____. "W. S. Gilbert, 1836-1936." *Stage* 14 (November, 1936): 101-3.

Shows appreciation for the full body of Gilbert's writings that serve to prove him as interesting a character as any he created for the theater. Makes the point that the creator of theatrical topsyturvydom found the model for that realm in himself. Tells how this notable humorist developed a paradoxical humorlessness toward his own works, and traces the roots of Gilbert's grudge against the world.

327. _____. "W. S. Gilbert's Topsy-Turvydom." *Bookman* 67 (April, 1928): 148-52. Reprinted in *W. S. Gilbert: A Century of Scholarship and Commentary*, John Bush Jones, (ed.), 1970, p. 135-46. See 386.

Analyzes Gilbert's personality, temperament, and attitudes by tracing his family history. Shows how Gilbert was neither a good nor representative Victorian; each of "the virtues" on which he prided himself was contested during his lifetime.

328. Golding, Victor. "Creatures of Impulse." *The Gilbert and Sullivan Journal* 10 (Spring, 1973): 9-10.

Transcribes recently discovered lyrics for the trio (Sergeant, Peter, and Pipette) in "a musical fairy tale," *Creatures of Impulse* by Gilbert (with score by Alberto Randeggar), performed at the royal Court Theatre in 1871.

329. _____. "The Evolution of *Utopia Limited*." *The Gilbert and Sullivan Journal* 9 (January, 1968): 134-36.

Identifies the genesis of *Utopia Limited* and traces its modifications from the original draft through some ten versions, noting changes in characters, settings and plot.

330. Goodwin, Noel. "Personal View." *The Musical Times* 101 (September, 1960): 551.

Offers personal opinions about the effects that the 1962 expiry of the G&S copyright may have on the D'Oyly Carte monopoly, on the attempts to give the operettas a "new look," and on the survivability of the G&S classics.

331. Granville-Barker, Harley. "Exit Planche--Enter Gilbert." *London Mercury* 25 (March, April, 1932): I: 457-66; II: 558-73. Also printed in *The Eighteen Sixties*. Edited by John Drinkwater. Cambridge: The University Press, 1932. p. 102-48.

Elaborates on the hall-mark qualities of Planché, the prodigiously industrious writer of extravaganzas, farces, comedies, melodramas, and librettos for opera, and compares the qualities and techniques of that other prolific playwright, W. S. Gilbert.

332. Gray, Donald Joseph. *Victorian Verse Humor: 1830-1870.* Unpublished Ph.D. Dissertation. The Ohio State University, 1956. 278 p.

Claims that Victorian verse humor and Victorian poetry traveled different roads to similar destinations. Notes the roles of Edward Lear, Lewis Carroll, and W. S. Gilbert in creating self-contained structures which seemed to make sense but did not quite do so.

333. Green, Martyn. "It Is Still a G&S World." *The New York Times Magazine* (November 11, 1962): 34-5. Illus.

Looks at the characters from the Savoy operas to show that the people G&S satirized did not die with the last century, but, with their clothes and speech changed but their follies intact, they are all around us today.

334. _____. "A Wand'ring Minstrel Sings of His First Love." *Theatre Arts* 37 (October, 1953): 30-2+. Illus.

Ponders what is going to happen to the G&S operettas when the copyright runs out, notes that they are in public domain in the U.S., comments on some modern adaptations, and recommends that G&S be accorded the reverence due them even as we stand on our heads to enjoy these gems of topsy-turveydom.

335. Grey, Rowland. "The Author of *Pinafore*; Sir W. S. Gilbert As I Knew Him." *The Century Magazine* 84 (October, 1912): 843-52. Illus.

Reminisces, upon Gilbert's death, about the dramatist's audacity in allying wit with purity, his claim to be regarded as a serious poet, his being in his element at Savoy rehearsals, and the legacy of invention, richness of vocabulary and new methods which will cause Gilbert to stand among the makers of the English language.

336. Grushow, Ira. "W. S. Gilbert." *Critical Survey of Drama.* (English Language Series). Edited by Frank N. Magill. Englewood Cliffs, N.J.: Salem Press, 1985. Vol. 2., p. 756-68.

Lists principal dramas, summarizes Gilbert's achievements, gives biographical information, and analyzes his writing, his themes, his satiric thrust, and the individual operas.

337. Guthrie, Sir Tyrone. "On Gilbert and Sullivan." *Monitor, An Anthology.* Huw Wheldon, (ed.). London: Macdonald, 1962. p. 136-41. Illus.

Offers a critique of G&S by one who has produced their operas and who admires them immensely. Claims that neither Gilbert nor Sullivan--alone-- was a great master, that Gilbert didn't aim high and that Sullivan was not known for original expression but for witty and scholarly parody. States that their genius showed as a team.

338. _____. "Should Gilbert Be Cut and Sullivan Swung?" *The New York Times Magazine* (May 3, 1959): 56+. Illus.

Questions whether it is desirable to preserve the G&S works of art without modernized versions and gives the opinion that a mummifying effect would follow such preservation. Identifies the topical nature of the librettos as their worst handicap. Gives a brief biography of G&S and reasons for concern about their utimate survival.

339. _____. "Yeomen, Pirates, and All." *The Listener* LXVII (February 8, 1962): 245.

Gives a brief history of Sir Guthrie's involvement with G&S operas; assesses Gilbert as one who, not a great satirist, chose "sitting ducks" as targets; and judges Sullivan as not highly original but having the good taste to base himself upon good models.

340. Hall, Robert A. "The Satire of *The Yeomen of the Guard.*" *Modern Language Notes* 73 (1958): 492-97. Reprinted in *W. S. Gilbert: A Century of Scholarship and Commentary,* John Bush Jones, (ed.), 1970, p. 217-25. See 386.

Investigates the question of why *The Yeomen of the Guard* does not fit into the general pattern of the other Savoy operas. Analyzes the characters as ordinary human beings rather than the usual G&S characters involved in stock tomfoolery.

341. Hamilton, Edith. "W. S. Gilbert: A Mid-Victorian Aristophanes."
     Theatre Arts Monthly XI (1927). Reprinted in *W. S. Gilbert: A Century
     of Scholarship and Commentary*, John Bush Jones, (ed.), 1970,
     p. 111-34. See 386.

     Describes the times and comedy of 5th-century Aristophanes,
     contrasts the circumstances of England's Victorian era, and judges
     Aristophanes and Gilbert to be quite similar in their essential genius
     and outlook.

342. Hammond, John W. "Gilbert's *Trial by Jury*." *The Explicator* 23
     (December, 1964): Item 34.

     Uses internal evidence to indicate that Gilbert intended this libretto
     to be an inversion of Oliver Goldsmith's "The Hermit." Shows
     similarities between the two works and points out the changes Gilbert
     made to give his satiric poniard an extra thrust.

343. Hankey, Julie. "Quiet, Unpumped and Everyday." *Times Literary
     Supplement.* (August 20, 1982): 901.

     Examines four forgotten stage successes of Tom Robertson to identify
     themes. Examines the astringent and cynical Gilbert (without
     Sullivan), looking at *Engaged, The Palace of Truth*, and several other
     plays to show the extremes of delight and disgust they provoked.
     Concludes that the wittier Gilbert seemed to need a shaping
     hand--perhaps Sullivan's.

344. Hargreaves, H. A. "Sir William Schwenck Gilbert and the Lure of the
     Fairies." *Gilbert and Sullivan*, James Helyar (ed.), 1971. p. 63-70.
     See 354.

     Examines Gilbert's complexity as opportunist, artist, and reformer
     through an analysis of the theme of fallen fairies which Gilbert
     created early and to which he returned four times during his career.

345. Hark, Ina Rae. "Writ of Habeas Corpus: Bodies as Commodities in the
     Bab Ballads." *Victorian Poetry* 26 (Autumn, 1988): 319-36.

     Provides background on body-as-object as a staple of comic
     representation, examines Gilbert's use of objectified bodies as victims
     of deplorable but inevitable human baseness, and looks at examples of
     ballads to show how, secure in his cynicism, Gilbert inscribed the
     commodified bodies into a comic discourse and collected the profits.

346. Harris, Roger. "Another Sullivan ' Trademark.' " *The Gilbert and
     Sullivan Journal* 8 (September, 1964): 247.

     Discusses a device used by Sullivan in which the orchestra
     recapitulates a theme previously heard only in the vocal part. Gives
     examples from the operas of the use of this "trademark."

347. _____. "The Artistry and Authenticity of the Savoy
     Overtures." *Gilbert and Sullivan,* James Helyar (ed.), 1971. p. 71-6.
     See 354.

     Defends Sullivan against the charge that his musical overtures were
     "perfunctory pot-pourris," shows the means by which Sullivan raised
     the artistic merit of the overtures, and discusses the overtures of
     most of the G&S operas.

348. _____. *"Patience--A* Dickens Ancestry." *The Gilbert and
     Sullivan Journal* 8 (May, 1965): 286.

     Gives reasons for thinking that the spiritual ancestry of the *Bab
     Ballad* "The Rival Curates" (and thus *Patience*) was from the first book
     by Charles Dickens, "Sketches by Boz." Pulls examples from Dickens
     and Gilbert to show the likelihood that Dickens' story provided the
     germ for Gilbert's characters and plot.

349. Hayter, Charles. *Gilbert and Sullivan.* (Modern Dramatists Series).
     New York: St. Martin's Press, 1987. xii, 186 p., 8 p. of plates, illus.,
     bibl., index.

     Gives an overview of the collaboration and the theatrical background.
     Analyzes several of the operas (*Mikado, Sorcerer, Pinafore, Patience*)
     and looks at *Gondoliers* as a retreat from satire. Assesses the operas'
     continued appeal to modern audiences.

350. Head, Thomas G. *Contract to Please: A Study of the Plays of W. S.
     Gilbert.* Unpublished Ph.D. Dissertation. Stanford University, 1970.
     139 p.

     Explains how Gilbert always thought of himself as a popular dramatist
     with a contract to please all classes of society. Shows how he
     simplified his characters to make them fit into a melodramatic mode.
     Traces his continued use of plots from his melodramas into his Savoy
     operas.

351. _____. "Gilbert, Sothern, and *The Ne'er-do-Weel.*"
     Nineteenth Century Theatre Research 4 (Autumn, 1976): 63-72.

     Summarizes the plot of *The Ne'er-do-Weel,* which Gilbert did not
     include in his collected works, and follows the complex set of
     circumstances that determined the play's form. Analyzes the many
     factors that contributed to the "complete failure" of the play.

352. _____. "Rank and Value in the Plays of W. S. Gilbert."
    Gilbert and Sullivan, James Helyar (ed.), 1971. p. 77-84.
    See 354.

    Examines Gilbert's intrigue with the theme of the foundling who
    miraculously finds out his true identity and is restored to his
    birthright. Looks at the concept of egalitarianism which was often
    motivated by self-interests, as with Sir Joseph in *H. M. S. Pinafore*.

353. Helperin, Ralph. "What's In a Name? Plenty!" *The Gilbert and
    Sullivan Journal* 9 (September, 1968): 178-79.

    Aims at the *raison d'etre*, the inner meaning, of the character whose
    appellation has never been satisfactorily explained: Ko-Ko in *The
    Mikado*. Submits slang expressions, of which Gilbert must have been
    aware, as a logical explanation so patly Gilbertian that it must be true.

354. Helyar, James (ed.). *Gilbert and Sullivan*. Papers Presented at the
    International Conference. Foreword by John Bush Jones. University of
    Kansas, 1970. Lawrence: University of Kansas Libraries, 1971.
    228 p.

    Presents a collection of 19 scholarly papers on the works and careers
    of Gilbert and Sullivan. Provides a record of the kinds of approaches
    that serious students and practitioners have begun to take to the
    study of G&S.

355. Henkle, Roger. "Hood, Gilbert, Carroll, Jerrold, and the Grossmiths:
    Comedy From Inside." *Comedy and Culture, England 1820-1900*.
    Princeton, N. J.: Princeton University Press, 1980. p. 185-237.

    Discusses the comic tone of the Victorian era, shows that Gilbert was a
    man bound by the anxieties and predilections of the affluent middle
    class, and examines the erratic flights of looniness that possess the
    secret lives of Gilbert's little people in the *Bab Ballads*.

356. Henshaw, N. W. "Gilbert and Sullivan Through a Glass Brightly." *The
    Texas Quarterly* 16 (Winter, 1973): 48-65.

    Identifies the salient features of Gilbert's style as paradox, inversion,
    incongruity, elegant absurdity, and sturdy common sense. Uses
    passages from the operas to focus on themes and techniques. Shows
    how Gilbert's characters, if they turn enough logical somersaults,
    will land right-side-up and will muddle through somehow.

357. Henshaw, W. A. "Gilbert's Opera *Ruddygore*." *The Texas Quarterly* 21 (Autumn, 1978): 108-23.

Analyzes how the characters in *Ruddygore* (the original version and spelling) handle their motives and roles as Gilbert turns moral order inside-out and every ideal and principle topsy-turvy in this most cynical (and yet cheerful) of the Savoy operas. Shows how the characters accept their fates without anxiety or shame in the face of absurdity.

358. Higbie, Robert. "Conflict and Comedy in W. S. Gilbert's Savoy Operas." *South Atlantic Bulletin* 45 (1980): 66-77.

Clarifies how Gilbert, unlike the satirist, treats conflicts in such a way that absolves us of the need to take them seriously, but also shows that there is a satiric edge in Gilbert. Identifies his techniques of under-cutting the sentimental and poetic, of preventing us from identifying too closely with his characters, and of blithe acceptance of contra-diction, all of which allow us to laugh at the conflicts they present.

359. Higgins, Regina Kirby. *Victorian Laughter: The Comic Operas of Gilbert and Sullivan.* Unpublished Ph.D. Dissertation. Indiana University, 1985. 209 p.

Explores the G&S comic operas with special regard to their great popularity among the Victorian middle class. Shows how Gilbert soothed the social fears and hopes of the newly affluent middle class.

360. Hilton, George W. "Early Thoughts for *The Gondoliers*." *The Gilbert and Sullivan Journal* 9 (January, 1969): 136.

Raises questions for research on the possibility of a rejected plot for *The Gondoliers*. Bases its plea for enquiry upon an American newspaper report of a plot for a forthcoming Savoy opera which seems to point to W. S. Gilbert as the librettist.

361. Hindle, E. B. "W. S. Gilbert, Playwright and Humorist." *Manchester Quarterly* 14 (January, 1885): 55-85.

Starts with a little personal history, examines the literary outputs from 1861 on, analyzes Gilbert's sense of humor in his poems, and discusses the various plays written before the G&S partnership and also the operas. Lists all of Gilbert's plays.

362. Hope-Wallace, Philip. "Who Stands Along?" *100 Years of D'Oyly Carte and Gilbert and Sullivan*, 1975? p. 6-7? (unpaged). Illus. See 143.

Asks the question: Is Sullivan on the way back? Looks at the changing tastes, at Sullivan's strength in eclecticism, the long neglect of his serious music, and the possibilities of modern generations developing a renewed appreciation of his "appropriate" music.

363. Howes, Frank. "Sullivan, Mackenzie, Cowen and Smyth." *The English Musical Renaissance*. London: Secker & Warburg, 1966. p. 50-67. Illus.

Observes that, outside the Savoy operas, little of Sullivan's work has survived, implying a lack of seriousness toward his art. Claims the root of his trouble was the infection of his music by his church training. Notes that the operas are another matter; Gilbert was salt, Sullivan sweet, and neither artist was successful without the other.

364. Huberman, Jeffrey H. "The Development of a Full-Length Farce." *Late Victorian Farce*. Ann Arbor, Mich.: UMI Research Press, 1986. p. 7-39, illus.

Examines Gilbert's two "entirely original farcical comedies," *Tom Cobb* and *Engaged*, looks at the devices used (farcical language, puns, accents, jokes, etc.), and notes the reception by British critics and audiences.

365. Hudson, Lynton. "Cyclones and Anticyclones." *The English Stage 1850-1950*. Westport, Conn.: Greenwood Press, 1972. p. 98-122.

Notes a remarkable resemblance between Gilbert's *Engaged* and Oscar Wilde's *The Importance of Being Earnest*, discusses the "heartless cynicism" and parallel scenes in both plays, and quotes Bernard Shaw's notice that in Wilde's play there is something inhuman enough to have been written by Gilbert.

366. Hughes, Gervase. "Bernard Shaw and *Utopia Limited*." *The Gilbert and Sullivan Journal* 8 (September, 1965): 300-1.

Analyzes Bernard Shaw's notice of *Utopia Limited*, published in *The World* four days after the first performance. Looks at Shaw's compliments and strictures, and considers Shaw's qualifications as music critic as well as drama critic.

367. _____. *The Music of Arthur Sullivan*. Reprint of the 1960 edition published by Macmillan, London. Westport, Conn.: Greenwood Press, 1973. vii, 180 p., illus. with music, index.

Provides a biographical survey of Sullivan alone and with Gilbert. Undertakes a comprehensive study of Sullivan's music as a whole, looking at the operettas and at Sullivan's weaknesses in perspective against the background of his sound musicianship. Includes index to Sullivan's compositions.

368. _____. "Sullivan." *Composers of Operetta.* New York:
St. Martin's Press, 1962. p. 187-99. illus. with music.

Rates Sullivan as standing head and shoulders above other British
composers of operettas, looks at the influences upon his music,
examines the qualities of the music in his works, and follows his
misfortunes as well as his successes.

369. Hunt, Marjorie Kate. "Moralisings in *H. M. S. Pinafore.*" *The Gilbert
and Sullivan Journal* 9 (September, 1968): 183-84.

Observes that Gilbert concocted a pottage of versified moralizing in
the Corcoran-Buttercup duet, and offers sources of epigrams,
proverbs, and fables in *Pinafore,* suggesting the breadth of Gilbert's
reading.

370. Hyde, Derek G. "A Real Red Herring?" *The Gilbert and Sullivan
Journal* 8 (September, 1961): 77.

Considers that in *Ruddigore* Gilbert may have aimed his shaft not at
the melodramatic stage, but at religious hypocrisy. Notes that Gilbert,
who hated hypocrisy and who backed his words with deeds, may have
over-stepped the mark by attacking the hypocritical standards of the
day.

371. "*Iolanthe*--Gilbert's Immortal Libretto." *Current Opinion* 55 (August,
1913): 97-101.

Explains why the G&S operetta, *Iolanthe,* remains perennially young,
how Gilbert was a prophet, and why there is room for a chapter on
G&S in any history of the English drama. Reprints several pages of
the dialogue from *Iolanthe.*

372. Isaacs, Lewis M. "W. S. Gilbert." *The Bookman* 16 (October, 1902):
150-57.

Examines Gilbert as a playwright, looking at the originality of design
of his opera librettos as well as his ability to catch the popular fancy
with his dramas. Discusses Gilbert's skill with dialogue, sense of
dramatic proportion, and literary workmanship.

373. "*Ivanhoe* at the Royal English Opera." *Spectator* 66 (February 7, 1891):
201-02.

Presents the contemporary critical judgment that the merit and
beauty of Sullivan's grand opera far outweigh its structural defects.
Recounts the disparagement of Sullivan for frittering away his talents
on comic operas and expresses the view that *Ivanhoe* deserves to
succeed.

374. Jacobs, Arthur. "Exit Sullivan; *Utopia* and *The Grand Duke*--the Last of
      G & S." *The Listener* 122 (December 7, 1989): 44-5.

      Uses the final programs of the British Radio 2's G&S series to reflect
      upon the *diminuendo* finale to the celebrated collaboration. Notes the
      wordiness and tiredness that set in these last two G&S operettas.

375. _____. "A Fair ' Trial '?" *Musical Times* 118 (October,
      1977): 814.

      States that *Trial by Jury* bears a special place in the canon, being the
      first G&S stage production associated with D'Oyly Carte. Observes
      ways that the music is different from that in following operas.
      Identifies a newly found autograph score that may help solve some
      puzzles about the composer's intentions.

376. _____. "The Mask of *The Mikado*." *Opera* 37 (August, 1988):
      882-86. Illus. with music.

      Shows how, in the most popular and longest-running of the Savoy
      operas, Gilbert adopts an allegorical mask. Explains that the pretty
      prose, the delicate steps, the exotic costumes, and even the
      characters' names have a more familiar application and interpretation.
      Looks at the familiar tunes and the plot of *The Mikado*.

377. _____. "*Mikado* and *Fledermaus*." *The Listener* LXVIII
      (December 13, 1962): 1028.

      Compares the approaches to operetta of the contemporaries G&S and
      Johann Strauss, and discusses Offenbach, who was the link between
      them. Observes differences and similarities in musical styles, and
      emphasizes that the greatest difference between Sullivan and Strauss
      was: Gilbert!

378. _____ . "Sullivan: A New Chapter." *Opera* 28 (March, 1977):
      239-42.

      Contradicts the notion that Sullivan is a fixed and well-defined figure,
      claiming that his life-story has not been properly told. Identifies
      treasure-troves of literary and musical materials that should occupy
      the researcher for years, and urges a re-scrutiny of the composer's
      career.

379. _____. "Sullivan, Gilbert, and the Victorians." *The Music
      Review* 12 (May, 1951): 122-32.

      Discusses how Sullivan's music lives today even if ignored by many
      cultured musicians, analyzes his non-theatrical output, tells how
      Gilbert's libretti both fettered and helped Sullivan, and evaluates
      Sullivan's musical achievements and his place in Victorian society.

380. Jenkins, William D. "Swinburne, Robert Buchanan, and W. S. Gilbert:
      The Pain Was All But a Pleasure." *Studies in Philology* 69 (July, 1972):
      369-87. Illus.

      Contends that Gilbert's model for Bunthorne in *Patience* was not Oscar
      Wilde, but rather Algernon Charles Swinburne, and the model for the
      "idyllic poet" Grosvenor was Robert Buchanan. Compares the
      sado-masochism of *Patience* to the pleasure/pain link of Swinburne
      and Grosvenor's dreadful doggerel to the highly moral stuff Buchanan
      contrived to publish.

381. Jones, John Bush. "Gilbert and His Ballads: Problems in the
      Bibliography and Attribution of Victorian Comic Journalism." *Studies
      in Bibliography* 25 (1972): 217-25.

      Identifies bibliographic problems relating to misstatements on dates
      by secondary sources, on attribution by external or internal evidence,
      and on reliance on works by Searle (see 972), Bulloch (see 912-913),
      and Ellis (see 600, 926). Raises questions about the overall method-
      ology in doing bibliographic studies on the Victorian era.

382. _____. "Gilbertian Humor: Pulling Together a Definition."
      Victorian Newsletter 33 (Spring, 1968): 28-31.

      Finds inadequate the common labelling of Gilbert's humor as
      "topsy-turvy (inversion) and builds on William Archer's identification of
      a strong logical faculty as the basis of the humor. Examines plots and
      characters to show that the method of humor-through-logic is the real
      basis for the comic inversion we call Gilbertian.

383. _____. "Gilbert and Sullivan's Serious Satire: More Fact
      Than Fancy." *Western Humanities Review* 21 (Summer, 1967):
      211-24.

      Refutes statements in an article by Paul J. Revitt in the *Western
      Humanities Review* (see 460) and examines Gilbert's use of comic
      methods--specifically satire and irony--for his far-reaching serious
      purposes and ends.

384. _____. "In Search of Archibald Grosvenor: A New Look at
      Gilbert's *Patience*." *Victorian Poetry* 3 (1965): 45-53. Reprinted in
      W. S. Gilbert: A Century of Scholarship and Commentary, John Bush
      Jones, (ed.), 1970. p. 243-56. See 386.

      Analyzes the poetry from *Patience* in an effort to identify the
      prototypes of the two rival poets, Bunthorne and Grosvenor.
      Concludes that Grosvenor's character is a composite of familiar
      aspects of the persons and poetry of William Morris and Coventry
      Patmore.

385. _____. "Mr. Gilbert and Dr. Bowdler: A Further Note on
     Patience." *Victorian Poetry* 12 (Spring, 1974): 65-66.

     Introduces a piece of evidence suggesting that Gilbert based the role
     of Grosvenor on an outlook, an attitude, a frame of mind, rather than
     on the earlier supposed persons of William Morris and Coventry
     Patmore. See 384.

386. _____. *W. S. Gilbert: A Century of Scholarship and
     Commentary.* Edited and with an introduction by John Bush Jones.
     Foreword by Bridget D'Oyly Carte. New York: New York University
     Press, 1970. xix, 321 p., bibl.

     Presents a collection of 18 articles and studies, written by major
     literary and drama critics, published between1869 and the 1960's
     and not easily available to Gilbert students. Articles of reminiscence
     and biography are not included.

387. Kennedy, Michael. "(Sir) Arthur (Seymour) Sullivan." *The New Oxford
     Companion to Music.* Denis Arnold, General Editor. Oxford and New
     York: Oxford University Press, 1983. Vol. 2., p. 1772-73. illus.

     Notes that Sullivan contributed to English music a distinctive style of
     light opera (with Gilbert); outlines his musical career; and comments
     on Sullivan's fertile ecclecticism and gifts for melody, parody and wit.

388. Kester, Dolores Ann. *Shaw and the Victorian "Problem" Genre: The
     Woman Side.* Unpublished Ph.D. Dissertation. University of Wisconsin
     (Madison), 1973. 457 p.

     Shows that the changes in Victorian law about women affected literary
     structure for 50 years before Shaw began his career. Considers
     statutory reforms after the 1830s and traces developments in the
     tradition of the literary "problem" genre with attention to such figures
     as Tennyson, W. S. Gilbert, Ibsen, and others.

389. Kirby, Harry L., Jr. "The Influence of Sancho's Barataria Adventure in
     the Gilbert and Sullivan Comic Opera *The Gondoliers.* " *Neohelicon* 9
     (1982): 233-42.

     Asserts that the plot of *The Gondoliers* (1889) was ingeniously
     adapted from Sancho Panza's adventure (Part II, *Don Quixote*). Looks
     at the origin of the place name, Barataria, and at the devices,
     techniques and roles of the G&S opera that indicate the fundamental
     influence of Sancho's adventure.

390. Kline, Peter. "Gilbert & Sullivan: Is It Opera?" *Opera Canada* 20, n. 3 (1979): 22-4.

Follows the efforts of Sullivan, the fair-haired prophet of the new English music in Victorian times, to keep English opera from dying out. Analyzes Sullivan's limitations as a "serious" composer, the superiority of his work with Gilbert, and the reasons why G&S opera has never gained proper recognition as part of the canon of true operatic literature.

391. Knight, G. Wilson. "Transitional." *The Golden Labyrinth, A Study of British Drama.* New York: W. W. Norton, 1962. p. 298-307.

Tells how, at the end of the 19th century, England's national imagination was enjoying a "renaissance." Speaks of the "buoyancy" of the G&S melodic dramas and their mastery of the sadistic by melody. Analyzes the human cruelty and sadistic complex in *The Mikado, Yeomen of the Guard,* and other operas.

392. Kresh, Paul. "Confessions of a Gilbert and Sullivan Addict, or, The Unrepentant Savoyard." *HiFi/Stereo Review* 18 (February, 1967): 51-8.

Describes the effects of G&S productions on the author as a growing boy and as an adult "addict." Analyzes why Gilbertian characters, lyrics and plots hold us enthralled.

393. Kresky, Jeffrey. "A Note on Gilbert by Sullivan." *The Music Review* 44 (May, 1983): 116-20. Illus. with music.

Analyzes how Sullivan achieved his musical rhythms when setting Gilbert's operetta verse, which is almost always strictly regular both in line-length and internal line-rhythm as well as rhyme-scheme. Rates Sullivan's Gilbert-inspired music above that of other composers of similar style and bent.

394. Kronenberger, Louis. "A Note on Gilbert and Sullivan." *The Thread of Laughter, Chapters on English Stage Comedy From Jonson to Maugham.* New York: A. A. Knopf, 1952. p. 203-8.

Explains how the English stage had become "stagey" and lagged seriously behind literature until the triumph of G&S's satire opened the way for the restoration of comedy. Appraises Gilbert as far from inspired as a librettist and a comparative failure at prose, but possessed with a gift for extravaganza and satirical nonsense.

395. Krutch, Joseph Wood. "The Creative Muddle." *The Nation* 143
     (October 24, 1936): 480+.

     Contends that Gilbert was, on the subjects of politics, morals and
     manners, completely muddled, having no consistent point of view.
     Claims Gilbert's paradoxes and sense of antithesis were the product of
     his not having the slightest idea what he was.

396. Lamb, Andrew. "*Ivanhoe* Revived at Last." *The Gilbert and Sullivan
     Journal* 10 (Autumn, 1973): 53-4.

     Evaluates Sullivan's *Ivanhoe* for its shortcomings in Sturgis' libretto, its
     complexity, its over-compression of material, and its lack of character
     development, upon its 1973 staging, the first in over 60 years.

397. _____. "A Tradition--and an Anomaly." *The Gilbert and
     Sullivan Journal* 9 (January, 1969): 196-97.

     Searches for the reason for the single anomaly of casting in the D'Oyly
     Carte tradition, an approach in which one seems to be watching the
     same characters regardless of whether the setting is Japan, Venice, or
     Rederring.

398. Lambton, Gervase. *Gilbertian Characters and a Discourse on W. S.
     Gilbert's Philosophy.* With a preface by Viscount Cecil of Chelwood.
     London: Philip Hall, 1931. 118 p.

     Analyzes the characters from *Yeoman of the Guard, Mikado*, and
     Pinafore, looks at the aesthetes and miscellaneous heroes and
     heroines, and presents short essays on topics such as Ugliness,
     Respectability, Snobbery, Modesty, and the English Girl.

399. Landis, John H. "The Music of *Utopia Limited.*" *The Gilbert and
     Sullivan Journal* 8 (May, 1965): 283-84.

     Rates the music of this opera (conceived in the most bitter years of
     both author and composer) as exhibiting excellent craftsmanship,
     taste and orchestration. Analyzes, song by song, each of the musical
     numbers and asserts that the vocal and orchestral writing is brilliant
     and indicative of the progress Sullivan had made in refining his style
     over the years.

400. Lassowsky, Jaropolk. *The Dramtic Function of Poetic and Musical
     Forms in a Savoy Opera Prototype (Vols. I & II).* Unpublished Ph.D.
     Dissertation. The Ohio State University, 1981. 839 p.

     Analyzes each discrete number in *H. M. S. Pinafore* to test two main
     perceptions: (1) The smallest structural dimensions which contain
     phonetically realistic word settings and the middle dimensions which
     please from a purely musical standpoint, and (2) formal coherence at
     the largest dimension achieved almost paradoxically without
     discarding the discrete numbers characteristic of the genre.

401. Lauterbach, Charles E. "Taking Gilbert's Measure." *The Huntington Library Quarterly* LXIX (February, 1956): 196-202. Reprinted in *W. S. Gilbert: A Century of Scholarship and Commentary*, John Bush Jones, (ed.), 1970. p. 207-15. See 386.

Calculates the "measure pay" to determine how much Gilbert was paid for his contributions of humorous verse, drama, drama criticism, and quips to the comic journal, *Fun.*

402. Lawrence, Elwood P. "The Banned *Mikado:* A Topsy-Turvey Incident." *The Centennial Review* 18 (Spring, 1974): 151-69.

Relates how the British government, preparing for an official visit by Prince Fushimi of Japan in 1907, banned all performances of G&S's *The Mikado.* Looks at the effects and effectiveness of the ban, the attitudes of Parliament and the press, and Gilbert's reaction.

403. _____. "*The Happy Land:* W. S. Gilbert as Political Satirist." *Victorian Studies* XV (December, 1971): 161-83.

Examines the contribution of W. S. Gilbert, writing under the pseudonym of F. Latour Tomline, to the 1873 sensation, *The Happy Land.* Analyzes Gilbert's political satire and traces both his negative and positive attitudes that mark him as a confirmed conservative.

404. Liebman, Arthur M. *The Works of W. S. Gilbert: A Study of Their Aristophanic Elements and Their Relationship to the Development of the Nineteenth and Twentieth Century British Theatre.* Unpublished Ph.D. Dissertation. New York University, 1971. 219 p.

Considers the philosophical ideas, intellectual outlook and methods of dramaturgy in the works of W. S. Gilbert as they relate to the comedies of Aristophanes, and evaluates Gilbert's contributions to the development of 19th- and 20th-century British drama.

405. Lynn, Harold W. "Topsy-Turvydom Refuted." *The Gilbert and Sullivan Journal* 10 (Spring, 1978): 297-98.

Contends that W. S. Gilbert has often been unjustly accused of creating dramatic situations which are illogical or topsy-turvy. Uses *H. M. S. Pinafore* to refute these charges and to show that Gilbert should be lauded as a dramatist who saw life as it was and described it with ultimate realism.

406. Mackenzie, Sir Alexander C. "The Life-Work of Arthur Sullivan."
     Sammelbande der Internationalen-Musik Gesellschaft. Jahrgang III,
     Heft 3. (1902): 539-64.

     Makes a survey of Sullivan's compositions to show that church and
     stage, the concert, platform and drawing room all had their share of
     his contributions. Comments on specific examples of his wide range
     of compositions and alludes to his talents of directness and
     conciseness of musical speech.

407. Macy, John. "Her Majesty's Jesters." *The Bookman* 73 (April, 1931):
     146-57.

     Examines how comic literature, journalism, and theater in general
     treated the gloomy Victorians in Merry England. Analyzes Gilbert and
     Sullivan's unique contributions in satirizing the conditions of the
     Englishman who had so much dignity he could afford to be silly.

408. Magill, Frank N. (ed.). "W. S. Gilbert." *Critical Survey of Drama.*
     (English Language Series). Englewood Cliffs, N.J.: Salem Press, 1985.
     Vol. 2, p. 756-68.

     Lists principal dramatic works, chronicles the comic opera
     achievements with Sullivan, and presents a biography of W. S.
     Gilbert. Analyzes each of the major Savoy operas, enunciating their
     topsy-turvy premises, the reduction of character and plot to a
     formula, Gilbert's ability as a lyricist, and his efforts to educate a
     generation of middle-class theatergoers to receive witty comedies.

409. Manheim, Leonard. "Strephon's Tipsy Lout': To Cut or Not to Cut."
     Gilbert and Sullivan, James Helyar (ed.), 1971. p. 107-11. See 354.

     Discusses the reasons that in Act II of *Iolanthe* a recitative and song
     for Strephon are usually deleted in versions of the libretto and the
     score after the 1882 version.

410. McElroy, George. "Meilhac and Halévy--and Gilbert: Comic Converses."
     Gilbert and Sullivan, James Helyar (ed.), 1971. p. 91-105. See 354.

     Considers the differences between Gilbert and his French
     predecessors whose works provided a source and challenge. Notes
     the antithetical nature of plots, characters, and comic methods.

411. _____. "Whose *Zoo;* or, When Did *Trial* Begin?" *Nineteenth
     Century Theatre Research* 12 (1984): 39-54.

     Documents historical events, dates and theatrical news items to form
     the basis for conjecture about whatever became of an announced
     forthcoming 2-act play by Sullivan, and when and how did *Trial by Jury*
     come into the picture.

412. McMullen, E. Wallace. "An Onomastic Review of Gilbert and Sullivan."
     Literary Onomastics Studies 1 (1974): 28-39.

     Analyzes titles of Gilbert's 14 Savoy operas (5 of which have alliter-
     ation) and 180 of his characters (of which 14 are alliterate). Shows
     how Gilbert was adept at exploiting word-sounds and how he used
     many acoustical tricks in choosing names. Selects examples from *The
     Mikado* to show how names can signify the personality of the
     character.

413. Meares, J. W. S. "An Old Addiction." *The Gilbert and Sullivan Journal*
     9 (January, 1969): 198-99.

     Observes that once one has an addiction for the Savoy operas, almost
     everything literary, political, or historic will call up some reference to
     the operas. Gives examples of ways we should use G&S as we explore
     the other arts.

414. _____. "Amongst the Blindfold Marriages." *The Gilbert and
     Sullivan Journal* 9 (May, 1967): 99-100.

     Joins the argument concerning how much of Vincent Wallace's opera,
     Maritana, W. S. Gilbert cribbed for *The Yeomen of the Guard*. Notes
     that Gilbert frequently parodied literature and theater, and identifies
     one case where the author believes there is a strong link to *Maritana*.

415. Meares, Stan. "*Ivanhoe*: Behind the Question-Marks." *The Gilbert and
     Sullivan Journal* 9. Part I (January, 1971): 339-40; Part II (May,
     1971): 352-54.

     Examines the issues about Sullivan's *Ivanhoe* (1895) being "grand'
     opera and being a "failure." Identifies problems of plot, Sullivan's
     responsibility, and various appraisals by critics.

416. _____. "A Victorian Legacy." *The Gilbert and Sullivan
     Journal* 10. Part I (Autumn, 1973): 57-8; Part II (Spring, 1974): 87-8.

     Analyzes act-by-act the strengths and weaknesses of Sullivan's opera,
     Ivanhoe, upon its revival. Judges that there is nothing to suggest
     it is "grand opera," recalls that Sullivan was an artistic compromiser,
     and suggests that *Ivanhoe* warrants occasional revivals.

417. Meisel, Martin. "Political Extravanganza: A Phase of Nineteenth-
     Century British Theatre." *Theatre Survey* 3 (1962): 19-31.

     Contends that, censorship notwithstanding, both topical and general
     politics had an important place in 19th-century English theater, and
     discusses, along with other playwrights, Gilbert's political satire and
     his battles with the censor over *The Happy Land*, which ridiculed not
     only exalted personalities but the whole ministerial system.

418. Midwinter, Eric. "W. S. Gilbert: Victorian Entertainer." *New Theatre Quarterly* 11 (1987): 273-79. Illus.

Analyzes the ingredients of the G&S operas which contributed to their popular success, describes the veritable industry of spin-offs which they generated, and assesses their contribution to the development of the "musical play." Notes that the musical plays, to which Sullivan contributed his inimitable scores, were careful and calculated blends of the theatrical resources Gilbert could command.

419. "Mr. Gilbert's New Play." *The New York Times* (December 31, 1871): 5.

Critiques Gilbert's mythological comedy, *Pygmalion and Galatea*, as displaying freshness of fancy and cleverness of manipulation. Claims any lack of success will be due to the subtleness of the theme, rather than to any deficiency of skill, of this blank verse play. Summarizes the story and lists the cast of the Haymarket Theatre production.

420. Mitchell, Jerome. "Sullivan's *Ivanhoe*." *The Walter Scott Operas, An Analysis of Operas Based on the Works of Sir Walter Scott.* [University]: The University of Alabama Press, 1977. p. 189-200, illus. with music and plates.

Analyzes Sir Arthur Sullivan's only full-fledged opera, *Ivanhoe* (with libretto by Julian Sturgis), which ran for over 150 consecutive performances in 1897, but generally has not seen revival since 1910. Gives historical information and contemporary reviews by critics.

421. Moulan, Frank. "The Humor of Gilbert and Shaw." *The Theatre* 31 (March, 1920): 158-60.

Reviews, from an actor's point of view, how Gilbert created the serio-comic role which was fun for both tragedian and comedian. Compares Gilbert's satiric perception with that of Shaw and tells the difference between a Gilbert audience and a Shaw audience.

422. "Mrs. Langry's Appearance and Gilbert's New Piece." *The New York Times* (January 2, 1882): 2.

Notes the first performance of *Foggerty's Fairy* at the Haymarket Theatre, critiques Mrs. Langtry's skills, and gives a negative review of Gilbert's farce in three acts. Claims the play is tedious, the humor grim, and, without Sullivan's music, Gilbert's dramatic *Bab Ballads* is unbearable. Gives a synopsis of the story of the play.

423. Munich, Adrienne A. " 'Capture the Heart of a Queen': Gilbert and
     Sullivan's Rites of Conquest." *The Centennial Review* 28 (1984):
     23-44. Illus.

     Argues that a basic conflict between powerful women and threatened
     patriarchal structures, embodied in the formulaic ritual of the G&S
     operas, was made particularly acute by the monarchy of Queen
     Victoria. Analyzes the arbitrary, irrational, jealous older woman of the
     operas as she demonstrates some resemblances to the popular image
     of the Queen.

424. "Musings Without Method." *Blackwood's Magazine* 190 (July, 1911):
     121-28.

     Reflects upon the life of the late W. S. Gilbert, the pitiless logician who
     was a plagiary of himself, and upon his pedestrian muse, dramas in
     blank verse, farce and satire, and the genius of his comic opera. Notes
     how he was more inspired with the comic spirit than anyone of his
     time and how his operas will interpret the Victorian age for historians
     in years to come.

425. Newey, Fred. "The Justice of Ahrimanes." *The Gilbert and Sullivan
     Journal* 10 (Autumn, 1977): 274.

     Judges that Gilbert victimized poor Mr. Wells in *The Sorcerer* when
     the decision was made he must die, this being a clear case of
     exploitation of the worker by the capitalist class and quite unnecessary
     according to the Book of Ahrimanes which provides the alternative of
     marriage.

426. Newman, Ernest. "Gilbert and Sullivan Operas." *The Living Age* 303
     (November, 1919): 433-36.

     Notes that Gilbert's success was not with professional writers, but the
     commoner who could enjoy the mechanical humor and too
     obvious verbal wiles. States that Sullivan made a small gift go far,
     scoring successes in humorous pieces but often failing in serious
     settings.

427. Newman, Jay. "Dimensions of Gilbert's Comedy." *The Gilbert and
     Sullivan Journal* 10 (Spring, 1980): 380-82.

     Investigates whether Gilbert's comedy is "classic" by analyzing his
     plots, characters, thought, diction, melody and spectacle.
     Concludes it is time to stop thinking of Gilbert as a mere critic of
     contemporary foibles and to recognize him as a multi-talented
     craftsman working in a classical literary tradition.

428. _____. "The Gilbertianism of *Patience*." *Dalhousie Review* 65 (Summer, 1985) : 263-82.

Speaks to the problems of interpreting (and modernizing) Gilbert's works, examines the plot of *Patience*, explains what the Aesthetic Movement was all about, takes on the question of Gilbert's models for Bunthorne, and examines Gilbert's purposes in the opera.

429. Newton, A. Edward. "A Dialogue Between Father and Son." *Atlantic Monthly* 131 (May, 1923): 591-604.

Uses the device of a conversation between father and son to comment on the plots, characters and lyrics of the various operas. Reminisces about the lives and personalities of G&S and about the various performances and productions of the operas.

430. Nicol, P. G. "Bab and His Ballads." *The Gilbert and Sullivan Journal* 9 (May, 1971): 358-59.

Argues that knowledge of the *Bab Ballads* is necessary to a full understanding of Gilbert's wit and fancy, traces the publication history of the ballads, and reviews *The Bab Ballads* by James Ellis (ed).

431. _____. "Sergeant Meryll's Song." *The Gilbert and Sullivan Journal* 9 (September, 1968): 180.

Reflects the modern interest in the song which Gilbert wrote for Sergeant Meryll, "A laughing boy but yesterday," that was deleted almost immediately after the first night of *The Yeomen of the Guard*. Prints the full words of the song and ponders the unknown fate of the orchestral score.

432. Nicoll, Allardyce. "Gilbert and Albery: Plays of the Seventies." *A History of English Drama 1660-1900. Vol. V: Late Nineteenth Century Drama 1850-1900*. Cambridge: The University Press, 1962. p. 132-47.

Traces the development of Gilbert's plays from *Dulcamara* through *Utopia, Limited*, identifies people and influences that shaped his writing, and uses passages from selected plays to reveal his techniques and aims.

433. Nightingale, Benedict. "Dramatist Dancing in Fetters." *New Statesman* 103 (January 29, 1982): 22-3. Illus.

Makes the point that G&S have become synonymous with all that's antiquated in the theater, notes the impishness of Gilbert's sniping at the Queen and others in power, and yet claims that there is much worth salvaging in the G&S works.

434. Noble, Karen Lavergne. *A View of Topical Adaptation of Gilbert and
     Sullivan Operettas.* Unpublished D. M. A. Dissertation. University of
     Washington, 1979. 290 p.

     Surveys and evaluates major topical adaptations of G&S operettas in
     the United States from 1911 through 1978 to measure the effects of
     innovations in staging, production, and topical references.

435. Parrott, Ian. "Arthur Sullivan (1842-1900)." *Music and Letters* 23
     (1942): 202-10.

     Argues that Sullivan, who is regarded as being "two distinct men"
     because he composed both "respectable" church music and
     "disrespectful" light opera, should be judged on the best works of each
     kind. Considers the unevenness of Sullivan's writing and identifies
     some of its characteristics which stand out.

436. _____. "*Iolanthe*." *Music Review* 34 (February, 1973):
     55-7. Illus. (with music).

     Rates the music of *Iolanthe* as an almost flawless masterpiece and
     urges critics not to dismiss Sullivan as a minor, not very original
     composer. Analyzes songs from the opera to show Sullivan's
     creativity.

437. Pascal, Roy. "Four Fausts: From W. S. Gilbert to Ferruccia Busconi."
     German Life and Letters 10 (July, 1957): 263-65.

     Comments on several modern versions of the Faust myth, including
     Gilbert's *Gretchen* (1878), which properly belong in a book entitled
     "The Misfortunes of Faust." Summarizes the plot of *Gretchen* to show
     how Gilbert turned Goethe's play into a crudely sentimental, crudely
     moralistic drama characteristic of the English tradition.

438. Payne, Anthony. "Sullivan." *The Musical Times* 108 (August, 1967):
     721-22.

     Notes that Sullivan's superb knack for setting Gilbert's metrical
     felicities has overshadowed the foundations of his serious orchestral
     music. Uses the occasion of a performance of the pre-G&S *Symphony
     in E* to sample and analyze the type of work Sullivan always dreamed of
     creating.

439. Perry, Henry Ten Eyck. "The Victorianism of W. S. Gilbert." *The Sewanee Review* 36 (1928): 302-9. Reprinted in *W. S. Gilbert: A Century of Scholarship and Commentary*, John Bush Jones, (ed.), 1970, p. 147-56. See 386.

Suggests that Gilbert's ideas were those of a conservative Victorian. Notes Gilbert's complacency with the Victorian regime and acceptance of British institutions even while making mild fun of their shortcomings and absurdities.

440. "Ph.D." *The Nation* 98 (March 19, 1914): 288.

Briefly reviews Gilbert's musical-comedy output, analyzes the nature of his self-made male characters, and states the hope that further inquiry will produce a Ph.D. thesis on this topic.

441. Phelps, Alice. "Gilbert & Sullivan As Required Literacy." *Music Journal Annual* (1967): 48+.

Points out why the ingredients unique with G&S constitute a complete art form, and argues the benefits of promoting the operas. Lists, with addresses, 21 official G&S societies.

442a."The Pirates of Penzance; or, Love and Duty." *The Theatre.* New Series. I (February, 1880): 107-9.

Reproduces the play-bill of the opera as first it was produced in makeshift fashion (for copyright purposes) at the Royal Bijou Theatre, Paignton. Summarizes the plot and comments on the difficulty of critiquing the play due to its hasty and imperfect performance.

442b."The Pirates of Penzance; or, The Slave of Duty." *The Theatre.* New Series. I (May 1, 1880): 305-9.

Observes the crowd of obstinate obstructionists who lay down a barrier of discontent about dramas and notes that two dramatic writers --Robertson and Gilbert--are firm enough in their saddles to overcome this. Notes the trial of criticism which Gilbert is undergoing and assesses *Pirates* as such a success that it will quiet the malcontents.

443. Pope, T. Michael. "Gilbert and Sullivan." *The Bookman* 61 (January, 1922): 207-8.

Observes that Gilbert has many followers but no successor in English comic opera. Recalls that Gilbert revived the English musical play, gave it a new form, and invested it with a dignity never attained before or since. Notes the serious purpose underneath the frivolities of his plays.

444. Powell, G. H. "The Gilbertian Libretto." *Temple Bar* 125 (January, 1902): 36-40.

Discusses Gilbert's pleasing nonsense and penetrating absurdity, the monotony of his plots in which every English child seems to have been changed at birth, and the application of the term "Aristophanic" to the ironical attitude characteristic of the topical or quasi-political libretti.

445. Prestige, Colin. "Elixir of *The Sorcerer.*" *The Gilbert and Sullivan Journal* 9 (May, 1970): 297-300.

Reveals that W. S. Gilbert based the plot of *The Sorcerer* (1877) upon one of his short stories, "An Elixir of Love." Details the history and plot of the short story and comments on how Gilbert adapted the thin material into material suitable for the stage.

446. _____. "Il Desdichado--The Disinherited Opera." *The Gilbert and Sullivan Journal* 10 (Autumn, 1973): 55-6.

Critiques Sullivan's "romantic opera," *Ivanhoe*, noting that the Sturgis libretto put Sullivan into a hopeless straightjacket, but that the orchestrations are a joy.

447. _____. "*Ruddygore*--With a ' Y '." *The Gilbert and Sullivan Journal* 8 (January, 1962): 92.

Asks why, in 1887, Gilbert selected a title that incurred the wrath of Victorian England. Conjectures that Gilbert outwardly directed his satire at transpontine melodrama, but beneath the surface was tilting at Shakespeare, wanting the acclaim accorded to *Hamlet*.

448. _____. "The Vocabulary of Aestheticism." *The Gilbert and Sullivan Journal* 10 (Spring, 1981): 421-22.

Identifies four kinds of verbal fun in *Patience* and discusses in particular the many examples of high flown language, medieval words and phrases, and aesthetic words and phrases. Points out that in this opera Gilbert's satire was both verbal and visual.

449. _____. "*The Yeomen of the Guard* Topsy-Turvy." *The Gilbert and Sullivan Journal* 8 (September, 1963): 186.

Describes the "dark clouds" passing over the Savoy scene in 1888 with pressures on Sullivan to eschew the frivolities of comic opera. Tells how Gilbert borrowed topsy-turvy features and worked them in this opera despite his yielding to the request to write a more serious opera.

450. Priestley, J. B. "From *Patience* to Pooter." *English Humour*. London: Heinemann, 1976. p. 91-99.

Discusses briefly W. S. Gilbert, that deft hand at witty or waggish lyrics, uses lines from *Patience* to show good bantering (but rubbish as far as satire goes), and denies Gilbert a secure place among English humorists while acknowledging that he did a service to late Victorian England as a comic librettist who inspired the best composer England ever had.

451. "*Pygmalion and Galatea*." *The Theatre*. New Series. III (January 1, 1884): 48-50.

Reviews a revival of Gilbert's Original Mythological Comedy and discusses the diametrically opposed views of critics and author. Cites Gilbert's assessment of this play and the ill-fated *On Guard* some years after the first productions.

452. Quiller-Couch, Arthur. "W. S. Gilbert." *Studies in Literature*, Third Series (1929): 217-40. Reprinted in *W. S. Gilbert: A Century of Scholarship and Commentary*, John Bush Jones, (ed.), 1970. p. 157-81. See 386.

Presents ten mini-essays on the art, the works, the personalities, and the inter-relationships of Gilbert and Sullivan.

453. Reed, Donald A. "Gothic Gilbert and Sullivan." *The Gilbert and Sullivan Journal* 8 (September, 1962): 120.

Gives the opinion that *Ruddigore* contains many Gothic touches and that Gilbert intended the opera, at least partly, as a satire on the Gothic romances.

454. Rees, Terence. "Burnand's Bandits." *The Gilbert and Sullivan Journal* 9 (May, 1968): 161.

Analyzes the Burnand/Sullivan two-act operetta *The Contrabandista* (and its revision 27 years later as *The Chieftain*) in regard to its origins, its very ordinary and unduly static plot, its characters, and its music.

455. _____. "Sullivan's *The Zoo*." *The Gilbert and Sullivan Journal* 9 (January, 1967): 74-5.

Peruses the score of Sullivan's little known "musical folly" to reveal some details of his methods and devices. Provides a brief biography of *The Zoo's* short life on the boards and Sullivan's own disappointed assessment of its potential.

456. _____. *Thespis, A Gilbert and Sullivan Enigma.* London: Dillon's University Bookshop, 1964. 150 p., Illus., index.

Traces the events leading to the performance of *Thespis* at the Gaiety in 1871, responds to the notion that *Thespis* was a failure, conjectures about the nature of the lost music, and presents a text that is thought to get as close as possible to the one performed in 1871 under Gilbert's personal supervision.

457. _____. "*Thespis* and Its Little Book." *The Gilbert and Sullivan Journal* 9 (September, 1971): 374-75.

Observes that the libretto to *Thespis*, having been hurried to the printer, was notoriously inaccurate as sold to the public. Cites the demand for the "little book" in the lighted auditoriums and ponders why the libretto came to be released in such a flawed state.

458. _____. "W. S. Gilbert and the London Pantomime Season of 1866." *Gilbert and Sullivan*, James Helyar (ed.), 1971. p. 149-73. Illus. See 354.

Describes the pantomime Christmas season of 1866 and lists (by title, author, place and date of first performance) 15 pantomimes and four extravaganzas. Investigates Gilbert's anonymous contribution to several of these works.

459. Rence, Robert Irving. *The Burlesque Techniques Employed by James Robinson Planché in His Dramatic Works and Their Relationship to the English Burlesque Tradition Between Joseph Fielding and W. S. Gilbert.* Unpublished Ph.D. Dissertation. University of Minnesota, 1967. 239 p.

Discusses Planché's techniques and methods of achieving the burlesque mode and describes the similar spirit of nonsense in Gilbert's works. Shows how Gilbert maintains the continuity from Planché through the use of puns, couplets, comic names, parodies of songs, and new lyrics to well-known songs.

460. Revitt, Paul J. "Gilbert and Sullivan: More Seriousness than Satire." *Western Humanities Review* 19 (Winter, 1965): 19-34

States that in all of Gilbert's libretti something is topsy-turvy, but beneath each situation is the Victorian principle that departure from the established order is fatal. Cites several operas to support the claim that Gilbert was probing seriously, not satirically. Concludes that, on the surface, it is clean fun, but fundamentally it is serious.

461. "The Revolutionary Satire of W. S. Gilbert." *The Living Age* 311
     (December 24, 1921): 795-98.

     Claims that Gilbert did more to cut away the props of the old world,
     to hasten that revolution in thought and manners, than did any who
     deliberately preached against the established order. Selects passages
     from the Savoy operas to show his onslaught upon politicians, the
     army, the law, and the ever-increasing flow of titles and official
     appointments of his time.

462. Reynolds, Richard R. "Gilbert's Fun with Shakespeare." *Mosaic* 9
     (Summer, 1976): 167-72.

     Shows that Gilbert, who pronounced Shakespeare's plays to be
     "ridiculously bad," found lines from the Bard to provide himself with
     ready material. Provides examples to show instances of parallel
     dialogue and to prove that Gilbert knew Shakespeare's plays
     thoroughly, using bits and pieces of them repeatedly for delightful
     comedy.

463. Rich, Alan. "Gilbert & Sullivan: Their Sun Never Sets." *The Music
     Journal* 23 (March, 1965): 60+.

     Examines those qualities which cause the G&S operas to have such
     vitality--Gilbert's texts full of zany joy in playing with words, his great
     weapon of satire, and Sullivan's brilliance in composing music on a
     level of operatic satire to match Gilbert's words.

464. Rogal, Samuel J. "The Hymn Tunes of Arthur Seymour Sullivan."
     Gilbert and Sullivan, James Helyar (ed.), 1971. p. 175-94. See 354.

     Provides historical and biographical information to show why Sullivan's
     often forgotten work as a writer of hymn tunes is important for
     understanding his full range of creative powers. Lists hymn tunes
     associated with Sullivan.

465. _____. " 'Onward, Christian Soldiers': A Reexamination."
     The Hymn 39 n. 1 (1988): 23-30. Illus. with music.

     Looks at the chronological and historic context of "Onward, Christian
     Soldiers," the hymn for which Arthur Sullivan composed the music.

466. Rowell, George. "The Return to Respectability." *The Victorian Theatre, A Survey.* Second Edition. Oxford: The Clarendon Press, 1978. p. 75-102. Bibl.

Discusses (among others) Gilbert and Sullivan, noting how in tone their work reflected clearly the growing refinement and respectability of the Victorian audience. Tells of Gilbert's apprenticeship in the traditional forms of mid-Victorian drama and his success with comic opera that has made the Savoy opera and Victorian theater almost synonymous. Includes a play-list.

467. _____. "Shaw and the Savoy Operas. *The Gilbert and Sullivan Journal* 9 (January, 1967): 77-8.

Refers to Bernard Shaw's generally known lack of interest in the G&S operas, but reveals evidence that there was a more active connection between Shaw and both Gilbert and Sullivan than was previously assumed.

468. Sahai, Surendra. "William S. Gilbert." *English Drama 1865-1900.* New Delhi: Orient Longman Ltd., 1970. p. 34-66.

Analyzes Gilbert's skills with lyrics, satire, irony and humor in the G&S operas, and examines his efforts as a developing playwright before his partnership with Sullivan.

469. Sawyer, Newell W. "Robertson, Gilbert, and a New Social Consciousness." *The Comedy of Manners from Sheridan to Maugham.* (A Perpetua Book). New York: A. S. Barnes, 1961. p. 64-94.

Explains how Tom Robertson and W. S. Gilbert brought the trinity of drama, acting and staging into harmonious operation, considers the under-current of social criticism that pervades the Gilbert plays and comic operas, and judges the indebtedness of English 19th-century comedy to these two showmen.

470. Schonberg, Harold C. "Two Victorians." *New York Times.* (January 15, 1961): Section 2, X-9.

Claims that Sullivan composed the only music worth talking about in a bad musical age, that the G&S partnership was unique in its chemical reaction that fizzed even as the two men looked upon each other with suspicion, and that the plot is the least consideration in a G&S opera. Says that G&S reflect their age and, in their satire, transcend it.

471. Seeley, Paul. "The Japanese March in *The Mikado.*" *Musical Times*
     126 (August, 1985): 454-56. Illus.

     Gives the history and evolution of the chorus song "Miya sama" which
     heralds the arrival of the Mikado and Katisha in Act II. Speculates how
     Sullivan discovered and modified the Japanese song for *The Mikado.*

472. "Serious Sullivan." *Music and Musicians* 25 (April, 1977): 18-19.

     Notes the traditional view that Sullivan was the musical equivalent
     of the clown wanting to play Hamlet and looks at efforts to give him
     the recognition he deserves. Chronicles the organization and efforts
     of the "Sir Arthur Sullivan Society" and at the choices of some of his
     serious music for revival.

473. Shaw, Bernard. "Sullivan." *The Great Composers, Reviews and
     Bombardments.* Edited by Louis Crompton. Reprinted from the
     Constable Standard Edition of Bernard Shaw's plays and prose.
     Berkeley: University of California Press, 1978. p. 326-33.

     Offers three of Shaw's criticisms on Sullivan, Gilbert and Sullivan, and
     the opera *Utopia, Limited.*

474. Sherlock, Ceri. "Here's a How-de-do!" *Opera News* 48 (March 17,
     1984): 8-10. Illus.

     Considers the transferability and viability of G&S for the small screen
     through the dozen operas filmed for video by Brent Walker
     Productions and aired on PBS. Examines the production philosophies
     and the quality of the finish products.

475. Sherr, Richard. "Schubert, Sullivan, and Grove." *Musical Times* 121
     (August, 1980): 499-500.

     Presents a transcription of Sullivan's "Notes on Schubert's Overture in
     Italian Style"--one of his few writings on music--and judges Sullivan,
     that great parodist, as having misunderstood the "put-on" nature of
     Schubert's style.

476. Shore, T. H. G. "Medicine in the Operas." *The Gilbert and Sullivan
     Journal* 10 (Spring, 1979): 337-38.

     Observes the various allusions of a medical or allied nature scattered
     throughout the operas and less well-known plays of Gilbert. Ties in
     these references to Gilbert's having a retired naval surgeon for a
     father and suffering himself from gout for many years.

477. Sichel, Walter. "The English Aristophanes." *The Fortnightly Review* XCVI (October, 1911): 681-704. Reprinted in *The Living Age* 271 (Dec 23, 30, 1911): 747-54; 778-87. Reprinted in *W. S. Gilbert: A Century of Scholarship and Commentary*, John Bush Jones, (ed.), 1970, p. 69-109. See 386.

Compares Aristophanes and W. S. Gilbert as poet-ironists who mocked the foibles of their societies. Uses selections from Gilbert's operas and dramas to illustrate how he used irony and paradox to earn his fame.

478. Silverman, Richard S. "Longfellow, Liszt, and Sullivan." *The Music Review* 36 (November, 1975): 253-60. Illus. with music.

Analyzes and evaluates the cantatas by Liszt and Sullivan that were based on Longfellow's *The Golden Legend*. Notes that, although Sullivan's work was highly praised at the time, posterity has not treated him with accuracy and has forgotten that Sullivan wrote music of power, beauty and sensitivity.

479. Siney, Marion C. "Victorian England Through Gilbert's Eyes." *Michigan Quarterly Review* 2 (Spring, 1963): 94-101.

Uses passages from the comic operas to show how Gilbert reflected views of the Victorian public on the usefulness of the royal family, the lack of reform in The House of Lords, the efficacy of the judicial system, the leadership of the Armed Forces, and the self-satisfaction and complacency of Englishmen.

480. "Sir Arthur Sullivan." *The Outlook* 6 (November 24, 1900): 528.

Reflects upon the life of the late Sir Arthur who, although not a great and earnest musical artist, brought wholesome pleasure to millions. Concludes that at times one *Utopia, Limited* is worth fifty *Tannhausers*, and that Sullivan caught the elements of the population for which he wrote.

481. "Sir Roderic and Sir Ruthven; Textual Changes in the Ghost Scene." *The Gilbert and Sullivan Journal* 8 (September, 1962): 126.

Examines Gilbert's pre-production prompt copy of *Ruddygore* to quote a duet deleted prior to the first night in 1887. Looks at other deletions and changes made before production.

482. "(Sir) W(illiam) S(chwenck) Gilbert 1836-1911." *Twentieth-Century Literary Criticism*. Edited by Sharon K. Hall. Detroit, Mich.: Gale Research, 1980. Vol. 3, p. 206-20. Bibl.

Prints excerpts from criticism of W. S. Gilbert by 15 authorities between 1869 and 1975. Gives an introductory biography of Gilbert and lists his principal works.

483. Smith, Geoffrey. *The Savoy Operas: A New Guide to Gilbert and Sullivan.* New York: Universe Books, 1985. 236 p., illus., bibl., index.

Offers biographical and historical information along with analysis of the Gilbert and Sullivan canon. Summarizes and discusses in detail each of the operas and contrasts the original productions with later versions.

484. Smith, Patrick J. "W. S. Gilbert and the Musical." *Yale/Theatre* 4 (Summer, 1973): 20-6.

Depicts Gilbert as a master versifier who must stand as godfather to a whole line of English and American lyricists. Shows how Gilbert interwove song and story into a unity, looks at his weaknesses in creating rounded characters, and examines his techniques of word use that, with Sullivan's music, planted the seeds for future musicals.

485. Stanton, Stephen S. "Ibsen, Gilbert, and Scribe's *Bataille de Dames.*" *Educational Theatre Journal* 17 (March, 1965): 24-30.

Documents how Ibsen and Gilbert drew upon the plot structure of the French "well-made" play in general and Augustin-Eugene Scribe's *Bataille de Dames* (1851) in particular. Points out similarities between Scribe's play and Gilbert's *Engaged* (1877) in which some of Scribe's devices are used and in which the Scribean triangle is reversed.

486. Stedman, Jane W. "Boz and Bab." *The Dickensian* LVIII (September, 1962): 171-78.

Notes how the mid-century stage teemed with Dickens adaptors and imitators, cites references to Dickens by his admirer, W. S. Gilbert, in various Savoy operas, and analyzes Gilbert's never-published play, *Great Expectations,* and reasons for its lack of success on the stage.

487. _____. "A Dose from *Dulcamara.*" *Opera News* 25 (December 24, 1960): 17-19.

Examines Donizetti's opera, *L'Elisir D'Amore,* and notes how Gilbert joined the trend toward travesties of currently popular operas by knocking off a burlesque of it in 1866. Follows Gilbert as he outgrew these conventional travesties and turned to a more subtle criticism of opera which he incorporated into nearly all his libretti.

488. _____. "From Dame to Woman: W. S. Gilbert and Theatrical Transvestism." *Victorian Studies* XIV (September, 1970): 27-46.

Discusses the English theatrical tradition of women playing men's roles and vice versa, notes how G&S broke this tradition, relates the unfavorable opinions about Gilbert's cruel depiction of his female roles, and gives a modern assessment on the matter.

489. _____. "General Utility: Victorian Author-Actors from Knowles to Pinero." *Educational Theatre Journal* 24 (October, 1974): 289-301.

Describes multi-dexterity as the Victorian dramatist's way of life, and documents, along with others, Gilbert's stage appearances, his coaching style and problems, and his extension of ensemble playing into the musical theater.

490. _____. "The Genesis of *Patience*." *Modern Philology* 66 (1968): 48-58. Reprinted in *W. S. Gilbert: A Century of Scholarship and Commentary*, John Bush Jones, (ed.), 1970. p. 285-318. See 386.

Traces passages from *Bab Ballads*, early operas, and manuscript fragments that foreshadow the plot and character relationships in *Patience*, and reconstructs the evolution of characters from clerics to poets.

491. _____. "A New Absurdity from Tomline: W. S. Gilbert's 'Dramatic Sell.' " *Nineteenth Century Theatre Research* 3 (Spring, 1975): 1-21. Illus.

Describes *The Blue-Legged Lady*, a one-act pot-boiler "joke-in" about the theater, written by Gilbert under his *nom de farce*, F. Latour Tomline, and never added to the Gilbert canon. Includes the text of the play.

492. _____. "The New Gilbert Lyrics." *Bulletin of the New York Public Library* 74 (November, 1970): 629-33.

Prints the "lost" lyrics and restores them to their proper places in *Our Island Home* which Gilbert wrote in 1870 for German Reed's Gallery of Illustration. Speculates why this work remained unpublished during Gilbert's lifetime.

493. _____. "The Verdict Was Rapture." *100 Years of D'Oyly Carte and Gilbert and Sullivan*, 1975? p. 8-9? (unpaged). Illus. See 143.

Cites reviews by critics to show that in the decade before Gilbert worked with Sullivan his reputation was so fixed that his first nights were theatrical events. Tells how *Trial by Jury* came to be, how the extraordinary staging was the result of Gilbert's skillful directing, and how the opera was received by audiences.

494. _____. "The Victorian After-Image of Samuel Johnson."
Nineteenth Century Theatre Research 11 (Summer, 1983): 13-27.

Shows how the Victorian comic writers, whose trade was mockery,
saw Dr. Johnson as a sanctity to violate, a style to parody. Discusses,
among others, Gilbert and his Arcadians as first seen in *Happy Arcadia*
(1872) and last seen in *Utopia, Limited* (1893).

495. Stedman, Jane W., et al. "The Sorcery of a Century." *The Gilbert and
Sullivan Journal* 10 (Autumn, 1977): 268-71.

Prints the responses of seven 20th-century scholars concerning what
appeals to them about *The Sorcerer* (1877) after its 100 years of
existence and performance.

496. Stephens, John Russell. "Political and Personal Satire." *The
Censorship of English Drama 1824-1901.* New York: Cambridge
University Press, 1980. p. 115-24.

Explains the rationale behind censorship of satire in personalized
form in the 19th-century theater, and tells how Gilbert and others
fought the Lord Chamberlain's office, laying the censors open to
ridicule and recrimination. Discusses the flap over Gilbert's *The
Happy Land.*

497. Stravinsky, Igor. "How Stravinsky Became a Gilbert and Sullivan Fan."
The New York Times (October 27, 1968): D-19. Illus.

Tells how and when the musician first became aware of the G&S
operas, explains his fascination with the way the music adjusts to the
rhyme, and states that, since the words and music are equally
important, Sullivan shows an incredibly self-effacing gift.

498. Sutton, Max Keith. "The Significance of *The Grand Duke.*" *Gilbert and
Sullivan,* James Helyar (ed.), 1971. p. 221-28. See 354.

Explains and defends the maligned and ignored last operetta that even
W. S. Gilbert called an "ugly misshapen little brat." Supports the
viewpoint that *The Grand Duke* was in many ways significant and
well-conceived.

499. "Symposium for the Brave New World; Thoughts on the Expiry of the
Gilbert Copyright." *The Gilbert and Sullivan Journal* 8 (January,
1962): 85-7.

Reprints the views of nine G&S authorities about the potential effects
of the removal of the Gilbert copyright on December 31, 1961.

500. Taubman, Howard. "The Best of G&S." *The New York Times* (September 17, 1961): Section 2, p. 1.

Uses the occasion of a Tyrone Guthrie production of *The Pirates of Penzance* to ponder the secret of G&S's durability. Claims the secret is not in the books, whose satire now seems like pinpricks, but in the felicitous songs of Sullivan. Calls the operas consistent works of art for the grace and gaiety of Gilbert's rhymes and Sullivan's brightest and fairest musical inspiration.

501. "The Theatre" [*On Guard*]. *The New York Times* (November 16, 1871): 5.

Critiques Gilbert's play, *On Guard*, with the observation that it is an evident imitation of Tom Robertson's pieces but without Robertson's expertness in construction and smartness of dialogue. Summarizes the story and criticizes Gilbert for outlining it in a fuzzy way and for drawing shadowy caricatures of characters.

502. Thorndike, Ashley H. "Sir William Schwenck Gilbert." *English Comedy*. New York: Macmillan, 1929. p. 540-59.

States that the "reviver of humour" on the English stage won his fame not by his comedies but by his operas. Follows Gilbert's progress through his plays and his operas, and analyzes his whimsicalities and seriousness in presenting comedy to a very proper Victorian audience.

503. Toye, Francis. "The Charm of Music, Some Thoughts on Gilbert and Sullivan." *The Illustrated London News* 194 (January 28, 1939): 147, illus, ports.

Uses the occasion of the film production of *The Mikado* to reflect upon the joint and respective contributions of G&S. Rates Gilbert as an uncommonly good satirist and writer of lyrics. Judges Sullivan's strength to be his ability to set our language to music with skill and sensitiveness.

504. Troubridge, St. Vincent. "Another Gilbert Borrowing." *Theatre Notebook* 10 (October-December, 1955): 20-1.

Relates how Gilbert appropriated the basic idea of a play, *A Duke in Difficulties*, by Tom Taylor to use in his last Savoy opera, *The Grand Duke* in 1896. Alleges this purloining was in retribution for an affront to Gilbert's father by Taylor some 27 years earlier.

505. _____. "Gilbert and Planché." *Notes and Queries* 180
     (March 22, 2941): 200-5.

     Quotes passages from the works of Gilbert and J. R. Planché (major
     works: 1825-1871) to show that Gilbert's borrowings from and
     parallels with Planché are sufficiently numerous and striking to
     deserve record. Notes that some borrowings include some "original"
     ideas for which Gilbert has received much praise.

506. _____. "Gilbert and Planché." *Notes and Queries* 180
     (July 12, 1941): 17-8.

     Extends further the study of Gilbert's borrowings from Planché (see
     505) by quoting three additional parallel sets of dialogue.

507. _____. "Gilbert's Sources." *Notes and Queries* 180 (March
     29, 1941): 224.

     Quotes a passage from "The Bancrofts" which appears to be the source
     of one of the Lord Chancellor's speeches in *Iolanthe*.

508. Turner, Harry B. "The Dating of *Iolanthe*." *The Gilbert and Sullivan
     Journal* 10 (Autumn, 1980): 401-5.

     Considers the anxieties of the Victorian society in which that keen
     observer of life, W. S. Gilbert, wrote. Tells how Gilbert understood
     his nation's problems and aimed his gun at the ineptitude and
     wastefulness of the aristocracy in one of his personally thoughtful
     works, *Iolanthe*.

509. "Two Victorian Humorists; Burnand and the Mask of Gilbert." *Times
     Literary Supplement* No. 1816. (November 21, 1936): 935-36. Illus.

     Shows parallels in the lives of these two contemporaries as in the
     sixties they sought to see the splendid scheme of things--standing on
     its head. Tells how these masters of the pun were led into the realm
     of burlesque but made their fame elsewhere. Analyzes the personality,
     interests, and skills of each man separately.

510. Vandiver, Edward P. "The Significance of *The Yeomen of the Guard*."
     Furman Studies, The Furman University Bulletin VII (November,
     1959): 1-5.

     Responds to perceived errors in an article by Robert A. Hall (see 340),
     gives arguments in defense of Colonel Fairfax, Elsie, and Jack Point,
     notes that Gilbert wrote more seriously and emotionally in the *Yeomen*
     due to Sullivan's insistence, and claims the collaborators would have
     produced more operas of this type if not for public indifference.

511. Vandiver, E. P., Jr. "W. S. Gilbert and Shakespeare." *The Shakespeare Association Bulletin* 13 (July, 1938): 139-45.

Argues that, contrary to legend, Gilbert did regard Shakespeare with proper respect and did actually chide Englishmen for not reading him more. Excerpts some of the more obvious examples of Gilbert's Shakespearean materials in his own works.

512. W. H. T. "On Descriptive Music; As Illustrated by *The Golden Legend.*" *The Living Age* 198 (August 12, 1893): 357-62.

Uses Sullivan's *The Golden Legend*, recognized by musicians as an excellent and beautiful work, as an example of how a composer can represent by musical expressions subjects which belong more properly to the poet, the orator, and the painter.

513. Walker, Ernest. "The English Renaissance." *A History of Music in England.* Third Edition. Revised and enlarged by J. A. Westrup. Reprint of the 1952 edition by Clarendon Press, Oxford. (Da Capo Music Reprint Series). New York: Da Capo Press, 1978. p. 316-43.

Writes about Sullivan (p. 316-25) as the most widely popular English composer of the 19th century, whose fame comes as master of the *buffo* style and genius of parody. Laments the "disgraceful rubbish" such as *The Lost Chord*, and severely criticizes Sullivan's attempts at serious music.

514. Walters, Michael P. "*Ruddigore* and *Hamlet.*" *The Gilbert and Sullivan Journal* 9 (May, 1968): 152-53.

Notes curious similarities between Gilbert's *Ruddigore* and Shakespeare's *Hamlet* and states that, indeed, almost all the characters in *Ruddigore* are Shakespearean caricatures. Looks at Robin Oakapple, Richard Dauntless, and others to show parallels with their counterparts in *Hamlet*.

515. Wands, John. "A Borrowing of W. S. Gilbert's." *Notes and Queries* 29 (August, 1982): 320-22.

Suggests that Gilbert's ballad "My Dream" (in which reality is inverted into topsy-turvydom) came to him not in a dream but from Joseph Hall's *Mundus Alter et Idem* (1605). Shows parallels between the two works and compares their literary merit.

516. Waters, Mary Watkins. *W. S. Gilbert and the Discovery of a Satiric Method for the Victorian Stage.* Unpublished Ph.D. Dissertation. Auburn University, 1974. 286 p.

Describes the various techniques and devices employed by Gilbert in his earlier works which were later developed in his Savoy operas as satiric fictions that allowed Gilbert to camouflage his satire and overcome the resistance of Victorian audiences to the ridicule of their follies.

517. Weisinger, Herbert. "The Twisted Clue." *The Agony and the Triumph* (1944). Reprinted in *W. S. Gilbert: A Century of Scholarship and Commentary,* John Bush Jones, (ed.), 1970, p. 227-41. See 386.

Examines the plots of Gilbert's libretti to disclose in them the presence of the paradigms of ritual and to portray them as exemplars of Christian belief. Claims that the wit of the words and the charm of the music divert the reader from the more profound meanings which are hidden in the text.

518. Whitsitt, Julia. "The Metaphorical Context of *The Mikado." Whimsy-II.* Proceedings of the 1983 WHIM Conference: *Metaphors Be With You: Humor and Metaphor.* Edited by Don L. F. Nilsen. Co-edited by Alleen Pace Nilsen. Tempe: English Department, Arizona State University, 1984. p. 189-92.

Notes that G&S used a kind of allegory--an alternative world against which we project our representations of the world. Analyzes three scenes to show how the humor derives from the ways the audience's interpretations differ from those of the characters.

519. Williamson, Audrey. *Gilbert and Sullivan Opera: An Assessment.* Rev. Edition. London and Boston: M. Boyars, 1982. xii, 292 p., 32 pages of plates, illus., index.

Assesses the merits and weaknesses of all aspects of the G&S operas (and *Cox and Box*)--humor, philosophy, lyrics, poetry, music, characterizations, themes and plots. Looks at contemporary drama criticism, traces the development and decline of artistic talents, and examines the place of the G&S operas in a world of changing styles and values.

520. Wilkinson, Clennell. "Gilbert and Sullivan." *The London Mercury* V (March, 1922): 494-505.

Looks into the appeal and popularity of the most obviously "dated" plays in the world and examines the qualities and methods of G&S that led to works that are immortal.

521. Williams, Henry B. "*Box and Cox* and Before." *The Gilbert and Sullivan Journal* 9 (May, 1967): 92-5.

Recalls the opening night in 1847 which saw the birth of one of the greatest farces in the English language, *Box and Cox*, an amusing one-act play which would have a profound significance on future British comedy. Summarizes the plot, identifies the brilliant merging of two dissimilar French plots, and notes its influence on W. S. Gilbert.

522. Wilson, A. C. "W. S. Gilbert." *The Manchester Quarterly* 51 (1925): 277-97.

Describes one man's wit that is so unique it has passed into the language in the form of an adjective--Gilbertian. Quotes from the *Bab Ballads* and operas to show the high caliber of workmanship and literary style of Gilbert's humorous verse. Sums up the essential characteristic of Gilbert's humor as incongruity of nonsensical ideas expressed in beautiful words and set to exquisite melodies.

523. Wilson, Edmund. "Gilbert Without Sullivan." *New Yorker* 23 (April 12, 1947): 110-16.

Reviews briefly the Random House edition of *Plays and Poems of W. S. Gilbert* and analyzes Gilbert's curious comic convention by which characters full of tender and noble sentiments nonetheless act from motives of self-interest. Considers Sullivan's contributions and assesses several of the operas.

524. Wolfson, John. *Final Curtain; The Last Gilbert and Sullivan Operas, Including the Unpublished Rehearsal Librettos and Twenty Unpublished Gilbert Lyrics.* London and New York: Chappell in association with Andre Deutsch, 1976. xiv, 293 p., illus. (some color), facsims., diagrs., bibl., index.

Tells the story of how the G&S partnership declined from the greatness that produced 11 popular operas to the state that produced *Utopia, Limited* and *The Grand Duke*, both "failures." Shows the difficulties in collaborating after the infamous "carpet quarrel," the bitterness and cynicism that seeped into Gilbert's librettos, and the degeneration from promising plots to production failures.

525. Woodfield, James. "The Censorship Saga." *English Theatre in Transition 1881-1914.* Totowa, N. J.: Barnes & Noble, 1984. p.108-31.

Outlines the history of dramatic censorship in England from 1543 and discusses Gilbert (among others), noting his 1873 clash over *The Happy Land* and the banning of *The Mikado* in 1907.

526. "Work of W. S. Gilbert." *The Nation* 92 (June 8, 1911): 586-87.

Evaluates Gilbert's contributions upon his death, notes that he was not
a great dramatist but that he had a powerful sense of both comic and
serious theatrical situation, and observes how he improved the British
theater by not pandering to low tastes.

527. "W. S. Gilbert--The Pervasive Spirit of Topsy-turveydom." *Current
Literature* 51 (July, 1911): 86-7.

Quotes critics from several newspapers in their assessment of the
recently deceased Gilbert, citing his fine humor, witty ridicule, and
coherent plots free of offense and vulgarity.

528. Wreford, Reynell J. R. G. "Gilbert and Sullivan." *The Nineteenth
Century and After* 96 (November, 1924): 698-704.

Examines the ingredients of G&S operas that cause their continued
performances in times of a miserable state of affairs for modern
theater. Considers *Iolanthe, Patience, Princess Ida* and *Yeomen of
the Guard* in regard to their plots and outstanding features. Concludes
that the "out of date" of the present is the historical of the future.

529. Yaffe, Carl William. "The Renaissance of Sir Arthur Sullivan." *College
Music Symposium* 21, n. 1 (1981): 24-32.

Observes that Sullivan is lightly passed over (or omitted) in most
serious music histories and examines the root of this problem. Looks
at the way that different writers/biographers have treated Sullivan,
uses selected musical passages to indicate his strengths and
weaknesses as a composer, and notes positive trends to place Sullivan
into a more fitting niche in musical history.

530. Young, Percy M. "Arthur Sullivan." *A History of British Music.* New
York: W. W. Norton, 1967. p. 505-13. Illus. with music.

Relates the professional history of the man who unwittingly saved
British music from sententiousness. Evaluates the merits of his
musical style and concludes that Sullivan was a completely professional
composer who accepted conventions as they were rather than trying
to reform them.

3. Concordances, Handbooks, & Dictionaries

531. Ayre, Leslie. *The Gilbert and Sullivan Companion.* Foreword by Martyn Green. Illustrated from the Raymond Mander and Joe Mitchenson Theatre Collection. New York: Dodd, Mead, 1972. 485 p., illus., bibl., index.

   Presents explanation and background information for hundreds of alphabetically listed items, including songs and speeches, allusions, obscure terms, characters, actors and other people, groups, places, and events. Gives synopsis of and passages from each of the operas, and outlines the separate and joint careers of G&S

532. Benford, Harry. "A Dozen Gilbertian Conversation Pieces." *The Gilbert and Sullivan Journal* 10 (Spring, 1980): 377-79.

   Presents several esoteric terms that puzzle Savoyards and suggests possible (but not absolute) meanings or interpretations for them.

533. _____. *The Gilbert and Sullivan Lexicon In Which Is Gilded the Philosophic Pill.* 1st Edition. (The Theater Student Series). Foreword by Isaac Asimov. Illustrated by Geoffrey Shovelton. New York: Richards Rosen Press, 1978. xv, 142 p., illus., bibl., index.

   Supplies a comprehensive lexicon of words, phrases and allusions which may be obscure to modern American audiences. Attempts to use the Victorian meanings Gilbert had in mind when writing his libretti. Covers the 14 G&S operas plus the Burnand-Sullivan *Cox and Box.*

534. _____. "A Second Dozen Gilbertian Conversation Pieces." *The Gilbert and Sullivan Journal* 10 (Autumn, 1980): 406-8.

   Presents another 12 debatable terms from the Savoy operas, supplying possible meanings while stating that the terms are still open for discussion and debate.

535. Colson, Warren A. *The Gilbert and Sullivan Concordance, Or, I've Got a Little List.* Drawings by Sarah Cole and W. S. Gilbert. 1st edition. Natick, Mass.: Feather's Press, 1986. viii, 352 p., illus.

   Uses alphabetically arranged key (unusual) words and semi-key (common) words to help locate lines of song and dialogue written by "Our Hero," Gilbert. Lists the character who says or sings the quote, identifies the opera and act in which it is located, and gives the page number from several books on which the quotation is printed.

536. Dixon, Geoffrey. *The Gilbert and Sullivan Concordance: A Word Index
     to W. S. Gilbert's Libretti for the Fourteen Savoy Operas.* (Reference
     Library of the Humanities, Vol. 702). New York: Garland Publ., 1987.
     2 vols., xx, 1877 p., 2 p. of plates, ports.

     Compiles over 60,000 entries in a word index to the 14 G&S Savoy
     operas. Gives a quoted context for each occurrence of every word
     together with its location in the full text.

537. Dunn, George E. (compiler). *A Gilbert and Sullivan Dictionary.*
     Reprint of the 1936 edition published by G. Allen & Unwin, London.
     Norwood, Pa.: Norwood Editions, 1976. 175 p.

     Provides identification, explanation or definition of terms, quotations,
     people, and things, alphabetically arranged, from the operas, and
     identifies which opera the entry is associated with.

538. "Gilbert, William Schwenck, 1836-1911." *The Dictionary of Humorous
     Quotations.* Edited by Evan Esar. Garden City, N.Y.: Doubleday, 1949.
     p. 81.

     Quotes nine humorous sayings from Gilbert's works.

539. Halton, Frederick J. *The Gilbert and Sullivan Operas: A Concordance.*
     With foreword by Rupert D'Oyly Carte. New York: Bass Publishers,
     1935. 183 p., front., plates, index.

     Defines and explains many of the obscure words and names, from
     "aceldama" to "Zoffany," as well as Gilbert's idiomatic references in 13
     of the G&S operas (excludes *Thespis*). Addresses the matter of
     misspellings and erratic pronunciations that Gilbert frequently
     forced upon his characters.

540. Hardwick, Michael. *The Drake Guide to Gilbert and Sullivan.* New
     York: Drake Publishers, 1973. 284 p., discog., bibl.

     Supplies a biography, a "who's who" listing 200-odd named characters,
     plot summaries followed by quotations from the works, index of first
     lines of songs, a "Gilbertian Glossary," and a listing of phonograph
     records.

541. _____. *The Osprey Guide to Gilbert and Sullivan.*
     New York: Drake Publishers, 1973. 284 p., discog., bibl.

     Identical to Hardwick, *The Drake Guide to Gilbert and Sullivan.* See
     540.

542. *Hoyt's New Cyclopedia of Practical Quotations.* Completely revised and greatly enlarged by Kate Louise Roberts. New York: Funk & Wagnalls, 1922. 1343 p. Index.

Scatters throughout the book under subject headings some dozen and a half quotations from the G&S operas. Provides the quotation, the source, and author identification.

543. Magill, Frank N. (ed.). *Magill's Quotations in Context.* Englewood Cliffs, N.J.: Salem Press, 1965. 2 vols., 1230 p. Index.

Includes, among 2,020 entires, a few quotations from *H. M. S. Pinafore, The Mikado,* and *The Pirates of Penzance.* Provides the quotation, the source, date of publication, and brief explanation of the context in which the line is found.

544. Moore, Frank Ledlie. *Crowell's Handbook of Gilbert and Sullivan.* (A Crowell Reference Book). Introduction by Dorothy Raedler. New York: Thomas Y. Crowell, 1962. 264 p. Plates, music, bibl.

Offers a detailed description of the G&S operas, biographies of Gilbert, Sullivan, and D'Oyly Carte, and factual information such as lists of original cast members of the Savoy Company, a chronology, index of roles, index of first lines and famous lines, and themes and texts of famous musical numbers.

545. _____. *The Handbook of Gilbert and Sullivan.* London : A. Barker, 1962. 264 p. Plates, music, bibl.

Identical to *Crowell's Handbook of Gilbert and Sullivan.* See 544.

546. Poladian, Sirvart (compiler). *Sir Arthur Sullivan: An Index to the Texts of His Vocal Works.* (Detroit Studies in Music Bibliography, No. 2). Detroit, Mich.: Information Service, Inc., 1961. 91 p.

Lists, in almost 3,000 entries, every title and first line, repeated catchy refrain, and important musical section in the operettas and other larger vocal works by Sullivan. Includes brief biographical sketch and alphabetically arranged list of first performances of Sullivan's major works.

547. "Sir William Schwenck Gilbert, 1836-1911." *Familiar Quotations; A Collection of Passages, Phrases and Proverbs Traced to Their Sources in Ancient and Modern Literature.* Fifteenth and 125th Anniversary Edition, Revised and Enlarged. John Bartlett. Edited by Emily Morison Beck. Boston: Little, Brown & Company, 1980. p. 627-30.

Prints 75 quotations from the Savoy operas, the *Bab Ballads,* and one play. Identifies the source, date, and place in the work where the quotation may be found.

548. "Sir William Schwenck Gilbert, 1836-1911." *The Oxford Dictionary of Quotations.* Second Edition. New York: Oxford University Press, 1955. p. 217-22.

Prints 185 quotations from the *Bab Ballads*, the operas, and various plays. Identifies the source of each quotation.

549. Taylor, Ian. *The Gilbert and Sullivan Quiz Book.* Text illustrated with drawings by W. S. Gilbert. London: William Luscombe, 1974. 92 p., illus.

Contains fifty 10-question topical quizzes (with answers) on a variety of themes such as Famous Names, Colors, First Lines, Characters, The Law, Ages, Artistes, Stage Directions, etc.

550. Walmisley, Guy H. and Claude A. Walmisley. *Tit-Willow; or, Notes and Jottings on Gilbert and Sullivan Operas.* [n.p.: Printed by R. G. Baker, 196-?]. 151 p., illus., ports., index.

Provides biographies of Gilbert and Sullivan, lists the G&S operas in chronological order, and supplies an introduction and notes for each opera.

551. Wilstach, Frank J. *A Dictionary of Similes.* New York: Grosset & Dunlap, 1924. 578 p. Index.

Includes, among 19,000 similes, some dozen and a half by W. S. Gilbert. Lists the simile under subject heading and identifies the author but not the source.

4. Production

552. Bassuk, Albert Oliver. *How to Present the Gilbert and Sullivan Operas.* Foreword by Sigmund Spaeth. New York: Bass Publishers, 1934. 195 p., illus. (incl facsims), plates, ports., bibl.

Offers practical hints for amateur production groups on selection of the opera, rehearsals, costumes, scenery, properties and lighting. Provides summaries of the stories of the operas.

553. Cox-Ife, William. *The Elements of Conducting.* With foreword by Sir Adrian Boult. London: J. Baker, 1964. 142 p., illus.

Discusses basic elements of conducting, addresses aspects such as rehearsals and final performances, and makes frequent references to the G&S operettas with suggestions for conducting them.

554. _____. *How To Sing Both Gilbert and Sullivan.* Foreword by Sir Thomas Armstrong. London: Chappell, 1961. 155 p.

Advises performers to pay meticulous attention to Sullivan's music as written and to the meaningful interpretation of Gilbert's libretti. Provides copious musical examples to illustrate suggested phrasing and dynamics. Gives a detailed study of ten operas (excluding *Thespis, The Sorcerer, Utopia, Limited,* and *The Grand Duke*).

555. _____. *Training the Gilbert and Sullivan Chorus.* Foreword by Bridget D'Oyly Carte. London: Chappell, 1955. 98 p. Illus. with music, diagrs.

Offers suggestions for improving the technical aspects of ensemble singing, discusses topics such as the patter refrain, music and movement, and the thought behind the words, and provides a working analysis for each of 11 G&S operas.

556. _____. *W. S. Gilbert: Stage Director.* (The Student's Music Library--Historical and Critical Series). Foreword by W. A. Darlington. London: Dobson, 1977. 112 p.

Deals with the issue of how to interpret and play Gilbert's comic roles, looks at problems of production before Gilbert when whims of actors carried more weight than the wishes of the director or writer, and examines Gilbert's recipe for comic acting.

557. Davis, D. Graham. "Gilbert and Sullivan Opera." *Theatre and Stage.*
     Edited by Harold Downs. London: Sir Isaac Pitman, 1951. Vol. II,
     p. 597-688.

     Considers acting requirements, the Savoy tradition and family tree,
     individual roles in light comedy leads, the heavy comedy parts, the
     individual roles for different voices, responsibility of the chorus, and
     problems of costume, musical requirements, and dancing.

558. Goffin, Peter. "Designing for Gilbert and Sullivan." *The Studio* 149
     (June, 1955): 161-67. Illus. (some color).

     Presents a view of changing designs of scenery and costumes for G&S
     operas in the first half of the 20th century, and illustrates more recent
     set and costume designs for various operas in modern revisions.

559. Grossman, Monroe. "Why Produce Savoy Operas?" *Music Journal* 31
     (April, 1973): 11+. Illus.

     Presents reasons why musical growth will be the benefit of having
     school amateur performances of the G&S operettas. Identifies four
     operas that most readily lend themselves to school performances and
     discusses the general appeal that the G&S operas have.

560. Kline, Peter. *Gilbert and Sullivan Production.* 1st ed. (The Theatre
     Student Series). New York: Richards Rosen Press, 1972. 299 p.,
     illus, bibl., discog.

     Discusses production style, characterizations, staging, costumes and
     scenery for each of the 14 G&S operas. Gives advice on forming a
     company, casting, rehearsals, and staging. Includes appendix with
     words and music to songs from the operas not otherwise in print.

561. Lucier, Mary. "From Meat Loaf to Pirates: A Sound Man's Lot Is Not a
     Happy One." *Theatre Crafts* 15 (June/July, 1981): 12-15+. Illus.

     Discusses problems and solutions to producing sound for the very
     contemporary production of *Pirates of Penzance* in New York City's
     Central Park. Includes a microphone chart and diagrams of sound
     dispersion.

562. Monroe, Paul Jordan. *Stage Director's Guide for Shreds and Patches
     from Gilbert and Sullivan.* Book and guide by Paul Monroe. Lyrics
     adapted from W. S. Gilbert. Music from Arthur Sullivan, arranged by
     Ira B. Wilson. New York: Lorenz Publishing, 1942. 20 p., diagr.

     Contains the stage business, action on songs, diagram of the stage,
     costume suggestions, and dramatic suggestions for the 2-act operetta
     Shreds and Patches from Gilbert and Sullivan (see 817).

563. Murphy, John M. "Savoy Operas as School Projects." *Music Journal* 25 (March, 1967): 48+

Gives opinions why *Pinafore* is the best choice for beginning a Savoy tradition of school productions. Looks at *Trial By Jury, Iolanthe, The Mikado,* and *Ruddigore,* and identifies the problem areas, amount of work, and joys associated with their presentation by school choruses.

564. Raedler, Dorothy. "A Training-School for Singers." *Music Journal* 17 (February, 1959): 14+

Warns against the assumption that the G&S operas are "inexpensive and easy to do" for amateur groups. Tells of the activities in the American Savoyards company and its apprenticeship program for young people.

565. Rickett, Edmond W. and Benjamin T. Hoogland. *Let's Do Some Gilbert & Sullivan; A Practical Production Handbook.* With illustrations by W. S. Gilbert. New York: Coward-McCann, 1940. xi, 238 p., incl. front. (facsim.), illus. (incl music), diagr.

Facilitates selection by discussing plot and cast of 13 G&S operas, looks at production matters (directors, staff, cast, orchestra, and scenery), and makes suggestions for dramatic and musical interpretation. Gives pointers for the guidance of the layman actor and notes for the director. Includes glossary of stage terms.

566. Stedman, Jane W. "Gilbert's Stagecraft: Little Blocks of Wood." *Gilbert and Sullivan,* James Helyar (ed.), 1971. p. 195-211. See 354.

Relates that Gilbert used a model stage and blocks of wood to work out the staging of his libretti. Details the endless pains Gilbert took as director to maintain control over actors, settings, and costumes.

567. Sugden, J. G. "The Production of Gilbert and Sullivan Operas in Schools." *Gilbert and Sullivan,* James Helyar (ed.), 1971. p. 213-20. See 354.

Elucidates the qualities of G&S operas that make them suitable for school production. Gives suggestions for adding polish to the productions.

568. Taylor, Ian. *How To Produce Concert Versions of Gilbert and Sullivan.* London: Hale, 1972. 249 p., illus.

Suggests producing G&S operas in concert versions to minimize cost and time. Provides notes for producing 11 of the operas and gives diagrams for stage arrangements and character positions. Makes suggestions for simple costumes.

569. _____. *Tarantara! Tarantara!* New York: Broadway Play
      Publishing, 1983. 98 p.

      Dramatizes the lives of Gilbert, Sullivan, D'Oyly Carte, Jessie Bond,
      George Grossmith, and "Joe, a stage hand" in a 2-act play which is
      interspersed with musical numbers from the operettas.

      Thane, Adele. See 877.

570. Tyson, George. "Notes on Characters in *The Sorcerer.*" *The Gilbert
      and Sullivan Journal* 8 (September, 1964): 243.

      Makes suggestions regarding the portrayal of John Wellington Wells,
      Dr. Daly, Alexis, Aline, and others in an amateur or professional
      performance.

571. Walsh, Shelford. *Operatics, Or, How to Produce an Opera, With
      Numerous Gilbertian and Other Anecdotes.* Liverpool: Littlebury Bros.,
      1903. 77 p., port.

      Gives suggestions on the formation and management of an operatic
      society, relates personal incidents and anecdotes, and quotes
      witticisms attributed to W. S. Gilbert. Lists operas for amateurs and
      suggests rules for an operatic society.

5. Juvenile

572. Botsford, Ward. *The Pirates of Penzance: The Story of the Gilbert and Sullivan Operetta.* Adapted by Ward Botsford. Illustrated by Edward Sorel. New York: Random House, 1981. 25 p., col. illus.

Retells in prose the story about a group of pirates who can't seem to make piracy pay, their apprentice who is a "slave of duty," and a major general and his daughters.

573. *Gilbert and Sullivan Songs for Young People.* (Whittlesey House Publication). Selected and arranged by Margaret Bush. Introduction and notes by J. R. de la Torre Bueno, Jr. Designed and illustrated by Erna M. Karolyi. New York: McGraw, 1946. 71 p., illus.

Gives brief introductory notes and the words and music of 19 ballads from 11 of the G&S operas.

574. *Gilbert and Sullivan's H. M. S. Pinafore.* Adapted by Robert Lawrence. Illustrated by Sheilah Beckett. Authorized by the D'Oyly Carte Company. New York: Grosset & Dunlap, 1940.

575. *Gilbert and Sullivan's The Gondoliers.* Adapted by Robert Lawrence. Illustrated by Sheilah Beckett. Authorized by the D'Oyly Carte Company. New York: Grosset & Dunlap, 1940.

576. *Gilbert and Sullivan's The Mikado.* Adapted by Robert Lawrence. Illustrated by Sheilah Beckett. Authorized by the D'Oyly Carte Company. New York: Grosset & Dunlap, 1940. 47 p., illus. (some color).

Gives a brief history of the operetta and tells the story in prose. Includes abridged music (words and melody) to songs at the appropriate spots in the story.

577. *The Gondoliers [by] W. S. Gilbert and Arthur Sullivan.* (A Curtain-Raiser Book). Told by Jean Blashfield. With drawings by Anne and Janet Grahame Johnstone. New York: Watts, 1967, c. 1965. Unpaged, color illus.

578. Harris, Paula. *The Young Gilbert and Sullivan.* Illustrated by Gloria Timbs. New York: Roy Publishing, 1965.

Presents, with much invented dialogue, the youthful years of the two gifted personalities and recreates life in Victorian England. Gives a brief history of the comic opera period of the partnership.

579. *H. M. S. Pinafore.* Story and music arrangements adapted from Gilbert
     and Sullivan by Opal Wheeler. Illustrated by Fritz Kredel. New York:
     Dutton, 1946. 96 p., illus. (incl color).

     Retells this favorite opera in prose and includes simplified musical
     arrangements

580. *Iolanthe [by] W. S. Gilbert and Arthur Sullivan.* (A Curtain-Raiser Book).
     Told by Jean Blashfield. With drawings by Anne and Janet Grahame
     Johnstone. New York: Watts, 1967, c. 1965. 1 vol., unpaged, color
     illus.

581. Lavine, Sigmund A. *Wandering Minstrels We: The Story of Gilbert and
     Sullivan.* New York: Dodd, Mead, 1954. 303 p., illus., facsims.

     Presents a fictionalized biography of the two disparate personalities.
     Integrates anecdotes, lyrics from the operas, and plot synopses into
     the story.

582. Mearns, Martha. *H. M. S. Pinafore [by] W. S. Gilbert and Arthur
     Sullivan.* Told by Martha Mearns. Drawings by Anne and Janet
     Grahame Johnstone. (A Curtain-Raiser Book). New York: F. Watts,
     1967. 26 p., col. illus.

     Retells the story of the operetta in which the crossed lives of a lowly
     sailor and the Lord of the Admiralty for the captain's daughter are
     finally put to rights by a faithful trinket-seller.

583. Miller, Margaret J. "W. S. Gilbert (1836-1911)." *Seven Men of Wit.*
     London: Hutchinson, 1960. p. 91-107. Bibl.

     Tells, with much imagined dialogue, the story of Gilbert's reading the
     libretto of *Trial by Jury* to Sullivan, who agreed forthwith to set it to
     music, and then relates how *H. M. S. Pinafore* came to be so popular.
     Concludes there has never been another partnership so successful in
     the history of light opera.

     Power-Waters, Alma Shelley. See Waters, Alma Shelley, 588.

584. Purdy, Claire Lee. *Gilbert and Sullivan: Masters of Mirth and Melody.*
     Illustrated by Eric Godal. New York: J. Messner, 1947. 276 p., illus.
     (incl music), bibl.

     Combines biography with synopses of the successful G&S operas.
     Includes quotations with music and descriptions of stage sets and
     costumes

585. Reiter, H. W. *The Merry Gentlemen of Japan.* A children's story by
     H. W. Reiter and Shepard Chartoc. Adapted from the Gilbert and
     Sullivan opera *The Mikado.* Illustrated by Philip Gelb. New York: Bass
     Publishers, 1935.

586. Sullivan, Sir Arthur Seymour. *Gilbert and Sullivan Song Book.*
     Selected by Malcolm Hyatt and Walter Fabell. Arranged by Irene
     Shannon. Illustrated by Margaret Ayer. New York: Random House,
     1955. 63 p., illus.

     Offers simplified arrangements for piano and voice of 26 songs from
     the seven best-known comic operas. Precedes each song with a story
     synopsis that explains the place of the song in the opera.

587. Untermeyer, Louis. *The Last Pirate: Tales from the Gilbert and
     Sullivan Operas.* Illustrated by Reginald Birch. New York: Harcourt,
     Brace, 1934. 319 p., illus.

     Adapts into narrative form the stories of seven G&S operas--*The
     Pirates of Penzance, The Mikado, The Gondoliers, Iolanthe, Patience,
     H. M. S. Pinafore,* and *Ruddigore.*

588. Waters, Alma Shelley. *The Melody Maker; The Life of Sir Arthur
     Sullivan, Composer of the Gilbert and Sullivan Operettas.* New York:
     E. P. Dutton, 1959. 220 p., bibl.

     Tells the story of the boy with the beautiful voice and musical talents
     who grew up to become Sir Arthur Sullivan. Relates how he created
     melodies of timeless appeal in spite of poor health, loneliness, and
     occasional failures.

589. Wells, Rosemary. *A Song to Sing, O! From the Yeomen of the Guard by
     W. S. Gilbert and Arthur Sullivan.* Set to pictures by Rosemary Wells.
     New York: Macmillan, 1968. 33 p., color illus.

     Uses drawings of three birds (Merryman, Merrymaid, and Popinjay) to
     interpret the popular G&S song for young children. Includes the
     melody, with words, at the end.

590. _____. *W. S. Gilbert's The Duke of Plaza Toro, From the
     Gondoliers.* Set to pictures by Rosemary Wells. New York: Macmillan,
     1969. 32 p., color illus.

591. Wymer, Norman. *Gilbert and Sullivan.* Portraits by John Pimlott. New
     York: E. P. Dutton, 1963, c. 1962. 157 p., illus, bibl.

     Uses the format of the novel to tell the life stories of the famous writer
     and composer. Incorporates dialogue based on actual words of G&S or
     on factual evidence.

6. Collected Librettos, Plays, & Poems

This section is intended to be representative, not comprehensive. Many of the books listed have gone through a number of editions, some as many a twenty. Gilbert himself had the habit of printing early and revising often making the identification of various editions somewhat difficult. Th researcher who needs to delve deeper into the variations will find authora tative materials listed in the section on Bibliography & Discography.

592. Allen, Reginald (ed.) *The First Night Gilbert and Sullivan: Containing Complete Librettos of the 14 Operas Exactly as Presented at Their Premier Performances.* Edited, with a prologue and copious descriptive particulars, by Reginald Allen. Illustrated with contemporary drawings. With a foreword by Bridget D'Oyly Carte. Rev. Centennial Edition. London: Chappell, [1975?]. xxi, 465 p., illus.

Presents an overview and, for each opera, an introduction and the first-night text plus a capsule comparison to the text in most recent librettos. Includes an "encore"--a list of first nights of first revivals.

593. *Asimov's Annotated Gilbert & Sullivan.* Text by William Schwenck Gilbert. Notes by Isaac Asimov. New York: Doubleday, 1988. xiv, 1056 p., illus., index.

Supplies the complete texts for all 14 operas and provides explanatory notes for words and allusions. Supplies, in a brief introduction, the historical perspective for each opera.

594. *Authentic Libretti of the Gilbert and Sullivan Operas As Presented by the D'Oyly Carte Opera Company During Their American Season.* (The Gilbert and Sullivan Library). Text by W. S. Gilbert. Music by Arthur Sullivan. With a foreword by Frederick Hobbs. New York: Crown Publishers, 1939. 202 p., illus. (incl music).

Presents the complete libretti plus selected songs (words and music) from 10 G&S operas (excludes *Thespis, The Grand Duke, Utopia, Limited,* and *The Sorcerer).* Includes famous musical selections and original "Bab" illustrations by Sir W. S. Gilbert.

595. Bradley, Ian (ed.). *The Annotated Gilbert and Sullivan.* London: Penguin, 1982. 463 p.

Presents the texts of five comic operas (*Mikado, Gondoliers, Iolanthe, Pinafore,* and *Pirates of Penzance*) and annotations which include details of other textual variants, "lost" songs and dialogue, performance anecdotes, production points, source references, and explanations of obscure terms.

596. Bradstock, Lillian. *Gilbert and Sullivan; A Romantic Prose Version of the Famous Operas.* London: C. Palmer, 1928. vii, 288p.

    Revised in 1933 as *Pooh-Bah and the Rest of Gilbert and Sullivan.* See 597.

597. Bradstock, Lillian. *Pooh-Bah and the Rest of Gilbert and Sullivan, A Story Version of the Famous Operas.* London: Figurehead Books, 1933. 238 p,, illus with 4 plates.

    Retells in prose the stories of eleven of the G&S operas (omits *Thespis, The Grand Duke,* and *Utopia, Limited*). Gives a brief introduction to "the trio," Gilbert, Sullivan, and D'Oyly Carte.

598. Bulla, Clyde Robert. *Stories of Gilbert and Sullivan Operas.* Illustrated by James and Ruth McCrea. New York: Thomas Y. Crowell, 1968. 246 p., illus.

    Gives a brief history of the G&S partnership and retells in prose the stories from 11 of the operas. Includes lyrics to the operas at the back.

599. Davidson, Gladys. *Stories from Gilbert and Sullivan.* London: Werner Laurie, 1952. 299 p., illus., index.

    Paraphrases the stories of the 14 G&S comic operas, using quoted passages. Includes biographies of Gilbert and Sullivan, a list of first lines of all songs, and a list of original cast members.

600. Ellis, James (ed). *The Bab Ballads.* Cambridge, Mass.: The Belknap Press of Harvard University Press, 1970. ix, 366 p., illus.

    Gives a history of the publishing of the ballads, analyzes Gilbert's personality, and prints more than 130 ballads attributed to Gilbert, along with several hundred of Gilbert's original illustrations. Provides notes to the ballads.

601. Geis, Darlene. *The Gilbert and Sullivan Operas.* New York: Abrams, 1983. 223 p., 270 illus. (incl 200 in full color), bibl.

    Presents a brief "overture" (biography/history) and then tells, in prose with frequent quoting of verse, the stories of 12 comic operas, including *Cox and Box.* Profusely illustrated with photographs from the George Walker Presentations television filmed in England and presented in the U.S. on PBS stations. Includes casts and credits for the television productions and a sampler of song lyrics.

602. Gilbert, W. S. *Additional Adventures of Messrs. Box and Cox, A Continuation of the Dramatic History of Box and Cox.* With an introduction by Ralph MacPhail, Jr. Bridgewater, Va.: The Parenthesis Press, 1974. 74 p., illus.

Fills in background on the original play, *Box and Cox,* describes sequels, and reprints the fanciful piece from Gilbert giving a continuation of the history of *Box and Cox.* Reprints the full text of *Penelope Anne,* F. C. Burnand's "second go" at the saga.

603. _____. *The "Bab" Ballads.* Complete Edition. With preface by W. S. Gilbert. With 215 illustrations by the author. New York: G. Routledge, n.d.   xiii, 309 p., illus., port.

Contains 79 poems which are the remainder after Gilbert thought it better to withdraw from previous editions such ballads as seemed to show evidence of carelessness or undue haste.

_____. *The Bab Ballads.* Edited by James Ellis. See 600.

604. _____. *Bab Ballads and Savoy Songs.* Philadelphia: Henry Altemus, 1894? 192 p., illus. [Published in several editions between 1894 and 19--?]

Contains 71 poems selected from among the *Bab Ballads* and various Savoy opera lyrics.

605. _____. *The Bab Ballads, Much Sound and Little Sense.* With illustrations by the author. London: John Camden Hotten, 1869. x, 224 p., advts.

606. _____. *The Bab Ballads, Much Sound and Little Sense.* With illustrations by the author. London and New York: G. Routledge, 1870. ix, 222 p.

607. _____. *"Bab" Ballads and More "Bab" Ballads, Much Sound and Little Sense.* With illustrations by the author. London: G. Routledge, 1874. viii, 202 p.

608. _____. *The Bab Ballads With Which Are Included Songs of a Savoyard.* 5th edition. London and New York: G. Routledge, 1902. xii, 563 p., illus. [Published in several editions between 1898 and 1902].

Includes 80 of the previously collected ballads along with 87 lyrics from the Savoy operas.

609. _____. *The Best Known Works of W. S. Gilbert.* (Cameo Classics). With Gilbert's own illustrations. New York: Grosset and Dunlap, 1932. 232 p., illus.

Contains the librettos for *H. M. S. Pinafore, The Pirates of Penzance,* and *The Mikado.* Also includes the 19 (the "best") of the *Bab Ballads.*

610. _____. *Book and Lyrics of the Best-Known Gilbert and Sullivan Operas and the Bab Ballads.* With Sir William Gilbert's own illustrations. New York: Windsor Press, 1932. 232 p.

Has same content as *The Best Known Works of W. S. Gilbert.* See 609.

611. _____. *The Complete Plays of Gilbert and Sullivan.* Illustrated by W. S. Gilbert. Reprinted from the 1941 edition published by the Garden City Publishing Co., New York. New York: W. W. Norton, 1976. 615 p., illus.

Offers the complete librettos for the 14 G&S operas. Includes a chronology from 1836 to 1911.

612. _____. *Fifty "Bab" Ballads, Much Sound and Little Sense.* With illustrations by the author. London: G. Routledge, 1877. xi, 255 p.

613. _____. *Foggerty's Fairy and Other Tales.* London: G. Routledge, 1890. viii, 366 p.

Contains *Foggerty's Fairy; An Elixir of Love; Johnny Pounce; Little Mim; The Triumph of Vice; My Maiden Brief; Creatures of Impulse; Maxwell and I; Actors, Authors, and Audiences; Angela; Wide Awake; A Stage Play; The Wicked World; The Finger of Fate; A Tale of a Dry Plate; The Burglar's Story; Unappreciated Shakespeare; Comedy and Tragedy;* and, *Rosencrantz and Guildenstern.*

614. _____. *Gilbert Without Sullivan.* Libretti by W. S. Gilbert. Illustrated by Leonard Lubin. New York: Viking Press, 1981. 112 p.

Contains the librettos for *H. M. S. Pinafore, The Pirates of Penzance, The Mikado,* and *The Gondoliers.*

615. _____. *H. M. S. Pinafore and Other Plays.* Introduction by Gilbert W. Gabriel. New York: Modern Library, 1925. 218 p.

Contains *H. M. S. Pinafore, Patience, The Yeomen of the Guard,* and *Ruddigore.*

616. _____. *H. M. S. Pinafore and Six Other Savoy Operas.*
(Dolphin Books C155). Garden City, N.Y.: Doubleday (Dolphin Books),
1961. 312 p.

Presents the librettos for *Trial by Jury, The Sorcerer, H. M. S.
Pinafore, The Pirates of Penzance, Patience, Iolanthe,* and *Princess
Ida.*

617. _____. *The Lost Stories of W. S. Gilbert.* Selected and
introduced by Peter Haining. Illustrated by "Bab." New York: Parkwest
Publications; London: Robson Books, 1985. 255 p., illus.

Anthologizes the never-before-collected short stories of W. S. Gilbert,
in which can be seen many of the themes and motifs that would be
developed in the Savoy operettas.

618. _____. *The Mikado and Five Other Savoy Operas.* (Dolphin
Books). Garden City, N.Y.: Doubleday (Dolphin Books), 1961. 386 p.

Contains *The Mikado, Ruddigore, The Yeomen of the Guard, The
Gondoliers, Utopia Limited,* and *The Grand Duke.*

619. _____ . *More "Bab" Ballads.* With illustrations by the author.
London: G. Routledge, 1873. viii, 224 p., advts.

620. _____. *New And Original Extravaganzas.* As first produced at
the London Playhouses. Edited by and with introduction by Isaac
Goldberg. Boston: John W. Luce, 1931. 180 p.

Gives a brief biography of Gilbert and analyzes his methods of
burlesque. Presents the texts for *Dulcamara, or, The Little Duck and
The Great Quack; La Vivandiere, or, True to the Corps; The Merry
Zingara, or, The Tipsy Gipsy and The Pipsy Wipsy; Robert the Devil,
or, The Nun, The Dun, and The Son of a Gun;* and *The Pretty
Druidess, or, The Mother, The Maid, and The Mistletoe Bough.*

621. _____. *Original Plays. First Series.* London: Chatto & Windus,
1926. 287 p. [Published in many editions between 1884 and 1926].

Contains *The Wicked World; Pygmalion and Galatea; Charity; The
Princess; The Palace of Truth; Trial by Jury;* and *Iolanthe.*

622. _____. *Original Plays. Second Series.* London: Chatto &
Windus, 1930. 338 p. [Published in many editions between 1881 and
1930].

Contains *Broken Hearts; Engaged; Dan'l Druce, Blacksmith; Gretchen;
Tom Cobb, or, Fortune's Toy; The Sorcerer; H. M. S. Pinafore, or, The
Lass That Loved a Sailor;* and *The Pirates of Penzance, or, The Slave
of Duty.*

623. _____. *Original Plays. Third Series.* London: Chatto & Windus, 1928. 453 p. [Published in many editions betwen 1895 and 1928].

Contains *Comedy and Tragedy; Foggerty's Fairy; Rosencrantz and Guildenstern; Patience, or Bunthorne's Bride; Princess Ida, or, Castle Adamant; The Mikado, or, The Town of Titipu; Ruddigore, or, The Witch's Curse; The Yeomen of the Guard, or, The Merryman and His Maid; The Gondoliers, or, The King of Barataria; The Mountebanks;* and *Utopia, Limited, or, The Flowers of Progress.*

624. _____. *Original Plays. Fourth Series.* London: Chatto & Windus, 1926. 499 p. [Published in many editions between 1911 and 1926].

Contains *The Fairy's Dilemma; The Grand Duke; His Excellency; Haste to the Wedding; Fallen Fairies; The Gentleman in Black; Brantinghame Hall; Creatures of Impulse; Randall's Thumb; The Fortune-Hunter; Thespis; The Hooligan;* and *Trying a Dramatist.*

625. _____. *Plays and Poems of W. S. Gilbert.* Preface by Deems Taylor. Illustrated by the author. Reprint of the 1932 edition. New York: Random House, 1946. lx, 1218 p., illus (incl. color front.).

Covers the history of Gilbert's career and the operas, and presents the complete texts of the G&S operas, three of Gilbert's plays (*The Palace of Truth; The Mountebanks;* and *His Excellency*), and "all" (86) of the *Bab Ballads,* including 6 "lost" ballads.

626. _____. *The Savoy Operas, Vol. I.* (The World's Classics Series). With an introduction by Lord David Cecil and notes on the operas by Derek Hudson. London and New York: Oxford University Press, 1962. xix, 396 p.

Presents the librettos for *Trial By Jury; The Sorcerer; H. M. S. Pinafore; Pirates of Penzance; Patience; Iolanthe; Princess Ida;* and the text for *Thespis.* Gives details of the history of the operas, first night performances, etc.

627. _____. *The Savoy Operas, Vol. II.* (The World's Classics Series). With an introduction by Bridget D'Oyly Carte and notes on the operas by Derek Hudson. London and New York: Oxford University Press, 1963. xv, 423 p.

Provides the librettos for *The Mikado, Ruddigore, The Yeomen of the Guard, The Gondoliers, Utopia, Limited,* and *The Grand Duke.* Gives details of the history of the operas, first night performances, etc.

628. _____. *The Savoy Operas, Being the Complete Texts of the Gilbert and Sullivan Operas As Originally Produced in the Years 1875-1896.* London: Macmillan; New York: St. Martin's Press, 1959. v, 698 p.

Contains the librettos for *Trial by Jury; The Sorcerer; H. M. S. Pinafore; The Pirates of Penzance; Patience; Iolanthe; Princess Ida; The Mikado; Ruddigore; The Yeomen of the Guard; The Gondoliers; Utopia, Limited;* and *The Grand Duke.*

629. _____. *Songs of a Savoyard.* Illustrated by the author. London: G. Routledge, 1894. 142 p., illus. [Published in several editions between 1890 and 1894].

Prints the lyrics to 69 songs found in 11 of the G&S operas (does not include *Thespis* nor the last two operas, *Utopia, Limited* and *The Grand Duke).*

630. _____. *Works of Gilbert and Sullivan.* Roslyn, N.Y.: Black's Readers Service Company, 1950. 320 p.

Contains the librettos for the 14 G&S operas and includes 19 of the *Bab Ballad* poems.

Goldberg, Isaac (ed.). See *New and Original Extravaganzas,* 620.

Green, Martyn. See *Martyn Green's Treasury of Gilbert and Sullivan,* 634.

631. Jefferson, Alan. *The Complete Gilbert & Sullivan Opera Guide.* New York: Facts on File, 1984. 352 p., illus. (some color), librettos, discog., bibl., index.

Provides a brief historical introduction to the 14 G&S operas, supplies the libretto, synopsis, and anecdotes about the creation of each work, and includes first reviews and descriptions of original costumes.

632. Lewis, Ross (ed). *The Corgi Book of Gilbert and Sullivan.* (A Corgi Book). London: Transworld Publishers, 1964. 397 p.

Includes brief synopses and complete librettos for *Trial By Jury, H. M. S. Pinafore, Pirates of Penzance, Patience, Iolanthe, The Mikado, Yeomen of the Guard,* and *The Gondoliers.* Includes some unaccompanied melodies.

633. Lubbock, Mark. "London." *The Complete Book of Light Opera*. With an American section by David Ewen. New York: Appleton- Century- Crofts, 1962. p. 467-575, illus.

Gives the condensed story with selected verse and music passages for each of the G&S operas and those done by the two artists in collaboration with other librettists/composers.

634. *Martyn Green's Treasury of Gilbert and Sullivan*. Edited and annotated by Martyn Green. Illustrated by Lucille Corcos. Arrangements by Dr. Albert Sirmay. New York: Simon and Schuster, 1961. 717 p., illus.

Contains the complete librettos of eleven operettas (omits *Thespis, The Grand Duke*, and *Utopia, Limited*) and the words and music of 102 favorite songs. Green's annotations deal extensively with production matters as well as content.

635. McSpadden, J. Walker. "Arthur Seymour Sullivan (1842-1900)." *Light Opera and Musical Comedy*. New York: Thomas Y. Crowell, 1936. p. 198-225.

Describes the cast, the argument, and the plot of *Cox and Box* and 12 of the G&S comic operas (excludes the last two).

636. Rowell, George (ed.). *Plays by W. S. Gilbert*. Cambridge: Cambridge University Press, 1982. ix, 189 p.

Presents the texts for plays written outside the Opera Comique and Savoy Theatres. Includes *Engaged; Rosencrantz and Guildenstern; The Palace of Truth; Sweethearts;* and, the libretto for *Princess Toto*, which had been set to music by Frederick Clay.

637. Stedman, Jane W. (ed.). *Gilbert Before Sullivan, Six Comic Plays by W. S. Gilbert*. Edited and with an introduction by Jane W. Stedman. Chicago: The University of Chicago Press, 1967. xi, 270 p., illus. (incl. music), 16 p. of plates, bibl., index.

Gives a 51-page historical account of the German Reed Gallery of Illustration entertainments of W. S. Gilbert, and presents the texts for *No Cards, Ages Ago* (followed by the musical score),*Our Island Home, A Sensation Novel, Happy Arcadia*, and *Eyes and No Eyes*. Provides a glossary of terms and two appendices.

638. Stevens, David. *All at Sea (A Gilbert and Sullivan Dream)*. Operetta in Two Acts. Boston: C. C. Birchard, 1921. 32 p.

Presents the libretto for an operetta that combines characters and songs from *H. M. S. Pinafore, Pirates of Penzance, The Mikado, Patience,* and *Iolanthe* all into one story. Gives a story outline, directions for setting the stage, and suggestions for costumes. For musical score, see 872.

7. Individual Librettos & Plays

This section is intended to be representative, not comprehensive. Those needing further information may wish to consult the section on Bibliography & Discography.

639. *Ages Ago; A Musical Legend.* Libretto by W. S. Gilbert. Music by Frederick Clay. London: A. S. Mallet, Printer, 1883. 16 p.

First produced in November, 1869, at the Gallery of Illustration.

Ages Ago. See 637.

Brantinghame Hall. See 624.

640. *Broken Hearts.* An Entirely Original Fairy Play. In Three Acts. By W. S. Gilbert. (French's Acting Edition). London: Samuel French, n.d. 35 p.

First produced in December, 1875, at the Royal Court Theatre.

Broken Hearts.. See 622.

641. *Charity:* An Entirely Original Play. In Four Acts. (French's Acting Edition). London: Samuel French, 18--? 44 p.

First produced in 1874, this melodrama was denounced as immoral and was subsequently withdrawn.

642. _____. ...With the Cast of Characters, Costume...etc. New York: Happy Hours Company, 187-? vi, 45 p., diagrs.

Charity. See 621.

643. *A Colossal Idea, An Original Farce.* By W. S. Gilbert. With introduction and decorations by Townley Searle. London and New York: G. P. Putnam's Sons, 1932. xi, 62 p.

Presents the text of one of Gilbert's plays that remains a mystery; it was found in an undated manuscript probably written between 1855 and 1870 and apparently never produced or published.

644. *Comedy and Tragedy.* An Original Drama in One Act, by W. S. Gilbert. (The Minor Drama Series). London and New York: Samuel French, 18--? 16 p.

First performed at the Lyceum Theatre, London, in January, 1884.

645. _____. (French's Acting Edition). London: Samuel French, 1884. 17 p.

Comedy and Tragedy. See 613, 623.

646. *The Contrabandista; or, The Law of the Ladrones.* Comic Opera in 2 Acts. Written by F. C. Burnand. Music by Arthur Sullivan. London: J. Mallett, 1867. 24 p.

First produced at St. George's Opera House in December, 1867.

Cox and Box. See 601-602, 635.

647. *Creatures of Impulse.* A Musical Fairy Tale in One Act. (Lacy's Acting Edition of Plays). London: T. H. Lacy, 18--? 20 p.

Music composed by Alberto Randegger. First performed in April, 1871, at the Royal Court Theatre.

648. _____. (French's Acting Edition). London: Samuel French, 1907. 20 p.

649. _____. In *Plays for Strolling Mummers.* Edited by F. Shay. New York: D. Appleton, 1926.

Creatures of Impulse.. See 613, 624.

650. *Dan'l Druce, Blacksmith.* A New and Original Drama in Three Acts. (French's Acting Edition). London: Samuel French, 187-? 42 p.

Melodrama first produced in September, 1876, at the Haymarket Theatre.

651. _____. In *The Golden Age of Melodrama: Twelve 19th Century Melodramas.* Edited by Michael Kilgarriff. London: Wolfe, 1974.

Dan'l Druce. See 622.

Dulcamara. See *A New and Original Extravaganza Entitled Dulcamara; or, The Little Duck and The Great Quack,* 687.

Dulcamara. See 620.

652. *Engaged.* An Entirely Original Farcical Comedy, in Three Acts. (French's Acting Edition). London: Samuel French, 18--? 48 p.

First produced in October, 1877, at the Haymarket Theatre.

653. _____. In *British Plays of the Nineteenth-Century: An Anthology to Illustrate the Evolution of the Drama.* Edited by J. O. Bailey. New York: Odyssey, 1966.

654. _____. In *English Plays of the Nineteenth Century. Vol. 3.* Edited by Michael R. Booth. New York: Oxford University Press.

655. _____. In *The Magistrate and Other Nineteenth-Century Plays.* Edited by Michael R. Booth. London: Oxford University Press, 1974.

Engaged. See 622, 636.

656. *An Entirely New and Original Aesthetic Opera, in Two Acts, Entitled Patience; or, Bunthorne's Bride.* Written by W. S. Gilbert. Composed by Arthur Sullivan. London: Chappell, 1881. 40 p.

First produced in April, 1881, at the Opera Comique. Became the first true Savoy opera when it was transferred to the new, electrically lighted Savoy Theatre.

657. *An Entirely New and Original Japanese Opera, in Two Acts, Entitled The Mikado; or, The Town of Titipu.* Written by W. S. Gilbert. Composed by Arthur Sullivan. London: Chappell, 18--? 48 p.

First produced in march, 1885, at the Savoy Theatre.

658. *An Entirely Original Comic Opera, in Two Acts, Entitled The Gondoliers; or,The King of Barataria.* Written by W. S. Gilbert. Composed by Arthur Sullivan. London: Chappell, 1889. 47 p.

First produced in December, 1889, at the Savoy Theatre.

659. _____. Philadelphia: T. Presser, 1930. 46 p.

660. *An Entirely Original Comic Opera, in Two Acts, Entitled The Mountebanks.* Written by W. S. Gilbert. Composed by Alfred Cellier. London: Chappel, 1892. 56 p.

First produced in January, 1892, at the Lyric Theatre.

661. *An Entirely Original Fairy Opera, in Two Acts, Entitled Iolanthe; or, The Peer and the Peri.* Written by W. S. Gilbert, composed by Arthur Sullivan. London: Chappell, 1882. 39 p.

First performed in November, 1882, at the Savoy Theatre.

662. *An Entirely Original Supernatural Opera, in Two Acts, Entitled Ruddygore; or, The Witch's Curse.* Written by W. S. Gilbert. Composed by Arthur Sullivan. London: Chappell, 1887. 48 p.

First produced in January, 1887, at the Savoy Theatre.

663. *Eyes and No Eyes; or, The Art of Seeing.* Written by W. S. Gilbert. Music by F. Pascal. London: Joseph Williams, 1896. 23 p.

Adapted from Hans Andersen's "The Emperor's New Clothes" and first presented in July, 1875, at St. George's Hall.

Eyes and No Eyes.. See 637.

The Fairy's Dilemma. See 624.

Fallen Fairies. See 624.

Foggerty's Fairy. See 613, 623.

The Fortune-Hunter. See 624.

664. *The Gentleman in Black.* An Original Musical Legend. Music composed by Frederick Clay. London: T. H. Lacey, 18--? 36 p.

First produced in May, 1870, in Charing Cross.

The Gentleman in Black. See 624.

The Gondoliers. See *An Entirely Original Comic Opera, in Two Acts, Entitled The Gondoliers; or, The King of Barataria,* 658.

The Gondoliers. See 592-593, 599, 611, 624, 627-628, 631.

665. *The Grand Duke; or, The Statutory Duel.* Written by W. S. Gilbert.
Composed by Arthur Sullivan. London: Chappell, 1896. 54 p.

This, the last collaborative effort of G&S, was first produced in March,
1896, at the Savoy Theatre.

The Grand Duke. See 592-593, 599, 611, 624, 627-628, 631.

666. *Gretchen.* A Play in Four Acts. By W. S. Gilbert. (French's Acting
Edition). London and New York: Samuel French, n.d.   50 p.

First produced in March, 1879, at the Olympic Theatre.

667. _____. London: Newman, 1879. iv, 122 p.

Gretchen. See 622.

Happy Arcadia. See 637.

668. *The Happy Land; A Burlesque Version of "The Wicked World."* By F.
Tomline [pseud.] and Gilbert A'Beckett. (French's Minor Drama, The
Acting Edition). London and New York: Samuel French, 187-? 24 p.

Gilbert collaborated under the pseudonym of F. Latour Tomline. First
performed in March, 1873, at the Court Theatre, and prohibited by
the Lord Chamberlain's office.

669. _____. London: J. W. Last, 1873. 28 p.

670. *Harlequin Cock-Robin and Jenny Wren; or, Fortunatus and the Water of
Life The Three Bears, The Three Gifts, The Three Wishes, and The
Little Man Who Woo'd the Little Maid.* London: The Music Publishing
Co., 1867. 23 p.

A grand comic Christmas pantomime first produced in December,
1867, at the Lyceum Theatre.

Haste to the Wedding. See 624.

His Excellency. See 624-625.

671. *H. M. S. Pinafore.* Dramatization of opera by W. S. Gilbert and A. S. Sullivan. Adapted by Adele Thane. *Plays* 33 (May, 1974): 81-92.

Adapts *Pinafore* for a 30-minute youth production with 13 male and 9 female characters. Gives production notes on costumes, properties, setting, lighting, and sound.

672. *H. M. S. Pinafore; or, The Lass That Loved a Sailor.* An Entirely Original Nautical Comic Opera, in Two Acts. Written by W. S. Gilbert. Composed by Arthur Sullivan. London: Chappell, n.d. 32 p.

First produced in may, 1878, at the Opera Comique.

673. _____ In *Preface to Drama.* Edited by Charles W. Cooper. New York: Ronald Press, 1955.

674. _____. In *Representative British Dramas: Victorian and Modern.* Revised Edition. Edited by Montrose Moses, Jr. Boston: Little, Brown, 1931.

675. _____. In *Nineteenth-Century British Drama.* Compiled by Leonard R. N. Ashley. Glenview, Ill.: Scott, Foresman, 1967.

H. M. S. Pinafore. See 592-599, 601, 609, 611, 614-616, 622, 626, 628-634, 638.

The Hooligan. See 624, 1005.

676. *Iolanthe.* Dramatization of opera by W. S. Gilbert and A. S. Sullivan. Adapted by Adele Thane. *Plays* 35 (October, 1975): 83-96.

Adapts *Iolanthe* for a 30-minute youth production. Gives production notes on costumes, properties, setting, lighting and sound.

677. _____. In *The Victorian Age.* Second edition. Edited by John Wilson Bowyer and John Lee Brooks. New York: Appleton-Century-Crofts, 1954.

678. _____. In *Modern Plays, Short and Long.* Edited by Frederick Houk Law. New York: Century, 1924.

679. _____. In *An Introduction to Drama.* Edited by Jay Broadus Hubbell and John Owen Beatty. New York: Macmillan, 1927.

Iolanthe. See *An Entirely Original Fairy Opera in Two Acts, Entitled Iolanthe; or, The Peer and the Peri,* 661.

Iolanthe. See 592-599, 601, 611, 616, 621, 625, 626, 628-634, 638.

680. *Ivanhoe, A Romantic Opera.* Adapted from Sir Walter Scott's novel. Words by Julian Sturgis. Music by Arthur Sullivan. London: Chappell, 1891. 36 p.

681. *The Medical Man.* In *Drawing-Room Plays and Parlour Pantomimes.* Edited by Clement Scott. London: S. Rivers, 1870.

682. *The Merry Zingara; or, The Tipsy Gipsy and The Pipsy Wipsy.* A Whimsical Parody on the "Bohemian Girl." By W. S. Gilbert. London: Phillips, 1868. 41 p.

First produced in March, 1868, at the Royalty Theatre.

The Merry Zingara. See 620.

683. *The Mikado.* Dramatization of opera by W. S. Gilbert and A. S. Sullivan. Adapted by Adele Thane. *Plays* 34 (November, 1974): 83-96.

Adapts *The Mikado* for a 40-minute youth production with 18 male and 10 female characters. Gives production notes on properties, costumes, setting, lighting and sound.

684. *The Mikado; or, The Town of Titipu.* Text by W. S. Gilbert. Music by Arthur Sullivan. (G. Schirmer edition of Gilbert and Sullivan librettos). New York: G. Schirmer, [between 1970 and 1978]. 31 p.

685. _____. In *Explorations in Literature.* Chicago: Lippincott, 1933-34. Vol. 2.

686. _____. In *Prose and Poetry for Appreciation.* (The Prose and Poetry Series). Edited by Harriet Marcelia Lucas, et al. Syracuse, N. Y.: Singer, 1950.

The Mikado. See *An Entirely New and Original Japanese Opera, in Two Acts, Entitled The Mikado; or, The Town of Titipu,* 657.

The Mikado. See 592-599, 601, 609-611, 614, 618, 623, 625, 627-634, 638.

The Mountebanks. See *An Entirely Original Comic Opera, in Two Acts, Entitled The Mountebanks,* 660.

687. *A New and Original Extravaganza Entitled Dulcamara; or, The Little Duck and The Great Quack.* London: Strand, 1866. 34 p.

A travesty of Donizetti's opera *Elixir of Love*, first produced in December, 1866, at the Theatre Royal St. James.

688. *A New and Original Opera, in Two Acts, Entitled The Yeomen of the Guard; or, The Merryman and His Maid.* Written by W. S. Gilbert. Composed by Arthur Sullivan. London: Chappell, 1888? 48 p.

First produced in October, 1888, at the Savoy Theatre.

No Cards. See 637.

689. *An Old Score.* An Original Comedy-Drama, in Three Acts. By W. S. Gilbert. (Lacy's Acting Edition). London: T. H. Lacy, n.d. 42 p.

First produced in July, 1869, at the Gaiety Theatre.

690. _____. (French's Acting Edition). London: Samuel French, 18--? 42 p.

691. *On Bail.* A Farcical Comedy, in Three Acts. Adapted from "Le reveillon." By W. S. Gilbert. (French's Acting Edition). London: Samuel French, n.d. 40 p.

First produced in February, 1877, at the Criterion Theatre.

692. *On Guard.* An Entirely Original Comedy, in Three Acts. By W. S. Gilbert. London: Samuel French, 18--? 47 p.

First produced in October, 1872, at the Court Theatre.

Our Island Home. See 637.

693. *The Palace of Truth.* A Fairy Comedy. In Three Acts. By W. S. Gilbert. (Lacy's Acting Edition). London: T. H. Lacy, n.d. 55 p.

First produced in November, 1870, at the Haymarket Theatre.

The Palace of Truth. See 621, 625, 636.

694. *Patience.* In *Types of Farce Comedy.* Edited by Robert Metcalf Smith and Howard Garrett Rhoads. New York: Prentice-Hall, 1928.

Patience. See *An Entirely New and Original Aesthetic Opera, in Two Acts, Entitled Patience; or, Bunthorne's Bride,* 656.

Patience. See 592-599, 601, 611, 615-616, 623, 626, 628-634, 638.

695. *The Pirates of Penzance.* Dramatization of opera by W. S. Gilbert and A. S. Sullivan. Adapted by Adele Thane. *Plays* 32 (May, 1973): 62, 78-88.

Adapts *Pirates of Penzance* for a 30-minute youth production with 5 male and 6 female characters plus police, pirates and daughters. Gives production notes about costumes, properties, setting, lighting and music.

696. *The Pirates of Penzance; or, The Slave of Duty.* An Entirely Original Comic Opera in Two Acts. Written by W. S. Gilbert. Composed by Arthur Sullivan. London: Chappell, 18--? 32 p.

First produced in December, 1879, at the Fifth Avenue Theater in New York.

697. _____. New York: Hitchcock Publishing, 1880. 39 p.

698. _____. Philadelphia, Pa.: J. M. Stoddart, 1880. 39 p.

The Pirates of Penzance. See 592-599, 601, 609-611, 616, 622, 625-626, 628-635, 638.

699. *The Pretty Druidess; or, The Mother, The Maid, and The Mistletoe Bough.* An Extravaganza (Founded on Bellini's opera *Norma*). By W. S. Gilbert. London: Phillips, 1869? 34 p.

First produced in June, 1869, at the Charing Cross Theatre.

The Pretty Druidess. See 620.

700. *The Princess.* A Whimsical Allegory. (Being a Respectful Perversion of Mr. Tennyson's Poem). By W. S. Gilbert. (Lacy's Acting Edition). London: T. H. Lacy, 18--? 44 p.

First produced in January, 1870, at the Olympic Theatre.

The Princess. See 621.

701. _____. London: Samuel French, 187-? 44 p.

702. *Princess Ida; or, Castle Adamant.* Words by W. S. Gilbert. Music by Arthur Sullivan. Philadelphia: J. M. Stoddart, 1884. 49 p.

First produced in January, 1884, at the Savoy Theatre.

703. _____. London: Chappell, 1884. 48 p.

Princess Ida. See 592-594, 596-599, 601, 611, 616, 623, 625-626, 628-631, 633, 634.

704. *Princess Toto.* Comic Opera in Three Acts. Written by W. S. Gilbert. Music by Frederick Clay. London: Metzler, n.d. 48 p.

First produced in October, 1876, at the Strand Theatre.

Princess Toto. See 636.

705. *Pygmalion and Galatea.* An Entirely Original Mythological Comedy, in Three Acts. By W. S. Gilbert. London & New York: Samuel French, n.d. 36 p.

First produced in December, 1871, at the Haymarket Theatre.

706. _____. London: J. W. Last, 1873. 40 p.

707. _____. (World Acting Drama). Chicago: Dramatic Publishing Company, n.d. 46 p.

708. _____. In *Chief British Dramatists.* Edited by J. B. Matthews and P. R. Lieder. Boston: Houghton Mifflin, 1924.

709. _____. In *Great Modern British Plays.* Edited by James William Marriott. London: Harrap, 1932.

Pygmalion and Galatea. See 621.

710. *Randall's Thumb.* An Original Comedy, in Three Acts. By W. S. Gilbert. (Lacy's Acting Edition). London: T. H. Lacy, 18--? 64 p.

First produced in January, 1871, at the Court Theatre.

711. _____. (French's Standard Drama). New York: Samuel French, 187-? 42 p.

Randall's Thumb. See 624.

712. *Robert the Devil; or, The Nun, The Dun, and The Son of a Gun.* An
Operatic Extravaganza. By W. S. Gilbert. London: Phillips, 1868?
40 p.

First produced at the opening of the New Gaiety Theatre in December,
1868.

Robert the Devil. See 620.

713. *Rosencrantz and Guildenstern.* A Tragic Episode in Three Tableaux,
Founded on an Old Danish Legend. (French's Acting Edition). London:
Samuel French, 189-? 24 p.

First produced in June, 1891, at the Vaudeville Theatre.

714. _____. In *Nineteenth-Century Burlesques.* Vol. 4.
Selected by Stanley Wells. London: Diplomatic Press, 1977.

715. _____. In *Nineteenth-Century Dramatic Burlesques of
Shakespeare: A Selection of British Parodies.* Edited by Jacob B.
Solomon. (A Facsimile Edition). Darby, Pa.: Norwood Editions, 1980.

Rosencrantz and Guildenstern. See 613, 623, 636.

716. *Ruddigore, or, The Witch's Curse.* Dramatization of opera by W. S.
Gilbert and A. S. Sullivan. Adapted by Adele Thane. *Plays* 35 (April,
1976): 38, 85-96.

Adapts *Ruddigore* for a 30-minute youth production. Gives
production notes on costumes, properties, setting, lighting and
sound.

Ruddigore. See *An Entirely Original Supernatural Opera, in Two Acts,
Entitled Ruddygore; or, The Witch's Curse,* 622.

Ruddigore. See 592-594, 596-599, 601, 611, 615, 618, 623, 625,
627-631, 633-634.

A Sensation Novel. See 637

717. *The Sorcerer.* Words by W. S. Gilbert. Music by Arthur Sullivan. London: Chappell, 1989. 40 p.

The Sorcerer. See 592-593, 596-599, 601, 611, 615, 618, 623, 625, 627-631, 633-634.

718. *A Stage Play.* In *Papers on Playmaking.* Edited by Brander Matthews. Introduction by William Archer. New York: Hill and Wang, 1957. p. 93-110.

Presents an article, written for *Comic Annual,* that gives Gilbert's views about how a play is made. Uses the fictional Mr. Horace Facile to show Gilbert's method, presenting dramatic conditions in a serious exposition with a whimsical flavor.

719. *Sweethearts, An Original Dramatic Contrast in Two Acts.* (French's Minor Drama Series, The Acting Edition). New York and London: Samuel French, 189-? 20 p.

Presents the text of Gilbert's play which was first produced at the Prince of Wales Theatre on November 7, 1874.

720. _____. (Sergel's Acting Drama). Chicago: Dramatic Publishing Co., 1874? 26 p.

721. _____. In *Representative Modern Plays.* Edited by Richard Albert Cordell. New York: Nelson, 1929.

722. _____. In *Typical Plays for Secondary Schools.* Edited by James Plaisted Webber and Hanson Hart Webster. Boston: Houghton Mifflin, 1929.

723. _____. In *The Drama: Its History, Literature, and Influence on Civilization.* Edited by Alfred Bates. London: Athenian Society, 1903-04. Vol. 16.

Sweethearts. See 636.

Thespis; or, The Gods Grown Old. See 592-593, 599, 611, 615-626, 630-631, 635.

724. *Tom Cobb; or, Fortune's Toy.* An Entirely Original Farcical Comedy, in Three Acts, by W. S. Gilbert. (French's Standard Drama). London and New York: Samuel French, n.d. 32 p.

First produced in April, 1875, at the St. James Theatre.

725. _____. In *English Plays of the Nineteenth Century; IV:
      Farces.* Edited by Michael R. Booth. Oxford: Clarendon Press, 1973.

      Tom Cobb. See 622.

726. *Topsyturvydom.* Original Extravaganza by W. S. Gilbert. Oxford: The
      University Press, 1931. 26 p.

      First produced in March, 1873, at the Criterion Theatre, but not
      published at that time. This edition was transcribed from a
      manuscript not in Gilbert's handwriting.

727. *Trial by Jury.* A Novel and Original Cantata by Arthur Sullivan and W. S.
      Gilbert. London: Walter Smith, 1875. 17 p.

      First produced in March, 1875, at the Royalty Theatre.

728. _____. Dramatization of opera by W. S. Gilbert and A. S.
      Sullivan. Adapted by Adele Thane. *Plays* 33 (December, 1973):
      90-96.

      Adapts *Trial by Jury* for a 25-minute youth production using 5 male
      and 6 female characters plus extras. Gives production notes on
      costumes, properties, setting, lighting and sound.

729. _____. In *Twenty-Three Plays; An Introductory Anthology.*
      Edited by Otto Reinert and Peter Arnott. New York: Little, Brown,
      1978.

      Trial by Jury. See 592-594, 596-599, 601, 611, 616, 625-626,
         628-634.

      Trying a Dramatist. See 624, 1009.

730. *Utopia, Limited; or, The Flowers of Progress.* Written by W. S. Gilbert.
      Composed by Arthur Sullivan. London: Chappell, 1893. 54 p.

      First produced in October, 1893, at the Savoy Theatre.

      Utopia, Limited. See 592-593, 599, 611, 618, 625, 627-628,
         630-631, 633-634.

731. *La Vivandiere; or, True to the Corps!* An Original Operatic
Extravaganza. London: H. Montague, 1868. 31 p.

First produced in June, 1867, at the St. James Theatre.

732. _____. An Operatic Extravaganza Founded on Donizetti's
Opera, "La Figlia Del Rigimento." Liverpool: Matthews Brothers, 1867.
30 p.

La Vivandiere. See 620.

733. *The Wedding March.* ("Le Chapeau de Paille d'Italie"). An
Eccentricity, in Three Acts. By W. S. Gilbert. (French's Acting
Edition). London & New York: Samuel French, 18--? 34 p.

First produced in November, 1873, at the Court Theatre.

734. *The Wicked World.* An Entirely Original Fairy Comedy, in Three Acts
and One Scene. By W. S. Gilbert. (French's Standard Drama). London
and New York: Samuel French, 18--? 42 p.

First produced in January, 1873, at the Haymarket Theatre.

735. _____. London: Judd, 18--? 44 p.

736. _____ With a cast of Characters, Costume...etc. (The Acting
Drama). New York: Happy Hours Co., 187-? iv, 44 p.

The Wicked World. See 613, 621.

737. *Yeomen of the Guard.* Dramatization of opera by W. S. Gilbert and A. S.
Sullivan. Adapted by Adele Thane. *Plays* 34 (April, 1975): 67-80.

Adapts *Yeomen of the Guard* for a 40-minute youth production with
7 male and 3 female characters. Gives production notes on
costumes, setting, properties, lighting and sound.

The Yeomen of the Guard. See *A New and Original Opera, in Two
Acts, Entitled The Yeomen of the Guard; or, The Merryman and His
Maid,* 688.

The Yeomen of the Guard. See 592-594, 596-599, 601, 611, 623,
625, 627-634.

8. Musical Scores

738. *The Authentic Gilbert and Sullivan Songbook.* Text by W. S. Gilbert. Music by Arthur Sullivan. Collected by Malcolm Binney and Peter Lavender. Selected and with plot summaries by James Spero. New York: Dover, 1971. 397 p.

Includes vocal score with piano accompaniment for 92 unabridged selections from all 14 G&S operas reproduced from early vocal scores authorized by Sir Arthur Sullivan. Provides plot summary for each opera.

739. *The Chieftain.* An Original Comic Opera in Two Acts. Written by F. C. Burnand. Music by Arthur Sullivan. London & New York: Boosey, 1895. 159 p.

Contains vocal score with piano accompaniment. Revision of *The Contrabandista.*

740. _____. An Original Comic Opera in Two Acts. Written by F. C. Burnand; composed by Arthur Sullivan. Reproduction of the Boosey edition of 1894. New York: Readex Microprint, 1979, microform.

Vocal score with piano reproduced on five microopaques.

741. *The Choruses of H. M. S. Pinafore, or, The Lass That Loved a Sailor.* Book by W. S. Gilbert; music by Arthur Sullivan. (Kalmus Vocal Score Series). New York: E. F. Kalmus, 196-? 48 p.

Presents the vocal scores for chorus with piano accompaniment.

742. *The Choruses of Iolanthe, or, The Peer and the Peri.* Book by W. S. Gilbert; music by Arthur Sullivan. (Kalmus Chorus Score Series). New York: E. F. Kalmus, 196-? 69 p.

Presents the vocal scores for chorus with piano accompaniment.

743. *The Choruses of The Mikado, or, The Town of Titipu.* Book by W. S. Gilbert; music by Arthur Sullivan. (Kalmus Vocal Series). New York: E. F. Kalmus, 196-? 44 p.

Presents the score for chorus with piano accompaniment.

744. *The Choruses of The Pirates of Penzance, or, The Slave of Duty.* Book by W. S. Gilbert; music by Arthur Sullivan. (Kalmus Vocal Series). New York: E. F. Kalmus, 196-?

Presents the vocal scores for chorus with piano.

745. *The Choruses of The Yeomen of the Guard, or, The Merryman and His Maid.* Book by W. S. Gilbert; music by Arthur Sullivan. Authentic version edited by Edmond W. Rickett. New York: G. Schirmer, 1954. 63 p.

Presents the scores for unaccompanied mixed voices.

746. *The Contrabandista; or, the Law of the Ladrones.* Comic Opera in Two Acts. Written by F. C. Burnand. Music by Arthur Sullivan. London: Boosey, 188-? 87 p.

Contains vocal score with piano accompaniment. First produced at St. George's Opera House in December, 1867.

747. *Cox and Box, or, The Long-Lost Brothers.* Triumviretta in One Act. Adapted to the lyric stage from J. Maddison Morton's farce of *Box and Cox.* By F. C. Burnand. Music by Arthur S. Sullivan. New York and London: Boosey & Hawkes, n.d. 58 p.

Contains vocal score and piano accompaniment.

748. _____. A Comic Opera in One Act. The book by F. C. Burnand. Music by Arthur S. Sullivan. Boston: Oliver Ditson, 19--? 56 p.

Contains vocal score and piano accompaniment.

749. *The Duke's Song from Patience.* Words by W. S. Gilbert [and] acc. by Arthur Sullivan. Melody reconstructed by Ian Bartlett. Banbury: Piers Press, 1967. 4 p.

Presents the vocal score with piano accompaniment for this excerpt.

750. *The Emerald Isle; or, The Caves of Carrig-Cleens.* A New and Original Comic Opera in Two Acts. Written by Basil Hood. Composed by Arthur Sullivan and Edward German. Arranged from the full score by Wilfred Bendall. London: Chappell, 1901. 230 p.

Contains vocal score and piano accompaniment. The music was completed by Edward German after Sullivan's death in 1900.

751. _____. Written by Basil Hood. Composed by Arthur
      Sullivan and Edward German. Arranged from the full score by Wilfred
      Bendall. Reprint of the Chappell 1901 edition. New York: Readex
      Microprint, 1969, microform.

      Presents the vocal score with piano accompaniment printed on three
      microopaques.

752. *An Entirely New and Original Aesthetic Opera in Two Acts, Entitled
      Patience; or, Bunthorne's Bride.* Written by W. S. Gilbert. Composed
      by Arthur Sullivan. London: Stoddart, 1881. 127 p.

      Contains vocal score and piano accompaniment.

753. *An Entirely New and Original Aesthetic Opera in Two Acts, Entitled
      Patience; or, Bunthorne's Bride.* Written by W. S. Gilbert. Music by
      Arthur Sullivan. Arranged from the full score by Berthold Tours.
      London: Chappell, 189-? 117 p.

      Contains vocal score and piano accompaniment.

754. *Gems from Gilbert and Sullivan.* Arranged for piano by Franz Mittler.
      Philadelphia: T. Presser, 1948. 48 p.

      Contains 25 favorite selections from the comic operas arranged for
      piano.

755. *Gilbert and Sullivan at Home.* (Whole World Series). Arranged for
      either playing or singing by Albert E. Wier. New York: Broadcast
      Music, 1944. 256 p.

      Presents the stories and vocal score with piano accompaniment for
      the most popular songs from *Trial by Jury, The Sorcerer, H.M.S.
      Pinafore,* and others.

756. *Gilbert and Sullivan's Famous Songs.* Arranged by Harold Dixon. New
      York: Robbins Music Corp., 1942. 64 p.

      Contains excerpts from various operas, arranged in vocal score with
      piano accompaniment.

757. *Gilbert and Sullivan's The Pirates of Penzance.* Highlights for concert
      band with optional mixed chorus. Arranged for band by Robert
      Russell Bennett. New York: Chappell, 1962, 22 p.

      Presents the condensed score with 65 parts.

758. *The Golden Legend.* (Novello's Original Octavo Edition). Adapted from the poem of Longfellow by Joseph Bennett. Music composed by Arthur Sullivan. Piano-forte arrangement by Berthold Tours. New York: Novello, Ewer, 1886? 137 p.

Contains the vocal score with piano accompaniment.

759. _____. Adapted from the poem of Longfellow by Joseph Bennett. Music composed by Arthur Sullivan. London: Novello, Ewer, 1887. 345 p.

Presents the full score of the cantata for soloists, chorus and orchestra. First performed at the Leeds Festival, 1886.

760. _____. Music by Arthur Sullivan. Words adapted from the poem of Longfellow by Joseph Bennett. New York: G. Schirmer, 19--? xi,137 p.

Presents vocal scores with piano accompaniment.

761. _____. Adapted from the poem of Longfellow by Joseph Bennett. Music composed by Arthur Sullivan. Edited by Roger Harris. Chorleywood, Herts., Eng.: R. Clyde, 1986. xiv, 355 p.

Presents a reprint of the 1887 Novello, Ewer score (see 759) with new editorial revisions and corrections.

762. *Gondoliers. Dance a Cachuca, Fandango, Bolero.* W. S. Gilbert and Arthur Sullivan. (Concord Series). Boston: E. C. Schirmer, 1925. 16 p.

Presents the Finale from *The Gondoliers* in four parts for men's voices with accompaniment for two pianos.

763. *The Gondoliers; or, The King of Barataria.* By W. S. Gilbert and Arthur Sullivan. Abridged and simplified by David Stevens. Boston: C. C. Birchard, 1940. 166p.

Contains vocal score with piano accompaniment.

764. _____. Text by W. S. Gilbert. Music by Arthur Sullivan. Authentic version edited by Bryceson Treharne. New York: G. Schirmer, 1941. 277 p.

Contains all the dialogue plus vocal score and piano accompaniment.

765. _____. By W. S. Gilbert and Arthur Sullivan. London: Chappell, 1950? 225 p.

Contains vocal score and piano accompaniment.

766. _____. Words by S. W. Gilbert, Music by Arthur Sullivan. (Kalmus Orchestra Library). Miami, Fla.: E. F. Kalmus, 1983? 273 p.

Presents the conductor's score.

767. _____. By W. S. Gilbert and Arthur Sullivan. East Aurora, N.Y.: Roycroft Editions, 198-?. 245 p.

Presents the vocal score with piano accompaniment.

768. _____. Libretto by W. S. Gilbert. Music by Arthur Sullivan. Edited by David Lloyd-Jones. London & New York: E. Eulenburg, 1984. xlii, 488 p.

Presents a miniature score. Preface in English and German.

769. *The Grand Duke; or, The Statutory Duel.* A Comic Opera in two acts. Written by W. S. Gilbert; composed by Arthur Sullivan. Arranged for the pianoforte by Wilfred Bendall. London: Chappell, 1896. viii, 93 p.

Arranged for piano solo.

770. _____. By W. S. Gilbert and Arthur Sullivan. New York: Chappell, 1911. 166 p.

Presents the complete vocal score with piano accompaniment.

771. _____. Arthur Sullivan. Arranged for symphony orchestra by Eugene Minor. (Kalmus Orchestra Library). Miami, Fla.: Kalmus, 1983. 32 p.

Presents the conductor's score, a photocopy of the arranger's manuscript.

The Grand Duke. See *Vocal Score of The Grand Duke; or, The Statutory Duel,* 893.

Haddon Hall. See *An Original Light English Opera, in Three Acts, Entitled Haddon Hall,* 821.

772. *Ho, Jolly Jenkin.* The Friar's Song from *Ivanhoe.* Words by Julian Sturgis; music by Arthur Sullivan. London: Chappell, 19--?. 7 p.

Presents the score of the Friar's Song for voice and piano.

773. *H. M. S. Pinafore, or, the Lass That Loved A Sailor.* Text by W. S.
Gilbert. Music by Arthur Sullivan. Boston: Oliver Ditson [19--]. 160 p.

Includes vocal score and piano accompaniment for this "entirely
original nautical opera."

774. _____. Text by W. S. Gilbert. Music by Arthur Sullivan.
London: J. B. Cramer, 1911. 150 p.

Provides vocal score and piano accompaniment for all songs and
recitatives.

775. _____. Written by W. S. Gilbert, music by Arthur Sullivan.
London: Metzler, 1920?. 150 p.

Presents vocal scores with piano accompaniment.

776. _____. Book by W. S. Gilbert. Music by Arthur Sullivan.
Boston: Oliver Ditson, 1927. 24 p.

Presents the score for the chorus parts from the opera.

777. _____. Text by W. S. Gilbert. Music by Arthur Sullivan.
Abridged and simplified by W. Norman Grayson. Boston: C. C. Birchard,
1934. 56 p.

Includes vocal score and piano accompaniment in an abridged version
of this "nautical operetta in two acts."

778. _____. Book by W. S. Gilbert, music by Arthur Sullivan.
Authentic version edited by Bryceson Treharne. New York: G.
Schirmer, 195-? 167 p.

Contains vocal score with piano accompaniment plus all the dialogue.

779. _____. Written by W. S. Gilbert; music by Arthur Sullivan.
London: Cramer, 197-?. 150 p.

Presents vocal scores with piano accompaniment.

780. *H. M. S. Pinafore.* By Gilbert and Sullivan. Evanston, Ill.:
Summy-Birchard, 1966. 64 p., illus.

Presents a new condensed version of the vocal score with piano
accompaniment. Includes stage directions and dialogue.

781. _____. *Operetta in Two Acts. Abridged Version for Schools.*
     Text and lyrics by W. S. Gilbert, adapted by Thomas M. Hayes. Music
     by Arthur Sullivan, arranged by Bryceson Treharne. Cincinnati: Willis,
     1946. 51 p., illus.

     Contains vocal score with piano accompaniment in abridged form.

     H. M. S. Pinafore. See *We Sail the Ocean Blue.* 897; *Selections
     from H. M. S. Pinafore,* 864.

782. *H. M. S. Pinafore, The Mikado.* " Libretto by W. S. Gilbert. Music by Sir
     Arthur Sullivan. *Light Opera at Home.* Arranged for either playing or
     singing by Arthur E. Wier. New York: Appleton, 1917. p. 70-98;
     121-136.

     Gives the story and most popular music in each of these two G&S
     favorites.

783. *Incidental Music to Shakespeare's Henry VIII.* Composed by Arthur
     Sullivan. London: J. Metzler, 1878. 47 p.

     Presents the full score.

     Incidental Music to Shakespeare's Tempest. See *The Music to
     Shakespeare's Tempest,* 819.

784. *Iolanthe, or, The Peer and the Peri.* Text by W. S. Gilbert. Music by
     Arthur Sullivan. London: J. M. Stoddart, 1882. 155 p.

     Presents the full score authorized copyright edition. Includes vocal
     score and piano accompaniment plus text.

785. _____. Written by W. S. Gilbert. Composed by Arthur
     Sullivan. Reprint of the 1882 Stoddart edition. New York: Readex
     Microprint, 1968, microform.

     Presents the vocal scores on 2 microopaques.

786. _____. Book by W. S. Gilbert; music by Arthur Sullivan.
     Boston: Ditson, 1929. 30 p.

     Presents vocal scores for chorus only.

787. _____. Text by W. S. Gilbert. Music by Arthur Sullivan. Abridged and simplified by Berta Elsmith. Boston: C. C. Birchard, 1935. 102 p.

Gives staging suggestions, vocal score, piano accompaniment, and text.

788. _____. By W. S. Gilbert and Arthur Sullivan. Rev. Ed. London: Chappell, 19--? 176 p.

Contains vocal score and piano accompaniment.

789. _____. Authentic version edited by Bryceson Treharne. New York: G. Schirmer, n.d. 208 p.

Contains the complete vocal scores, piano accompaniment, and all the dialogue.

Iolanthe. See *The Choruses of Iolanthe,* 742; *The March of the Peers,* 802.

790. *Ivanhoe.* A Romantic Opera Adapted from Sir Walter Scott's Novel. Words by J. Sturgis, Music by A. Sullivan. Arranged for the pianoforte by Ernest Ford. London: Chappell, 1891. 261 p.

Contains the vocal score with piano accompaniment.

791. _____. A Romantic Opera Adapted from Sir Walter Scott's Novel. Words by J. Sturgis, music by A. Sullivan. Arranged for the pianoforte by Ernest Ford. Reprint of the 1891 Chappell edition. New York: Readex Microprint, 1969, microform.

Presents the vocal scores on 3 microopaques.

792. *Kenilworth, A Masque of the Days of Queen Elizabeth As Performed at the Birmingham Festival.* Words by Henry F. Chorley, music by Arthur S. Sullivan. Op. 4. London: Chappell, 187-? 72 p.

Contains the vocal score with piano accompaniment.

793. _____. Words by Henry F. Chorley, music by Arthur Sullivan. Op. 4. Reprint of the Chappell edition of 187-? New York: Readex Microprint, 1969, microform.

Presents the vocal score on one microopaque.

794. *The Light of the World, An Oratorio First Performed at the
     Birmingham Musical Festival August 27, 1873.* The words compiled
     from the Holy Scripture. The music composed by Arthur Sullivan.
     New York: G. Schirmer, 190-? xiv, 264 p.

     Contains the vocal score with piano accompaniment.

795. _____. Arthur Sullivan. Oxford: Bodleian Library, 1986,
     microform.

     Presents one manuscript score (approx. 300 p.) on 35mm microfilm.

796. *The Lost Chord.* Part Song for Men's Voices. [Words by] Adelaide A.
     Procter. [Music by] Arthur Sullivan. Arranged by Austin M. Beattie.
     Boston: Oliver Ditson, 1926. 11 p.

     Contains the vocal parts for men's voices and organ or piano
     accompaniment.

797. _____. Sir Arthur Sullivan. Arranged by Howard Stube.
     (Belwin Ensemble Series). Rockville Centre, N.Y.: Belwin, 1946. 4 p.

     Presents a score for cornet or trumpet quartet in four parts.

798. _____. Sir Arthur Sullivan. (Belwin Ensemble Series).
     Rockville Centre, N.Y.: Belwin, 1946. 4 p.

     Presents an arrangement for trombone quartet.

799. _____. Sir Arthur Sullivan. Arranged by Irvin Cooper.
     Words by Adelaide Proctor. New York: Fischer, 1951. 9 p.

     Arranged for Junior High School chorus featuring cambiata (changing
     voice), soprano, alto and baritone with piano or organ.

800. _____. Sir Arthur Sullivan. Arranged by Beldon Leonard.
     Melville, N.Y.: Belwin Mills, 1973. 4 p.

     Presents the score arranged for E-flat alto clarinet solo with piano
     accompaniment.

801. *Madrigal Mikado.* Sir Arthur Sullivan. Arranged by Leigh Martinet.
     Baltimore: Baltimore Horn Club, 1981. 2 p.

     Presents the music for French horn ensemble to "Brightly dawns our
     wedding day."

802. *March of the Peers.* From *Iolanthe* (1882). Sir Arthur Sullivan. Arranged by Merle J. Isaac. (Highland/Etling Concert Orchestra Series). Norwalk, Cal.: Highland/Etling Publishing, 1983. 32 p.

Presents an arrangement in 51 parts for concert orchestra.

803. *The Martyr of Antioch: Sacred Musical Drama.* The words selected and arranged from Milman's poem. The music composed by Arthur Sullivan. The accompaniment arranged for the pianoforte from the full score by Eugene d'Albert. London: Chappell, 1880. 216 p.

Contains the vocal score with piano accompaniment. Performed for the first time at the Leeds Triennial Musical Festival October 15, 1880.

804. *The Mikado.* Operetta in two acts, with libretto by W. S. Gilbert and music by Arthur Sullivan. Introduction by Gordon Jacob. Farnborough, Hants., Eng.: Gregg International Publishers, 1968. 391 p.

Reproduction in facsimile of Sullivan's autograph score in the Library of the Royal Academy of Music, London.

805. *The Mikado. Easy Piano Picture Book.* Text by Kenneth Lillington after W. S. Gilbert; music by Arthur Sullivan, arranged by Alan Gout. Illustrations by Jenny Tylden-Wright. London: Faber & Faber in association with Faber Music, 1988, 32 p.

Presents arrangements for the piano of selections from *The Mikado.*

806. *Mikado Melange.* Arthur Sullivan. Arranged by Leigh Martinet. Baltimore, Md.: Baltimore Horn Club, 1988. 6 p.

Presents selections from *The Mikado* arranged for four horns.

807. *The Mikado, or, The Town of Titipu.* By W. S. Gilbert. Music by Arthur Sullivan. Arrangements for the pianoforte by George Lowell Tracy. London & New York: Chappell, 1885? 193 p.

Contains the vocal score with piano accompaniment.

808. _____. Text by W. S. Gilbert. Music by Arthur Sullivan. Abridged and simplified by W. Norman Grayson. Boston: C. C. Birchard, 1935. 95 p.

Provides vocal score, piano accompaniment, and text for *The Mikado.*

809. _____. Text by W. S. Gilbert. Music by Arthur Sullivan.
Authentic version edited by Bryceson Treharne. New York: G.
Schirmer, n. d. 231 p.

Contains complete vocal scores, piano accompaniment, and all the
dialogue.

810. _____. Written by W. S. Gilbert; composed by Arthur Sullivan.
Boston: Tracy Music Library, 1947. 189 p, illus.

Presents vocal score with piano; includes libretto. Authentic version
edited by Percival B. Metcalf, containing pictures of the D'Oyly Carte
Opera Company.

811. _____. [Text by] W. S. Gilbert; [music by] Arthur Sullivan.
(Kalmus Orchestra Library). New York: Edwin F. Kalmus, 197-?.
335 p.

Presents the score for orchestra.

812. _____. By W. S. Gilbert and Arthur Sullivan. Arranged for
school performance by Christopher Le Fleming. London: J. B. Cramer,
1975. 105 p.

Presents the vocal score without accompaniment.

813. _____. W. S. Gilbert and Arthur Sullivan. (Kalmus Vocal
Scores). Miami, Fla.: CPP Belwin, 198-?. 231 p.

Presents vocal scores with piano; includes the dialogue.

814. _____. Book by W. S. Gilbert; music by Arthur Sullivan.
Authentic version edited by Bryceson Treharne. [s.l.]: G. Schirmer.
Milwaukee: Distributed by Hal Leonard Publ. Corp., 198-?. 231 p.

Presents the vocal scores with piano accompaniment and all the
dialogue.

815. _____. Book by W. S. Gilbert; music by Arthur Sullivan. East
Aurora, N.Y.: Roycroft Editions, 198-?. 231 p.

Presents vocal scores with piano accompaniment.

816. _____. [Text by] W. S. Gilbert and [music by] Arthur Sullivan.
(Kalmus Vocal Scores Series). Melville, N.Y.: Belwin Mills, 198-?.
231 p.

Presents vocal scores with piano accompaniment; includes dialogue.

The Mikado. See *The Choruses of The Mikado,* 743; *Madrigal Mikado,* 801; *Our Great Mikado,* 825; *Overture to the Mikado,* 829; *Songs from Michael Todd's Hot Mikado,* 867. *Vocal Score of The Mikado,* 894;

817. Monroe, Paul Jordan. *Shreds and Patches from Gilbert and Sullivan; An Operetta for High Schools and Adults.* Book by Paul Jordan Monroe. Lyrics adapted from W. S. Gilbert. Music adapted from Arthur Sullivan by Ira B. Wilson. New York: Lorenz Publishing, 1942. 84 p. See 562.

Supplies vocal score, piano accompaniment and dialogue for a 2-act operetta, the lyrics and music being adapted from half a dozen G&S operas and worked into a story of a 19th-century opera company whose manager is Mr. Coyly and whose tenor is Mr. Darte.

818. *The Music to Shakespeare's Tempest.* Composed by Arthur S. Sullivan. [Op. 1. Arranged from the score by Franklin Taylor.] London: Novello, Ewer, 186-? 106 p.

Includes the vocal score for SATB with piano accompaniment.

819. _____. Arthur Sullivan. New York: Kalmus, 198-?. 204 p.

Presents the score for orchestra with soloists and chorus.

820. *On Shore and Sea; A Dramatic Cantata.* Words by Tom Taylor. Music by Arthur S. Sullivan. New York: G. Schirmer, 1898. vi, 55 p.

Contains the vocal score with piano accompaniment. Composed for and performed at the opening of the London International Exhibition May 1, 1871.

821. *An Original Light English Opera, in Three Acts, Entitled Haddon Hall.* Written by Sydney Grundy. Composed by Arthur Sullivan. Arranged from the full score by King Hall. London: Chappell, 1892. 169 p.

Contains the vocal score with piano accompaniment.

822. _____. Written by Sydney Grundy. Composed by Arthur Sullivan. Arranged from the full score by King Hall. Reprint of the 1892 Chappell edition. New York: Readex Microprint, 1969, microform.

Presents the vocal score with piano accompaniment on two microopaques.

823. *Orpheus With His Lute.* Words from Shakespeare's Henry VIII. Music by Arthur Sullivan. Boston: Oliver Ditson, 188-? 7 p.

Includes the song with piano accompaniment.

824. _____. Words from Shakespeare's "Henry VIII." Music by Arthur Sullivan. Edited by Bainbridge Crist. New York: Fischer, 1918. 7 p.

Presents four songs for low voice with piano.

825. *Our Great Mikado.* From *The Mikado.* Sir Arthur Sullivan. Boston: E. C. Schirmer, 1960. 11 p.

Presents the piano-vocal score for this excerpt from the opera.

826. *Overture di Ballo.* Composed by Arthur Sullivan. London: Novello, Ewer, 1889. 80 p.

Presents the full score for orchestra.

827. *Overture in C (In Memoriam).* Composed by Arthur Sullivan. London & New York: Novello, Ewer, 1867? 74 p.

Written on his father's death and first performed at the Norwich Festival October 30, 1886. Includes the full score for orchestra.

828. _____. Arthur Sullivan. Edited by Roger Harris. Reprint of the 1889 Novello, Ewer edition, with new editorial revisions and corrections. Chorleywood, Herts., Eng.: R. Clyde, 1985. ii, 95 p.

Presents the full orchestra score.

829. *Overture to the Mikado.* Sir Arthur Sullivan. Transcribed by R. D. King. North Easton, Mass.: Music for Brass, 195-? 12 p.

Presents the score to the overture arranged for band.

830. *Overture to The Yeomen of the Guard.* Arthur Sullivan. Edited by David Lloyd-Jones and Sir Charles Mackerras. London: Ernst Eulenberg, 1979. 34 p.

Presents a miniature score for orchestra.

831. *Patience, or, Bunthorne's Bride.* Written by W. S. Gilbert. Composed by Arthur Sullivan. Authorized copyright edition. Philadelphia: J. M. Stoddart, 1881. 117 p.

Contains the vocal score with piano accompaniment.

832. _____. Text by W. S. Gilbert. Music by Arthur Sullivan.
Abridged and simplified by David Stevens. Boston: C. C. Birchard,
1935. 114 p.

Includes vocal score, piano accompaniment, text, and stage directions
for this two-act opera.

833. _____. Book by W. S. Gilbert. Authentic version
edited by Edmond W. Rickett. New York: G. Schirmer, 1950. 193 p.

Contains vocal score with piano accompaniment plus all the dialogue.

834. _____. [Text by] W. S. Gilbert and [music by] Arthur Sullivan.
(Kalmus Vocal Scores Series). Melville, N.Y.: Belwin Mills, 1970?
166 p.

Presents the vocal score with piano accompaniment.

835. _____. Words by W. S. Gilbert. Music by Arthur Sullivan.
(Kalmus Orchestra Library Series). New York: E. F. Kalmus, 1981?
192 p.

Presents the score in 18 parts.

Patience. See *An Entirely New and Original Aesthetic Opera in Two
Acts, Entitled Patience; or, Bunthorne's Bride,* 752; *The Duke's Song
from Patience,* 749.

836. *Pianoforte Arrangement of Princess Ida, or, Castle Adamant.* By W. S.
Gilbert and Arthur Sullivan. Arranged by George L. Tracy. Boston:
C. C. Birchard, 19--? 31 p.

Presents vocal scores for chorus parts with piano.

838. *The Pirate Movie.* [s.l.]: Columbia Pictures Publications, 1982. 87 p.,
illus. (some color).

Presents the score of a movie based loosely on *The Pirates of
Penzance* by Gilbert and Sullivan.

839. *Pirates of Penzance.* Freely adapted from Gilbert and Sullivan by
Shubert Fendrich and Jerry Waldrop. Denver: Pioneer Drama
Service, 1984. 26 p.

Presents the text with voice parts for young people.

840. *The Pirates of Penzance, or, The Slave of Duty.* An Entirely Original
      Comic Opera in Two Acts. Written by W. S. Gilbert. Composed by
      Arthur Sullivan. London: Chappell, 1880? 135 p.

      Contains the vocal score with piano accompaniment.

841. _____. An Entirely Original Comic Opera in Two Acts. Text
      by W. S. Gilbert. Music by Arthur Sullivan. London: J. M. Stoddart,
      1880. 141 p.

      Contains the complete vocal score, piano accompaniment, and all the
      dialogue.

842. _____. Book by W. S. Gilbert. Music by Arthur Sullivan.
      Philadelphia: Ditson, 1927.

      Presents the vocal score for chorus parts.

843. _____. By W. S. Gilbert and Arthur Sullivan. New York:
      Chappell, 1931, 174 p.

      Presents the vocal scores with piano accompaniment.

844. _____. Text by W. S. Gilbert. Music by Arthur Sullivan.
      Abridged and simplified by David Stevens. Boston: C. C. Birchard,
      1935. 116 p.

      Contains abridged text plus vocal score and piano accompaniment.

845. _____. Book by W. S. Gilbert. Music by Arthur Sullivan.
      Authentic version edited by Bryceson Treharne. New York: G.
      Schirmer, 1940? 213 p.

      Contains vocal score with piano accompaniment plus all the dialogue.

846. _____. Written by W. S. Gilbert; composed by Arthur Sullivan.
      New York: Hitchcock, 1946, 141 p.

      Presents the vocal scores with piano accompaniment.

847. _____. [Text by] W. S. Gilbert and [music by] Arthur Sullivan.
      East Aurora, N.Y.: Roycroft Editions, 198-? 213 p.

      Presents the vocal scores with piano accompaniment.

848. _____. Text by W. S. Gilbert. Music by Arthur Sullivan.
      (Kalmus Orchestra Library Series). Miami, Fla.: E. F. Kalmus, 1984?
      188 p.

      Presents the score for orchestra.

849. _____. Book by W. S. Gilbert; music by Arthur Sullivan.
(Kalmus Vocal Scores Series). New York: E. F. Kalmus, 198-? 213 p.

Presents the vocal scores with piano accompaniment.

The Pirates of Penzance. See *The Choruses of The Pirates of
Penzance,* 744; *Gilbert and Sullivan's The Pirates of Penzance,* 757;
Three Pieces from The Pirates of Penzance, 883; *Vocal Highlights
from the Pirates of Penzance,* 892; *When the Foeman Bears His
Steel,* 898.

850. *Princess Ida, or, Castle Adamant.* By W. S. Gilbert and Arthur Sullivan.
[Washington, D.C.?]: J. M. Stoddart, 1884. 133 p.

Present the vocal scores with piano.

851. _____. By W. S. Gilbert and Arthur Sullivan. London:
Chappell, 1911. 138 p.

Contains vocal score with piano accompaniment.

852. _____. By W. S. Gilbert and Arthur Sullivan.
Arrangement for pianoforte by George Lowell Tracy. Boston: Oliver
Ditson, 1884. 133 p.

Contains the vocal score with piano accompaniment.

853. _____. Libretto by W. S. Gilbert. Based on Tennyson's The
Princess. Music by Arthur Sullivan. Melville, N.Y.: Belwin Mills, 198-?
138 p.

Presents the vocal scores with piano accompaniment.

Princess Ida. See *Pianoforte Arrangement of Princess Ida,* 836.

854. *The Prodigal Son, An Oratorio.* The words selected entirely from the
Holy Scriptures. The music composed by Arthur S. Sullivan. The
orchestral accompaniments arranged for the pianoforte by Franklin
Taylor. London: Boosey, n.d. 113 p.

First performed at the Worcester Musical Festival September 8, 1869.
Contains the vocal score with piano accompaniment.

855. _____. The words selected entirely from the Holy
     Scriptures. The music composed by Arthur S. Sullivan. Boston:
     O. Ditson, 19--? 128 p.

     Presents the vocal scores with piano.

856. *The Rose of Persia; or, The Story-Teller and the Slave.* New Comic
     Opera Written by Basil Hood. Composed by Arthur Sullivan. Arranged
     from the full score by Wilfred Bendall. London: Chappell; New York:
     Boosey, 1900. 254 p.

     Contains the vocal score with piano accompaniment.

857. _____. New comic opera written by Basil Hood. Composed
     by Arthur Sullivan. Arranged from the full score by Wilfred Bendall.
     Reprint of the 1900 Boosey edition. New York: Readex Microprint,
     1969, microform.

     Presents the vocal score with piano on three microopaques.

858. *Ruddigore; or, The Witch's Curse.* By W. S. Gilbert and Arthur Sullivan.
     Arrangements for pianoforte by George Lowell Tracy. London:
     Chappell, 1887. 129 p.

     Contains all the dialogue, vocal score with piano accompaniment, and
        brief plot sketch.

859. _____. Text by W. S. Gilbert. Music by Arthur Sullivan.
     G., Schirmer Edition. Authentic version edited by Edmond W.
     Rickett. New York: G. Schirmer, 1953. 220 p.

     Contains all the dialogue, vocal score with piano accompaniment, and
        brief plot sketch.

860. _____. (Laurel Edition Standard Operas). Boston: C. C.
     Birchard, 191-? 23 p.

     Contains chorus parts for 1-5 voices.

861. _____. By W. S. Gilbert and Arthur Sullivan. (Kalmus Vocal
     Series). Melville, N.Y.: Belwin Mills, 197-? 141 p.

     Presents the vocal scores with piano.

862. _____. By W. S. Gilbert and Arthur Sullivan. (Kalmus
     Orchestra Library Series). New York: Edwin F. Kalmus, 198-?

     Presents one score in 19 parts for orchestra.

863. _____. By W. S. Gilbert and Arthur Sullivan. London &
     New York: Chappell, 198-? 141 p.

     Presents the vocal scores with piano.

864. *Selections from H. M. S. Pinafore.* Arthur Sullivan. Arranged by Leigh
     Martinet. Baltimore, Md.: Baltimore Horn Club, 1988. 4 p.

     Arranged for four horns.

865. *Songs.* Arthur Sullivan. Edited by Alan Borthwick and Robin Wilson.
     London: Stainer & Bell; New York: Galaxy Music, 1986.

     Presents the score for medium voice; includes The Lost Chord; O Fair
     Dove; Orpheus With His Lute; Tears, Idle Tears; and others.

866. *Songs from Gilbert and Sullivan.* (Cole's Library of Familiar Music).
     Chicago: M. M. Cole, 1940. 64 p.

     Presents the vocal scores with piano for songs from the operas.

867. *Songs from Michael Todd's Hot Mikado.* The new musical hit based
     on the Gilbert and Sullivan classic. Modern rhythm adaptations by
     Charles L. Cooke. New York: Robbins Music Corporation, 1939. 28 p.

     Presents the vocal scores with piano.

868. *Songs of Two Savoyards.* Words and illustrations by W. S. Gilbert.
     Music by Arthur Sullivan. Second Edition. London: Routledge & K.
     Paul, 1948. 267 p. Illus.

     Contains vocal score with piano accompaniment. All choruses or
     concerted pieces have been arranged for a single voice.

869. *The Sorcerer.* An Original Modern Comic Opera in Two Parts. Words
     by W. S. Gilbert. Music by Arthur Sullivan. London: Metzler, 1920?
     137 p.

     Contains the vocal score with piano accompaniment.

870. _____. Vocal Gems. W. S. Gilbert and Arthur Sullivan.
     London: Chappell, 1950, 27 p.

     Presents vocal scores with piano for selections from the opera.

871. _____. W. S. Gilbert and Arthur Sullivan. (Kalmus Vocal
     Series). Melville, N.Y.: Belwin Mills, 19--? 137 p.

     Presents the vocal scores with piano.

872. Stevens, David. *All at Sea (A Gilbert and Sullivan Dream)*. Operetta in Two Acts. Music arranged and adapted by Harvey Worthington Loomis. Boston: C. C. Birchard, 1921. 92 p.

Provides the vocal score with piano accompaniment for songs and choruses from *H. M. S. Pinafore, Pirates of Penzance, Patience, The Mikado*, and *Iolanthe* which are integrated as part of this opera adaptation. For libretto, see 638.

873. "Sullivan, Sir Arthur (1842-1900)." *A Dictionary of Opera and Song Themes*. Compiled by Harold Barlow and Sam Morgenstern. New York: Crown, 1976. p. 362-75.

Provides words and melody to convey the principal song themes from eleven G&S operas plus a few of Sullivan's miscellaneous compositions.

874. *Symphony in E for Orchestra*. By Arthur Sullivan. Full score. London: Novello, 1915. 204 p.

Contains the full score for orchestra.

875. _____. By Arthur Sullivan. New York: Edwin F. Kalmus, 196-? 204 p.

Presents the score for orchestra.

876. *Te Deum Laudamus and Domine Salvam fac Reginam.* For soprano, solo, chorus, orchestra, organ and military band (ad libitum) composed for the festival held at the Crystal Palace May 1, 1871, in celebration of the recovery of H. R. H. the Prince of Wales. By Arthur S. Sullivan. London: Novello, Ewer, 187-? 77 p.

Contains the vocal score with piano accompaniment.

877. Thane, Adele. *Gilbert and Sullivan Operettas Adapted for Half-Hour Performance*. Boston: Plays, Inc., 1976. 330 p.

Presents plot summaries, libretti and music in condensed form for royalty-free performance by youth amateur music and drama groups. Includes *The Mikado, H. M. S. Pinafore, Trial By Jury, The Pirates of Penzance, The Yeomen of the Guard, Iolanthe*, and *Patience*.

878. *Thirty Minutes on H. M. S. Pinafore*. Based on the popular Gilbert and Sullivan opera. New York: Belwin, 1940. 21 p.

Provides vocal score and piano accompaniment, production notes, and dance routines for an abbreviated version of G&S's third opera.

879. *Thirty Minutes with Iolanthe.* Based on the popular Gilbert & Sullivan opera, by Arthur Johnson and May Van Dyke. New York: Boosey, Hawkes, Belwin, 1942. 21 p., diagr.

Provides the vocal score and piano accompaniment, production notes, and dance routines for this abridged version of the opera.

880. *Thirty Minutes with The Gondoliers.* Based on the popular Gilbert & Sullivan opera by Arthur Johnson and May Van Dyke. New York: Boosey, Hawkes, Belwin, 1942. 21 p., diagr.

Provides the vocal score and piano accompaniment, production notes, and dance routines for this abridged version of the opera.

881. *Thirty Minutes with The Mikado.* Based on the popular Gilbert & Sullivan opera by Arthur Johnson and May Van Dyke. New York: Belwin, 1940. 20 p.

Provides the vocal score and piano accompaniment, dance routines and production notes for this abbreviated version of the opera.

882. *Thirty Minutes with The Pirates of Penzance.* Based on the popular Gilbert & Sullivan opera by Arthur Johnson and May Van Dyke. New York: Belwin, 1940. 20 p.

Provides the vocal score and piano accompaniment, dance routines, and production notes for this abbreviated version of the opera.

883. *Three Pieces from The Pirates of Penzance.* Arthur Sullivan. Arranged for string orchestra by Nicholas Hare. London: Chester Music, 1983. 7 p.

Presents the score for string orchestra; includes The policeman's song, Poor wand'ring one, and With cat-like tread.

884. *Trial by Jury.* A Novel and Original Dramatic Cantata by Arthur Sullivan & W. S. Gilbert. London: Chappell, 188-? 53 p.

Presents the vocal scores with piano.

885. _____. By W. S. Gilbert and Arthur Sullivan. Abridged and simplified by Berta Elsmith. Evanston, Ill.: Summy-Birchard Publ. Co., 1960. 79 p.

Presents abridged vocal scores with piano.

886. _____. An opera in one act. Sir Arthur Sullivan. Words by W. S. Gilbert. Edited by John Bauser. (Kalmus Orchestra Library Series). New York: E. F. Kalmus, 1981. 124 p.

Presents the score for orchestra.

887. _____. Text by W. S. Gilbert. Music by Arthur Sullivan.
     Authentic version edited by Bryceson Treharne. New York:
     G. Schrimer, 1941. 89 p.

     Provides plot, vocal score and piano accompaniment.

888. *Utopia Limited; or, The Flowers of Progress.* An Original Comic Opera,
     in 2 Acts, Written by W. S. Gilbert. Composed by Arthur Sullivan.
     Vocal score. Arranged by Ernest Ford. London: Chappell, 1893.
     155 p.

     Contains the vocal score with piano accompaniment.

889. _____. By W. S. Gilbert and Arthur Sullivan. London &
     New York: Chappell, 1970. 155 p.

     Presents the vocal scores with piano.

890. _____. By W. S. Gilbert and Arthur Sullivan. (Kalmus Vocal
     Series). Melville, N.Y.: Belwin Mills, 1981? 155 p.

     Presents the vocal scores with piano.

891. *Vocal Gems from the New Opera Patience; or, Bunthorne's Bride.*
     Written by W. S. Gilbert. Composed by Arthur Sullivan. London:
     Stoddart, 1881. 49 p.

     Contains the vocal score with piano accompaniment.

892. *Vocal Highlights from The Pirates of Penzance.* Words by W. S.
     Gilbert; music by Arthur Sullivan. Lynbrook, N.Y.: Joe Goldfeder
     Music, 1981. 95 p., illus.

     Presents the vocal scores with piano accompaniment.

893. *Vocal Score of The Grand Duke; or, The Statutory Duel.* By W. S.
     Gilbert and Arthur Sullivan. London & New York: Chappell, 1896.
     166 p.

     Contains the vocal score with piano accompaniment.

894. *Vocal Score of The Mikado; or, The Town of Titipu.* By W. S. Gilbert
     and Arthur Sullivan. Arrangement for pianoforte by George Lowell
     Tracy. London: Chappell, 1885. 152 p.

     Contains the vocal score with piano accompaniment.

895. _____. By W. S. Gilbert and Arthur Sullivan. London &
     New York: Chappell, 1986? 193 p.

     Presents the vocal scores with piano accompaniment.

896. *Vocal Score of The Pirates of Penzance, or, The Slave of Duty.* Text by
W. S. Gilbert. Music by Arthur Sullivan. London: Chappell, [19--].
174 p.

Provides vocal score and piano accompaniment for all songs and for
all roles.

897. *We Sail the Ocean Blue.* From *H. M. S. Pinafore.* W. S. Gilbert and
Arthur Sullivan. Adapted and arranged by Ruth Artman. Chapel Hill,
N.C.: Hinshaw Music, 1982. 15 p.

Presents the vocal score for three-part male choir (TBB) with piano.

898. *When the Foeman Bears His Steel.* From *The Pirates of Penzance.*
Words by W. S. Gilbert. Music by Arthur Sullivan. Arranged by Irvin
Cooper. New York: Fischer, 1953. 13 p.

Presents the score for 1st and 2nd soprano, cambiata, and baritone
with piano.

899. *The Window, or, The Songs of the Wrens.* A set of songs written by
Alfred Tennyson; with German translation by Willy Kastner;
composed by Arthur Sullivan. London: Joseph Williams; New York:
Edw. Schuberth & Co., 1900. 55 p.

Presents the vocal score for high voice with piano; words in English
and German.

900. *The World's Best Gilbert & Sullivan Operas.* Compiled and edited by
E. M. Schumann. New York: Amsco Music, 1939.

Contains a collection of vocal scores with piano accompaniment.

901. *The Yeomen of the Guard; or, The Merryman and His Maid.* By W. S.
Gilbert and Arthur Sullivan. London: Chappell, 192-? 184 p.

Presents the vocal scores with piano.

902. _____. Book by W. S. Gilbert, music by Arthur Sullivan.
Authentic version edited by Edmond W. Rickett. New York:
G. Schirmer, 1954. vi, 238 p.

Contains the vocal score with piano accompaniment plus all the
dialogue.

903. _____. Words by W. S. Gilbert. Music by Arthur Sullivan.
Edited by John Bauser. (Kalmus Orchestra Library Series). New York:
E. F. Kalmus, 1979. 275 p.

Presents the score for orchestra.

904. _____. Book by W. S. Gilbert. Music by Arthur Sullivan.
     Authentic version edited by Edmond W. Rickett. New York:
     G. Schirmer, 198-? 238 p.

     Presents the vocal scores with piano and all the dialogue.

905. *The Yeomen of the Guard Overture.* Arthur Sullivan. New York:
     Edwin F. Kalmus, 1981? 20 p.

     Presents the score for orchestra for the overture to this opera.

     Yeomen of the Guard. See *The Choruses of The Yeomen of the
     Guard,* 745; *Overture to the Yeomen of the Guard,* 830.

9. Bibliography & Discography

906. Allen, Reginald. *W. S. Gilbert: An Anniversary Survey and Exhibition Checklist With Thirty-Five Illustrations.* Reprinted from *Theatre Notebook* 15 (1961): 118-28. Charlottesville: Bibliographic Society of the University of Virginia, 1963. 82 p., illus., ports., facsims.

Lists and describes bibliographically the literary products of W. S. Gilbert's career as presented in the Grolier Club Anniversary Exhibition of 600 items, including librettos, manuscripts, programs, playbills, posters, copies, letters, and "Bab" sketches. Includes printed record of Gilbert's works and record of production.

907. _____. "What, Never? No! Never!" *Saturday Review* 43 (April 30, 1960): 56. Illus.

Reviews a London recording of *H. M. S. Pinafore,* the first ever available with complete dialogue.

908. Ardoin, John. "G&S: After the Carpets." *Saturday Review* (April 16, 1966): 69+.

Gives a brief history of the period following the "carpet quarrel" that caused Gilbert to promise never to work with Sullivan again, and evaluates recordings made of *The Mountebanks* and *Utopia, Limited.*

909. _____. "Gilbert & Sullivan: Two Views." *Saturday Review* (March 12, 1966): 127+

Gives a brief history of G&S on records and evaluates the stereo remakes of *Princess Ida* and *Pirates of Penzance.*

910. Atkins, Sidney H. "*Utopia Limited* Recorded." *The Gilbert and Sullivan Journal* 8 (May, 1965): 285.

Reviews and evaluates a recording by the Lyric Theater Company in Washington.

911. Bristow, Mary R. *A Gilbert and Sullivan Bibliography.* Second Edition.
Bel Air, Md.: Published by the author, 1968. Various paging (16 p. +
addendum).

Lists, without annotations, dozens of books, newspapers, periodicals,
recordings, vocal scores and organizations. Gives leads to many
obscure sources, although in very incomplete form. Contains many
errors.

912. Bulloch, John Malcolm. "The Anatomy of the '*Bab Ballads.*' " *Notes and
Queries* 171 (November 14, 1936): 344-48.

Explains the difficulties in following the chronology of the *Bab Ballads,*
summarizes the book editions in which they have appeared, and lists
ballads which had appeared serially in *Fun* and elsewhere.

913. _____. "The *Bab Ballads* by Titles." *Notes and Queries* 172
(May 22, 1937): 362-67.

Gives a summary of the different editions of the *Bab Ballads* from
1869 to 1932 and lists 143 ballads, giving publication date and name
of journal, dates of reprints, and notes on changes and background.

914. Canby, Edward Tatnall. "G&S a la Carte." *Audio* 73 (May, 1989): 15+.

Explains that G&S is that series of comic operas in which were
combined the work of three wildly diverse talents: Gilbert, Sullivan,
and D'Oyly Carte. Tells of the record reviewers' early infatuation
with the operas and comments on comparisons between the early 78s
and the modern LP record versions of various works.

915. Cantrell, Scott. "*Concerto for Cello, D Major.*" *Ovation* 9 (September,
1988): 43-5.

Reviews an Angel compact disc recording which includes Sullivan's
Concerto for Cello and Orchestra in D Major. Notes that Sullivan,
before Gilbert, was recognized as a formidably talented "serious"
composer, but judges the *Cello Concerto* (1866) to be slim fare.

916. Carpenter, Charles A. "Gilbert, William Schwenck." *Modern Drama
Scholarship and Criticism 1966-1980; An International Bibliography.*
Toronto: University of Toronto Press, 1986. p. 104-5.

Identifies, without annotations, recent works (monographs and
journal articles) of analysis on W. S. Gilbert, including some foreign
language entries.

917. _____. "Modern Drama Studies: An Annual Bibliography."
Modern Drama 31 (June, 1988): 184-308.

Records current scholarship, criticism and commentary of importance
to students of dramatic literature and, to a lesser extent, of theater
history. Contains a section on British studies that usually includes
some entries about W. S. Gilbert. [Note: Published annually starting in
1974].

918. Cohen, Edward H. (ed.). "Victorian Bibliography for 1988." *Victorian
Studies* 32 (Summer, 1989): 611-734.

Divides material into 6 sections, of which the most pertinent to the
person seeking information on W. S. Gilbert would be (I) Bibliographic
Materials and (VI) Individual Authors. [Note: Published annually
starting in 1957].

919. Connor, Billie M. and Helene G. Mochedlover. "Gilbert, William
Schwenck 1836-1911 [and Sullivan, Sir Arthur Seymour, composer]."
Ottemiller's Index to Plays in Collections. Seventh edition, revised
and enlarged. Metuchen, N. J.: The Scarecrow Press, 1988. p. 89.

Identifies anthologies in which various plays and operas of W. S. Gilbert
can be found.

920. Conolly, L. W. and J. P. Wearing. "Gilbert, Sir William Schwenck
(1836-1911)." *English Drama and Theatre, 1800-1900, A Guide to
Information Sources.* Detroit, Mich.: Gale Research, 1978. p. 165-85.

Lists, with evaluative annotations, monographs and articles classified
into (1) collected works, (2) acted plays, (3) bibliographies, (4)
biographies, and (5) critical studies.

921. _____. "Nineteenth-Century Theatre
Research: A Bibliography for 1974." *Nineteenth Century Theatre
Research* 3 (Autumn, 1975): 97-126.

Supplies for Gilbert (p. 107) a list of theater and drama studies done
during or just before 1974, and a comprehensive list on other authors
and subjects. [Note: The bibliography is updated annually through
1986].

922. Crick, R. G. D. "*The Chieftain*--Sullivan's Rare Opera." *The Gilbert and
Sullivan Journal* 10 (Spring, 1981): 430.

Reviews a Rare Recorded Edition album of the Burnand/Sullivan opera,
The Chieftain.

923. DuBois, Arthur E. "Additions to the Bibliography of W. S. Gilbert's
     Contributions to Magazines." *Modern Language Notes* XLVII (May,
     1932): 308-14.

     Attempts to supplement and correct Townley Searle's 1931
     bibliography (see 972) which contained some "eccentric" selections,
     omissions, and inaccuracies. Reconstructs the entire *Bab Ballad* series
     in chronological order.

924. Dyer, Richard. "A Gilbert and Sullivan Discography, Part I." *High
     Fidelity and Musical America* 27 (May, 1977): 52-8.

     Gives an overview of recorded G&S singles, complete operas, and
     series from 1898 to the present. Identifies and evaluates the
     recordings of the operas of the time period 1875-1884 (*Trial by Jury*
     through *Princess Ida*).

925. _____. "A Gilbert and Sullivan Discography, Part II." *High
     Fidelity and Musical America* 28 (February, 1978): 50-9.

     Identifies and comments on recordings of *The Mikado* (1885),
     Ruddigore (1887), *Yeomen of the Guard* (1888), *Utopia, Limited*
     (1893) and *The Grand Duke* (1896). Gives background information
     about the plots, scores, characters, and performers.

926. Ellis, James D. "*Bab Ballads* Lost and Found." *Gilbert and Sullivan*,
     James Helyar, (ed.), 1971. p. 43-51. See 354.

     Describes the problems involved in collecting, collating and annotating
     137 poems for a new edition. Explains the acceptance of new entries
     or the rejection of previous attributions.

927. Firkins, Ina Ten Eyck. "Gilbert, Sir William Schwenck, 1836-1911."
     Index to Plays 1800-1926. New York: H. W. Wilson, 1927. p. 65-7.

     Lists alphabetically Gilbert's plays and comic operas, emphasizing early
     editions and collections.

928. _____. "Gilbert, Sir William Schwenck, 1836-1911."
     Index to Plays, Supplement. New York: H. W. Wilson, 1935. p. 29-30.

     Lists Gilbert's plays and comic operas that can be found in collections,
     series, and anthologies, as well as early editions of individual titles.

929. Francis, John W. N. "The Gilbert and Sullivan Operettas on 78's,
      Complete Sets and Abridgements, 1906-1950--Discography."
      Association for Recorded Sound Collections--Journal 20 (Spring,
      1989): 24-81. Bibl.

      Gives a history of acoustic recordings of the Savoy operas in the
      context of the D'Oyly Carte Opera Company. Documents, year by year,
      the production of 29 complete recordings of 10 G&S operettas
      published on 78's, including contents, casts, dates, playing times,
      producers, and technical details.

930. Fuld, James J. "Gilbert and Sullivan." *The Book of World-Famous
      Music, Classical, Popular, and Folk.* Revised and enlarged edition.
      New York: Crown, 1971. p. 64-5 and various other pages.

      Gives the first line of music for each of 8 Sullivan compositions and
      traces the printing history of each, identifying first known printings of
      piano-vocal scores, sheet music, etc. Supplies information on first
      performances and explains the problems in dating the G&S
      piano-vocal scores.

931. Gammond, Peter. "(Sir) Arthur Sullivan." *The Illustrated
      Encyclopedia of Recorded Opera.* London: Salamander Books, 1979.
      p. 190-97. Illus.

      Includes a thumbnail biography, the plots of the G&S operas plus
      three others, the titles of well-known arias in each opera, and lists of
      recordings with casts.

932. "Gilbert, Sir William Schwenck." *The National Union Catalog,
      Pre-1956 Imprints.* London: Mansell Information/Publishing, 1972.
      Vol. 199, p. 503-25.

      Presents several hundred entries from a cumulative author list
      representing Library of Congress printed cards and titles by other
      American libraries.

933. "Gilbert, Sir William Schwenck (1836-1911)." *The Player's Library
      and Bibliography of the Theatre.* London: Faber and Faber, 1950.
      p. 271-73.

      Lists Gilbert's plays and operettas, individually and in collections, and
      gives single-word descriptors for settings, costumes, number of acts,
      number of main characters, etc.

934. "Gilbert, Sir William Schwenck, Playwright, 1836-1911." *Cumulated Dramatic Index 1919-1949. A Cumulation of the F. W. Faxon Company's Dramatic Index.* Boston: G. K. Hall, 1970. Vol. l, p. 537.

Lists, without annotations, titles of books and articles about W. S. Gilbert, as well as cross-references to individual opera and play titles.

935. "Gilbert, William Schwenck." *English Drama of the Nineteenth Century; An Index and Finding Guide.* Compiled and edited by James Ellis. New Canaan, Conn.: Readex Books, 1985. p. 105-6.

Lists, in alphabetical order, the plays and comic operas published by W. S. Gilbert. Gives publisher, date and place of publication, and number of pages for each entry.

936. Gilder, Eric and June G. Port. "Sullivan, Sir Arthur/1842-1900/Great Britain." *The Dictionary of Composers and Their Music.* New York and London: Paddington Press, 1978. p. 199-200.

Lists in chronological order the compositons of Sir Arthur, starting with*The Tempest* incidental music and going through the posthumous *The Emerald Isle.* Identifies the nature of the work and, when applicable, the name of the librettist.

937. Goldsmith, Harris. "Gilbert and Sullivan Glories Recalled." *Opus* 1 n. 6 (1985): 27-9.

Offers analysis and history of G&S's *Princess Ida* and reviews recordings of that opera, an abridged *Pirates of Penzance,* and G&S opera excerpts.

938. Gordon, Eric. "Early and Late Sullivan." *The Gilbert and Sullivan Journal* 8 (September, 1961): 72.

Reviews the first recording of *Cox and Box* and a complete recording with dialogue of *The Gondoliers* by the D'Oyly Carte Opera Company, both issued by Decca Records.

939. Gower, J. Antony. "Ida Is Her Name." *The Gilbert and Sullivan Journal* 9 (January, 1966): 6.

Reviews Decca recordings of *Princess Ida.*

940. _____. "Overtures and Abridged Versions." *The Gilbert and Sullivan Journal* 10 (Autumn, 1973: 59.

Assesses the long-playing stereo set of seven overtures and abridged versions by the Gilbert and Sullivan For All Company. Includes *Pirates of Penzance, The Mikado,* and *Yeomen of the Guard.*

941. Grandsen, K. W. and P. J. Willetts. "Papers of W. S. Gilbert." *The British Museum Quarterly* 21 (June, 1958): 67-9.

Describes a large collection of manuscripts acquired by The Museum, including Gilbert's correspondence and various autograph manuscript synopses and drafts which reveal how the final work emerged from the original idea.

942. Grimsditch, H. B. "Sir William Schwenck Gilbert (1836-1911)." *The Cambridge Bibliography of English Literature*. Edited by F. W. Bateson. Cambridge at the University Press, 1966. Vol. III 1800-1900, p. 610-13.

Provides bibliographic entries under the headings of collected and separate plays, collected and separate operas with and without Sullivan, and biography and criticism.

943. Hawes, Arthur. "Sung With a Sigh and a Tear in the Eye." *The Gilbert and Sullivan Journal* 8 (January, 1965): 268.

Appraises the skill with which the spirit of the opera *The Yeomen of the Guard* has been captured on a Decca recording.

944. Hedgegrove, Quentin. "Inside the Old Savoy." *The Gilbert and Sullivan Journal* 10 (Autumn, 1973): 60.

Discusses a set of 3 Pearl Records *(The Art of the Savoyard: Recordings 1900-1922)* featuring singers who sang at the Old Savoy during Gilbert's lifetime, with Henry Lytton dominating the album.

945. _____. "Vintage Recordings: Strange Magic." *The Gilbert and Sullivan Journal* 10 (Spring, 1977): 254-55.

Reviews reissues by Pearl Records of 20 songs sung by Charles H. Workman, the 1924 cast of *Princess Ida* with Henry Lytton, and the 1926 cast of *The Mikado*.

946. "*H. M. S. Pinafore* and *The Mikado*." (Famous Operas No. 29, Junior Etude Series). *The Etude* 52 (February, 1934): 135.

Presents a brief introduction to G&S and lists several recordings of the two operas on the Victor label. [Note: Juvenile level].

947. Jacobs, Arthur. "On Video." *Opera* 38 (December, 1987): 1465-66.

Reviews the Brent Walker television versions of *The Sorcerer, Princess Ida,* and *Ruddigore,* commenting on the overall quality and the aspect of having them produced with an eye toward the American market.

948. Jacobson, Robert. "Recordings: Gilbert Without Sullivan." *Saturday Review* 54 (February 27, 1971): 58.

Gives a brief biography of Frederic Clay, who composed the music for Gilbert's *Ages Ago* (1869), and reviews a recording of this seldom-issued light opera.

949. _____. "Recordings: Souped-Up Savoyards." *Saturday Review* 54 (November 27, 1971): 80.

Assures us that the D'Oyly Carte Company has ably survived two world wars but has now entered still another epoch, geared to capture the breed of modern G&S addict. Reviews the London Phase 4 recording of *H. M. S. Pinafore*.

950. Jones, John Bush. " 'Bab' and *Punch*: Gilbert's Contributions Identified." *Gilbert and Sullivan*, James Helyar (ed.), 1971. p. 85-89. See 354.

Uses the ledgers on contributions to *Punch* to identify as Gilbert's some anonymous verse and prose.

951. _____. "The Printing of *The Grand Duke*: Notes Toward a Gilbert Bibliography." *Papers of the Bibliographic Society of America* LXI (1967): 335-42. Reprinted in *W. S. Gilbert: A Century of Scholarship and Commentary*, John B. Jones (ed.), 1970, p. 273-84. See 386.

Notes the unreliability and inaccuracy of Townley Searle's 1931 bibliography (see 972) and presents a tentative model for a complete description of first-edition Chappell librettos. Uses *The Grand Duke* as an example of issues in separating and describing editions and impressions.

952. _____. *The Uncollected Verse of W. S. Gilbert: A Critical Edition.* Unpublished Ph.D. Dissertation. Northwestern University, 1970. 318 p.

Presents the critically edited texts of 54 positively identified contributions to periodicals by W. S. Gilbert which he did not include in his own published collection of poems. Establishes criteria for the identification and inclusion of verses. Gives a historical introduction to Gilbert's journalistic career.

953. _____. "W. S. Gilbert's Contributions to *Fun*, 1865-1874." *Bulletin of the New York Public Library* LXXIII (April, 1969): 253-66.

Works from the Proprietor's Copy of *Fun* to identify Gilbert's uncollected verses. Provides a chronology of contributions to regular weekly issues and special numbers, and describes the type of contribution, i.e., review, cartoon, verse, column, etc.

954. Joseph, Tony. "Towards a 'G&S' Bibliography." *Library Review* 23 (Winter, 1971): 135-40.

Examines the need for a comprehensive bibliography, gives an overview of publications by and about Gilbert and Sullivan, and identifies and comments on the major biographies, histories, and books of critical analysis available at that time.

955. Keller, Dean H. "Gilbert, William Schwenck, 1836-1911." *Index to Plays in Periodicals.* Revised and expanded edition. Metuchen, N. J.: The Scarecrow Press, 1979. p. 248.

Lists and directs the reader to several of Gilbert's plays and comic operas that can be found in periodicals.

956. Kinard, Epsie. "Take Advantage of the Gilbert and Sullivan Recording Boom." *House Beautiful* 105 (March, 1963): 30+

Examines a new crop of stereo albums from Angel Records and London Records upon the expiration in 1961 of the last British copyright.

957. Kresh, Paul. "Sir Arthur Sullivan's *Zoo Story.*" *Stereo Review* 43 (July, 1979): 107. Illus. (port).

Reviews the story of the 1875 operetta by B. C. Stephenson (Bolton Rowe) with music by Arthur Sullivan and critiques a London recording that does full justice to "Sullivan's stunning orchestration."

958. _____. "Very Model Records of the Major Gilbert & Sullivan." *High Fidelity* 37 (June, 1987): 56-8. Illus, ports.

Examines the part of the folklore of serious record collecting that states that old is always better, and reviews the D'Oyly Carte recordings between 1927 and 1932.

959. Kupferberg, Herbert. "They Shall Have Music. Five Operas Better Than They Seemed." *The Atlantic* 217 (April, 1966): 136-38.

Reviews recordings that rescue G&S's *Princess Ida* from desuetude and gives a brief review of the shortcomings and virtues of this seldom-performed opera. Also reviews recordings of four other operas by composers other than G&S.

960. Lamb, Andrew. "The Music of Sullivan." (Gramophone Collection, No. 10.) *Gramophone* 56 (November, 1978): 847-48.

Identifies, with explanatory and evaluative comments, phonograph recordings of Sullivan's music, including that of the G&S operas.

961. Leyburn, James G. "Words by W. S. Gilbert." *Yale University Library Gazette* 17 (1943): 53-4.

Describes the contents of a new collection presented to the Library, most of the material consisting of first editions of the operas. Presents an opportunity to examine the libretti of those operas in which Sullivan did not collaborate with Gilbert.

962. Mercer, Ruby. "*The Gondoliers*." *Opera Canada* 30, n. 1 (1989): 52.

Reviews a videocassette recording (Connaisseur VHS) of *The Gondoliers*, noting the skills of the performers, the quality of the sets, and the caliber of the conducting and musical arrangements.

963. _____. "*The Mikado*." *Opera Canada* 29, n. 3 (1988): 52.

Reviews a videocassette recording (Connaisseur VHS) of *The Mikado*, which was performed and recorded at the Stratford Festival's Avon Theatre.

964. "Music for Pleasure." *The Gilbert and Sullivan Journal* 9 (September, 1966): 48.

Reviews recordings of highlights of *The Gondoliers*, *The Yeomen of the Guard*, and *The Mikado*.

965. Mutch, Marie L. "Little G, Little S." *Saturday Review* 30 (December 27, 1947): 43.

Reviews the current situation of small availability of G&S recordings in the post-war period and identifies the available staples of the repertory.

966. Pence, James Harry. "Gilbert, Wm. Schwenck." *The Magazine and the Drama.* New York: Burt Franklin, 1896. Reprinted by Lennox Hill, New York, 1970. p. 71-2.

Lists periodical articles up to 1895 which deal with Gilbert's career and personal life, as well as the operettas done with Sullivan.

967. Randall, David A. "Gilbert and Sullivan's *The Gondoliers* and *Princess Ida*." *Papers of the Bibliographical Society of America* 59 (1965): 293-98; 322-26. Reprinted in *W. S. Gilbert: A Century of Scholarship and Commentary*, John Bush Jones (ed.), 1970. p. 257-72. See 386.

Examines the problem of accurately describing pre-publication and first-night or first edition texts of G&S librettos. Analyzes in detail the alterations in *The Gondoliers* and *Princess Ida*, using American librettos for comparison.

968. Sackville-West, Edward and Desmond Shawe-Taylor. "Sullivan, Sir Arthur (1842-1900)." *The Record Guide.* Revised edition. Westport, Conn.: Greenwood Press, 1978. p. 757-60.

Presents a short essay on the continued popularity (and cultishness) of the G&S operas and lists recordings from the comic operas by categories of complete recordings, excerpts, overtures, and arrangements.

969. Samples, Gordon. "Gilbert, William Schwenck, 1836-1911." *The Drama Scholar's Index to Plays and Filmscripts: A Guide to Plays in Selected Anthologies, Series, and Periodicals.* Metuchen, N. J.: The Scarecrow Press, 1980. Vol. 2, p. 205-6.

Lists Gilbert's plays and operas by title and indicates various anthologies in which each can be located.

970. _____. "Gilbert, William Schwenck, 1836-1911." *The Drama Scholar's Index to Plays and Filmscripts: A Guide to Plays and Filmscripts in Selected Anthologies, Series, and Periodicals.* Metuchen, N. J.: The Scarecrow Press, 1986. Vol. 3, p. 98-9.

Lists Gilbert's plays and operas by title and indicates anthologies in which they may be found.

971. Sams, Jeremy. "*The Gondoliers.*" *Opera* 36 (August, 1985): 880-81.

Identifies and discusses a miniature score, *The Gondoliers* (see 768), edited by David Lloyd-Jones (Eulenburg), commenting on the music of the opera being a triumph in spite of Gilbert.

972. Searle, Townley. *Sir William Schwenck Gilbert: A Topsy-Turvy Adventure.* With decorations by the author and an introduction by R. E. Swartwout. London: Alexander-Ouseley, 1931. 105 p., col. front., illus., plates, facsims.

Lists and describes works by Gilbert (including the G&S operas), books illustrated by him, books and magazine articles about him, and the separate musical selections from the operas, etc. Often described by modern scholars as incomplete and inaccurate, the Searle work represents the first important effort to compile a bibliography on Gilbert.

973. "Sir William Schwenck Gilbert 1836-1911." *The New Cambridge Bibliography of English Literature.* Edited by George Watson. Cambridge: Cambridge University Press, 1969. Vol. 3, p. 1159-64.

Lists, without annotations, works by and about Gilbert, grouped under bibliographies, collected works and collected biography and critical studies.

974. Stedman, Jane W. "Gilbert, Sir W(illiam) S(chwenck)." *Great Writers of the English Language: Dramatists.* Edited by James Vinson. London: Macmillan, 1979. p. 245-50.

Lists publications under the headings of collections, plays, fiction, and other. Gives also a biography/analysis of Gilbert's career and works.

975. "Sullivan." *American Record Guide* 44 (April, 1981): 35-40.

Describes the rush to release new and old recordings of the D'Oyly Carte Opera Company. Lists and describes the merits of recordings of *The Yeomen of the Guard, H. M. S. Pinafore, The Pirates of Penzance, The Mikado,* and *The Gondoliers.*

976. "Sullivan Concerto Resurfaces." *Ovation* 7 (December, 1986): 10.

Tells of the reconstruction of Sullivan's *Concerto for Cello, D Major* (1866) which was thought to be irretrievably lost, and its recording on an Angel release.

977. "Sullivan, Sir Arthur." *Index to Record Reviews.* Compiled and edited by Kurtz Myers. Boston: G. K. Hall, 1978. Vol. 3, p. 128-33.

Indicates publications in which reviews of recordings of the G&S operas can be located.

978. "Sullivan, Sir Arthur (1842-1900)." *BBC Music Library Choral and Opera Catalogue I: Composers.* London: British Broadcasting Corp., 1967. p. 443-45.

Lists the BBC Music Library's holdings of Sullivan's choral and operatic publications, listed alphabetically with title, name of arranger, publisher and, when available, date of publication.

979. "Sullivan, Sir Arthur (1842-1900)." *BBC Music Library Song Catalogue II: Composers L-Z.* London: British Broadcasting Corp., 1966. p. 1107-10.

Lists the BBC Music Library's holdings of Sullivan's songs arranged alphabetically and including title, arranger, key, and publisher.

980. "Sullivan, Sir Arthur (1842-1900)." *Choral Music in Print, Vol. I: Sacred Choral Music.* Edited by Thomas R. Nardone, James H. Nye, and Mark Resnick. Philadelphia: Musicdata, 1974. p. 561.

Provides an index to Sullivan's sacred choral works with generic information about the compositions and specific information pertaining to editions in print.

981. "Sullivan, Sir Arthur (1842-1900)." *Choral Music in Print: Vol. II: Secular Choral Music.* Edited by Thomas R. Nardone, James H. Nye, and Mark Resnick. Philadelphia: Musicdata, 1974. p. 516-17.

Provides an index to Sullivan's secular choral works with generic information and specific information about editions in print.

982. "Sullivan, Sir Arthur Seymour." *The National Union Catalog, Pre-1956 Imprints.* London: Mansell Information/Publishing, 1978. Vol. 576, p. 80-122.

Lists several hundred entries from a cumulative author list representing Library of Congress printed cards and titles reported by other American libraries.

983. "Theatrical Material in the British Museum." *Theatre Notebook* XVII (Autumn, 1962): 10-11.

Lists theatrical materials existing in the British Museum, including *Papers of W. S. Gilbert.*

984. Way, Geoffrey. "*The Gondoliers* on Record." *The Gilbert and Sullivan Journal* 9 (September, 1966): 45-6.

Discusses the artistic and technical qualities of five recordings of *The Gondoliers* made between 1918 and 1961.

985. Wearing, J. P. "Gilbert, Sir William Schwenck (1836-1911), English Dramatist." *American and British Theatrical Biography: A Directory.* Metuchen, N.J. and London: The Scarecrow Press, 1979. p. 411.

Identifies more than 20 seldom-cited reference sources for biographical information about Gilbert.

986. _____. "Sullivan, Sir Arthur (1842-1900), English Composer." *American and British Theatrical Biography: A Directory.* Metuchen, N.J. and London: The Scarecrow Press, 1979. p. 889.

Directs the reader to a small number of infrequently cited reference sources of biographical materials on Sullivan.

987. Wolfson, John. *The Savoyards on Record: The Story of the Singers Who Worked with Gilbert and Sullivan and the Records They Made.* Chichester, West Sussex: Packard, 1985. x, 96 p., illus., bibl., discog.

Lists all the known recordings (some as early as 1898) of every artist who performed under the personal direction of Gilbert or Sullivan, and who subsequently made records. Gives a brief biography of each artist. Lists complete recordings 1917-1936 by The Gramophone Company and reissues by Pearl Records.

10. Unclassified

This section contains items which could not be obtained, examined, annotated and classified in time to meet the publication deadline.

988. Abeshouse, Benjamin S. *A Medical History of Sir Arthur Sullivan.* Edited by Eaton Laboratories from an original manuscript by Benjamin S. Abeshouse, M.D. Norwich, N.Y. : Eaton Laboratories, 1966. 26 p.

989. Allvine, G. "Future of Gilbert & Sullivan." *Variety* 225 (January 10, 1962): 235.

990. Beckerman, M. "The Sword on the Wall: Japanese Elements and Their Significance in *The Mikado.*" *Musical Quarterly* 73 n. 3 (1989): 303-19.

991. Beerbohm, Max. *A Note on "Patience."* London: Miles & Company, 1918. 8 p., illus.

992. Bessey, M. A. "Age Ten and Up." *Scholastic* 25 (November 3, 1934): 7-9+, illus.

993. Botsford, W. "Gilbert and Sullivan: *The Grand Duke; or, The Statutory Duel.*" *American Record Guide* 41 (November, 1977): 15.

994. Bowman, Walter P. "Gilbert Without McMullen." *Pubs, Place-Names, and Patronymics: Selected Papers of the Names Institute.* Edited by E. Wallace McMullen. Madison, N.J.: Fairleigh Dickinson University Names Institute, 1980. p. 160-70.

995. Boyer, Robert D. "The 'Perfect Autocrat': W. S. Gilbert in Rehearsal." *Theatre Studies* 1979-1981, v. 26-27. p. 64-78.

996. Burton, Nigel. "100 Years of a Legend." *The Musical Times* 127 (October, 1986): 554-57.

997. Carlile, J. B. "*Ivanhoe.*" *The Theatre.* Fourth Series XVII (May, 1891): 158-61.

998. Ellis, Horace. "Sir Arthur Sullivan." *Music* 19 (1901): 301-3.

999. Farnsworth, Dean B. *Satire in the Works of W. S. Gilbert.* Unpublished Ph.D. Dissertation. University of California, Berkeley, 1950. 196 p.

1000. *Favorite Melodies from Gilbert and Sullivan.* Arranged by Bryceson Treharne. New York: G. Schirmer, 1948. 146 p.

1001. Field, Kate. "W. S. Gilbert." *Scribner's Monthly* 18 (September, 1879): 751-55.

1002. Finck, H. T. "Sir Arthur Sullivan." *Independent* 52 (December, 1900): 2921-23.

1003. Fitzgerald, Percy. *The Savoy Opera and the Savoyards.* London: Chatto & Windus, 1894. xv, 248 p., illus.

1004. Gilbert, W. S. *Awakening of Galatea.* Illustrated romantic statue scene from the play *Pygmalion and Galatea.* Arranged by and posed under the direction of Helen Merci Schuster. Cincinnati: E. S. Werner, 1906. 16 p., Illus.

1005. _____. *"The Hooligan.* A Character Study." *The Century Magazine* 83 (November, 1911): 97-102.

1006. _____. *Poems.* Selected by William Cole. Illustrated by W. S. Gilbert, "Bab." New York: Crowell, 1967. 163 p. Illus.

1007. _____. *The Story of The Mikado.* Told by W. S. Gilbert. Illustrated by Alice B. Woodward. New York: A. A. Knopf, 1924. xi, 114 p., illus., color plates.

1008. _____. "Thumbnail Sketches in the London Streets." *London Society* 8 (February, 1868): 132-36.

1009. _____. *"Trying a Dramatist.* An Original Sketch in One Act." *The Century Magazine* 83 (December, 1911): 179-89.

1010. "Gilbert and Sullivan." *American Organist* 33 (June, 1950): 188.

1011. *Gilbert and Sullivan; An Operatic Glossary.* The Gilbert and Sullivan Society, 1975.

1012. Grau, R. "When *Pinafore* Was the Craze." *New England Magazine* 44 (July-August, 1911): 663-65.

1013. Herget, Kurt. "Fehlgeleitetes Lachen: Kritische Invention und Exotische Camouflage in der Gilbert-and-Sullivan opera, Besonders in *The Mikado."* *Anglistik & Englischunterricht* 17 (1982): 83-109.

1014. Hope-Wallace, Philip. "The Gilbert and Sullivan Phenomenon." *Observer Magazine* (April 27, 1975): 12-15.

1015. Jacobs, Arthur. *"The Golden Legend."* *The Musical Times* 126 (April, 1985): 232-33.

1016. _____. "Sir Arthur Sullivan." *Musical America* 71 (February, 1951): 15+.

1017. _____. "A Sullivan Archive." *The Musical Times* 128 (April, 1987): 206.

1018. Keshian, Katherine. *Gilbert and Sullivan: Soprano Heroines.* Unpublished M. A. Thesis. Hofstra University, 1976. 61 p.

1019. Knapp, Shoshana. "George Eliot and W. S. Gilbert: *Silas Marner* into *Dan'l Druce*. *Nineteenth-Century Fiction* 40 (March, 1986): 438-59.

1020. Kronenberger, Louis (ed.). *An Anthology of Light Verse.* New York: The Modern Library, 1935. p. 131-47.

1021. "Land of Gilbert and Sullivan." *Life* 25 (October 11, 1948): 86-7. Illus.

1022. Landauer, Bella C. *Gilbert and Sullivan Influence on American Trade Cards.* New York: Privately Printed, 1931. 15 p.

1023. Lovat, L. "On the Operas of Gilbert and Sullivan." *Gramophone* 27 (June, 1949): 3.

1024. Magor, Cliff and Edna. *The Song of a Merryman: Ivan Menzies of the D'Oyly Carte Gilbert and Sullivan Operas.* London: Grosvenor Books, 1976. 108 p.

1025. March, Ivan (ed.). *The Great Records.* Chosen by Michael Cox and others. Blackpool, Lanc.: The Long Playing Record Library, 1967. viii, 201 p. [Contains a G&S section.]

1026. Metcalf, J. S. "Survival of Gilbert and Sullivan Operas." *Life* 72 (December 19, 1918): 936.

1027. "Musical Work of Gilbert." *Outlook* 98 (June 10, 1911): 277-78.

1028. *Nineteenth-Century Autograph Music Manuscripts in the Pierpont Morgan Library.* New York: Pierpont Morgan Library, 1982. 53 p.

1029. Otten, A. L. "D'Oyly Carte Ends Long Gilbert & Sullivan Run." *Wall Street Journal* 62 (February, 1982): 22.

1030. Parrott, Ian. "Arthur Sullivan (1842-1900)." *Music and Letters* 23 (1942): 202-10.

1031. Pearsall, Ronald. *Victorian Popular Music.* Detroit, Mich.: Gale Research, 1973. 240 p., illus., bibl., index. [Scattered references to G&S throughout the book.]

1032. "The Pedigree of the Savoy Operas." *Observer* (January 20, 1907): 6.

1033. Raynor, H. "Sullivan Reconsidered." *Monthly Music Record* 89 (September/October, 1959): 163-70.

1034. Rees, Terence (ed.). *Uncle Baby.* A Comedietta. London: Privately Printed, 1968. 30 p.

1035. Rees, Terence and Roderick Spencer (eds.). *Sing With Sullivan; A New Anthology of Music for Voice.* Selected and edited by Terence Rees and Roderick Spencer. London: J. B. Cramer; New York: A. Broude, 1977. 79 p.

1036. Riewerts, Sally Jo. *A Study of the Operetta as a Teaching Device in the Junior High School Music Program with Special Attention to the Adaptation of "The Mikado" by W. S. Gilbert and Arthur Sullivan.* Unpublished M. A. Thesis. Northeast Missouri State University, 1973. 91 p.

1037. Ronning, Robert Thomas. *The Development of English Comic Farce in the Plays of Sir Arthur Pinero.* Unpublished Ph.D. Dissertation. Wayne State University, 1972. 316 p. [It is reported to discuss the early farces of W. S. Gilbert.]

1038. Rowell, George and Kenneth Mobbs (adaptors). *Engaged!; or, Cheviot's Choice.* A Comic Opera in Three Acts. By W. S. Gilbert. London: Chappell, 1963. 179 p. [vocal score]

1039. _____. *Engaged!; or, Cheviot's Choice.* A Comic Opera in Three Acts. By W. S. Gilbert. London: Chappell, 1963. 57 p. [libretto]

1040. "The Rush to Stage G&S." *Music and Musicians* 10 (January, 1962): 15+., illus.

1041. Schumann, E. M. (ed). *Everybody's Favorite Gilbert and Sullivan Album; World Famous Songs from Gilbert and Sullivan's Most Popular Operas Arranged for Voice and Piano and Containing the Complete Story of Each Opera.* (Everybody's Favorite Series). Edited by E. M. Schumann. New York: Amsco Music Sales, 1938. 208 p.

1042. Scott, Nan C. *Five Little-Known Operas of Gilbert and Sullivan.* Unpublished M. A. Thesis. University of Kansas, 1965.

1043. Searle, Townley (ed.). *Lost Bab Ballads.* By W. S. Gilbert. Collected, edited and illustrated by Townley Searle. London and New York: G. P. Putnam's Sons, 1932. x, 127 p.

1044. Shaw, Bernard. "Light Entertainment." *Shaw on Music; A Selection from the Music Criticism of Bernard Shaw Made by Eric Bentley.* New York: Doubleday and Company, 1955. p. 195-220. [6 essays on Gilbert and Sullivan]

1045. Shipley, J. T. "Gilbert and Sullivan, Peerless Pair of Comic Opera."
      Drama 16 (December, 1925): 87-9.

1046. Simcoe, H. Augustine. *Sullivan v. Critic; Or Practice v. Theory, A Study
      in Press Phenomena.* London: Simpkin, Marshall, 1906. 150 p., illus.,
      music.

1047. Slade, F. T. "Gilbert and Sullivan." *Central Literary Magazine* 40
      (December, 1966): 51-6.

1048. Smith, J. Fletcher. *H. M. S. Pinafore; or, The Lass That Loved a Sailor.*
      Adapted from Gilbert and Sullivan by J. Fletcher Smith. Illustrated by
      Griswold Tyng. Boston: L. C. Page, 1935. ix, 106 p., illus., plates.

1049. Stedman, Jane W. *W. S. Gilbert: His Comic Techniques and Their
      Development.* Unpublished Ph.D. Dissertation. University of Chicago,
      1956. 139 p.

1050. Swinton, Marjory. *Lyrics from Gilbert & Sullivan Operas; Favorite
      Selections from the Lyrics of W. S. Gilbert.* Chosen and introduced by
      Marjory Swinton. London: Collins Press, 1964. 160 p., index.

1051. Thompson, Hilary. *The Savoy Operas as Metatheatre: A Study of
      Characterization in the Libretti.* Unpublished Ph.D. Dissertation.
      University of Alberta, 1972. 240 p.

1052. Vallillo, S. M. "Battle of the Black Mikados." *Black American
      Literature Forum* 16 (Winter, 1982): 153-57.

1053. Williamson, A. "Sullivan the Craftsman." *Monthly Musical Record* 81
      (March-April, 1951): 69-73

1054. Wilson, Frederic W. *An Introduction to the Gilbert and Sullivan
      Operas from the Collection of the Pierpont Morgan Library.*
      New York: Pierpont Morgan Library in association with Dover
      Publications, 1989. 112 p., illus. (some color).

1055. _____ (ed.). *The Gilbert and Sullivan Birthday Book.* Dobbs
      Ferry, N.Y.: Cahill, 1983. 172 p.

1056. Wojtowicz, Jeanette O. "Bravo, Opera!" *Instructor* 8 (March, 1981):
      62-65+. [Suggested student activies for elementary school studies
      of *The Mikado* and two other operas.]

Chronology

This section presents the year of first performance or publication for the works of Gilbert and Sullivan. The left column contains works by Gilbert alone or in collaboration with composers other than Sullivan. The right column contains the works by Sullivan alone or in collaboration with librettists other than Gilbert. The middle column contains those works of the Gilbert and Sullivan collaboration.

W. S. Gilbert [b. Nov. 18, 1836]	Gilbert & Sullivan	Arthur S. Sullivan [b. May 12, 1842]
1861 First published contribution to *Fun*		
1862		Incidental Music to The Tempest
1863 "My Maiden Brief"		Princess of Wales' March
1864		Kenilworth, A Masque L'Ile Enchante (ballet) The Sapphire Necklace
1865		
1866 Ruy Blas (unacted?)		Symphony in E Concerto in D
1867 Allow Me to Explain Highly Probable Robinson Crusoe La Vivandiere Harlequin, Cock-Robin, and Jenny Wren		The Contrabandista Cox and Box Marmion Overture
1868 The Merry Zingara Robert the Devil		O Fair Dove (song)
1869 No Cards Pretty Druidess An Old Score Ages Ago The "Bab" Ballads	[G&S met for the first time]	The Prodigal Son

Gilbert	Gilbert & Sullivan	Sullivan
1870 The Princess Gentleman in Black Palace of Truth A Medical Man An Elixir of Love		Overture "Di Ballo"
1870 Our Island Home		
1871 Randall's Thumb A Sensation Novel Great Expectations Creatures of Impulse Pygmalion & Galatea The Brigands	Thespis	On Shore and Sea Incidental Music to Mercant of Venice Onward, Christian Soldiers
1872 On Guard Happy Arcadia		Festival "Te Deum"
1873 The Wicked World The Happy Land The Wedding March More "Bab" Ballads A Stage Play The Realm of Joy A Colossal Idea		The Light of the World
1874 Charity Ought We to Visit Her? Topsy-Turvydom Committed for Trial Sweethearts "Bab" Ballads and More "Bab" Ballads The Blue-Legged Lady		Incidental Music to Merry Wives of Windsor
1875 Tom Cobb Eyes and No Eyes Broken Hearts	Trial by Jury	The Zoo
1876 Dan'l Druce Princess Toto		
1877 On Bail Fifty "Bab" Ballads Engaged		Incidental Music to Henry VIII

	Gilbert	Gilbert & Sullivan	Sullivan
1878	The Ne'er-do-Weel Ali Baba and the Forty Thieves	H.M.S. Pinafore	The Lost Chord
1879	Gretchen	Pirates of Penzance	
1880			The Martyr of Antioch
1881	Foggerty's Fairy	Patience	
1882		Iolanthe	
1883		[5-year contract among G, S, & D'Oyly Carte]	[Sullivan knighted]
1884	Comedy & Tragedy	Princess Ida	
1885		The Mikado	
1886			Overture in C (In Memoriam) Ode for Opening of Colonial & Indian Exhibition
1887		Ruddigore	
1888	Brantinghame Hall	Yeomen of the Guard	Incidental Music to Macbeth
1889		The Gondoliers	
1890	Foggarty's Fairy and Other Tales	["carpet quarrel"]	
1891	Rosencrantz and Guildenstern Songs of a Savoyard		Ivanhoe (grand opera)
1892	The Mountebanks Haste to the Wedding	[new contract between Gilbert & Sullivan]	Incidental Music to The Foresters Haddon Hall
1893		Utopia, Limited	

Gilbert	Gilbert & Sullivan	Sullivan
1894 His Excellency		The Chieftain Incidental Music to King Arthur
1895		
1896	The Grand Duke	
1897 The Fortune Hunter [revivals of Savoy operas]		Victoria and Merrie England (Ballet)
1898	[final meeting between Gilbert and Sullivan]	The Beauty Stone
1899		The Rose of Persia
1900		[d. November 22]
1901	[last of the G&S operas at the Savoy for a few years]	The Emerald Isle [completed by E. German]
1902		
1903		
1904 The Fairy's Dilemma		
1905		
1906	[Yeomen revived]	
1907 [Gilbert knighted]		
1908 The Pinafore Picture Book		
1909 Fallen Fairies		
1910		
1911 The Hooligan Trying a Dramatist		
[d. May 27]		

Title Index

A

B

C

T

U

V

W

XYZ

Name Index

This section includes the names of persons responsible for any intellectual or artistic contribution-- authors, editors, compilers, adaptors, selectors, translators, arrangers, and illustrators.

A

A'Beckett, Gilbert   668
Abeshouse, Benjamin   988
Adams, William Davenport   215-216
Aldford, Edward   2, 217-218
Aldredge, James   3
Allen, Reginald   4-6, 219, 592, 906-907
Allvine, G.   989
Archer, William   7, 89, 222-225, 718
Ardoin, John   908-909
Armstrong, Sir Thomas   554
Arnold, Denis   387
Arnott, Peter   729
Artman, Ruth   897
Ashley, Leonard R. N.   227
Ashley, R. N.   675
Asimov, Isaac   533, 593
Atkins, Sidney   8, 910
Atkinson, Neville   228
Ayer, Margaret   586
Ayre, Leslie   531

B

Baily, J. O.   653
Baily, Leslie   9
Baker, George   10-11, 229
Baker, H. Barton   12
Bargainnier, Earl F.   13, 230-234
Baring, Maurice   235
Barker, Frank Granville   14
Barlow, Harold   873
Barnby, Muriel   15
Barrington, Rutland   16-18
Bartlett, Ian   264, 749
Bassuk, Albert Oliver   552

194

D

E

I

J

M

S

S

W

XYZ